Ghosts
and poltergeists

Ghosts
and poltergeists
TRUE STORIES FROM BEYOND THE GRAVE

Paul Roland
and
Rupert Matthews

ARCTURUS

The techniques and exercises described in this book should never be attempted while under the influence of alcohol or drugs of any kind. Nor should they be attempted by anyone who has or is currently suffering from any form of psychological disturbance, abnormal grief or trauma. The publisher and author accept no liability for harm caused by or to anyone as a result of the misuse of these exercises. If you are in doubt you should seek medical advice before attempting any of these exercises.

All efforts were made to secure permission for reproducing the quotes from C. G. Jung's book *Memories, Dreams, Reflections*.

ARCTURUS

This edition published in 2015 by Arcturus Publishing Limited
26/27 Bickels Yard, 151–153 Bermondsey Street,
London SE1 3HA

Copyright © Arcturus Holdings Limited

ISBN: 978-1-78404-875-4
AD004765UK

Printed in China

CONTENTS

POLTERGEISTS

INTRODUCTION

The evidence for the existence of ghosts and poltergeists and things that go bump in the night, would at first appear to be overwhelming. Eyewitness accounts abound, photographic evidence proliferates and scholarly tomes record hauntings, manifestations and seemingly inexplicable happenings. In view of this, can we simply dismiss them all as hallucinations or figments of the imagination? The short answer is no because people are usually quite genuine in what they report as having seen, although there is a vast difference in what one perceives or what one believes one has seen and what was actually seen. It is in the examination of this difference that most answers can be found.

Ghosts are associated with hauntings, they manifest themselves in a vague sort of 'feeling' which adheres to places or occasionally to objects. Then we have poltergeists or 'noisy spirits' as they are sometimes called, they can cause great concern when they appear for no apparent reason in any household. Furniture appears to move of its own accord, objects fly across a room, lights and electrical appliances turn on and off without human hands manipulating the switches and household articles mysteriously and spontaneously break.

A far cry from the predictable fireside stories, this book investigates well-documented ghost hauntings and the poltergeist phenomenon, attested to by multiple eyewitnesses. Thoroughly researched and lending equal weight to both investigation and skepticism, this dazzling book re-examines a fascinating assortment of recorded sightings from as far back as Roman times; the authors present a serious look at ghosts and poltergeists, not as chain-rattling spooks or cold clouds of vapour, but as actual entities with which we share a greater reality.

GHOSTS
by Paul Roland

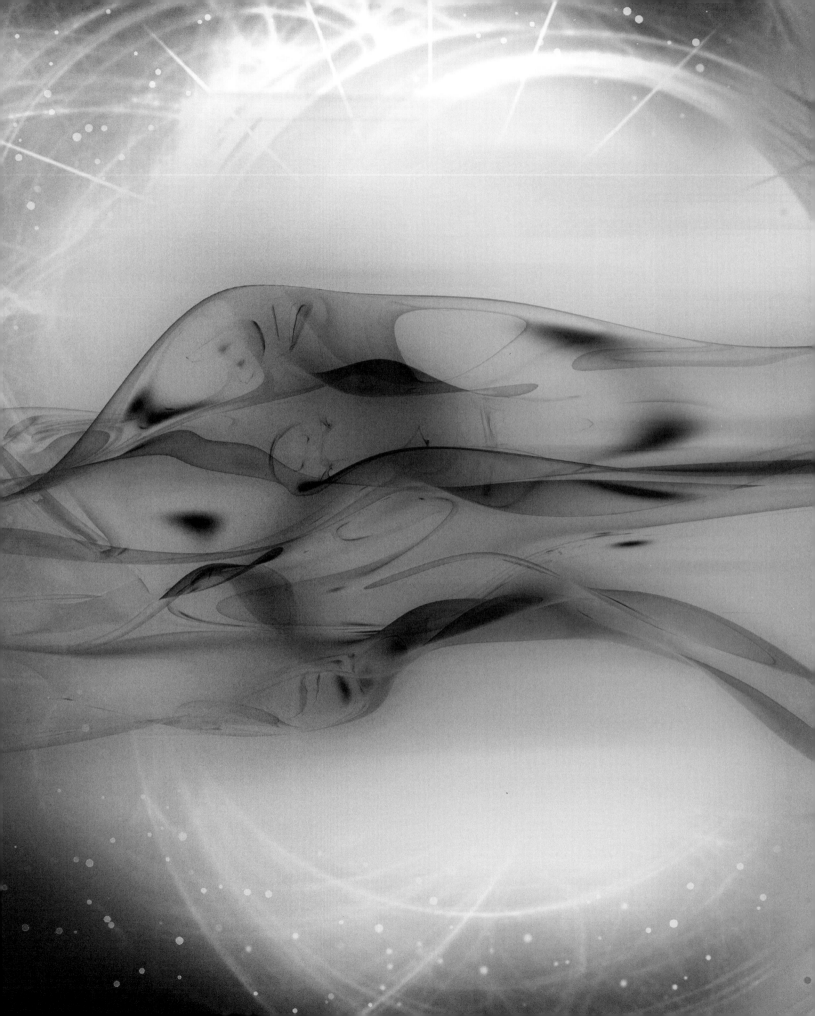

CHAPTER 1

Belief in the Soul

The belief in an immortal human soul and its survival after death dates back to prehistoric times and is common to almost every culture around the world.

Evidence for a belief in immortality can be found in ancient burial customs which reveal that our ancestors had an expectation of an afterlife and a respect for the memory of the dead. This reverence for the departed, which dates back to the Stone Age and possibly beyond, is the clearest evidence that primitive man possessed self-awareness long before he had formed the means of

expressing it in words. Prehistoric cave paintings from Africa to Australia support the belief that early man had a strong intuitive link with the spirit world and attempted to communicate both with his ancestors and with animals through tribal elders, shamans, medicine men and, later, the high priests of the first civilizations. Despite, by present standards, the inherent cruelty and

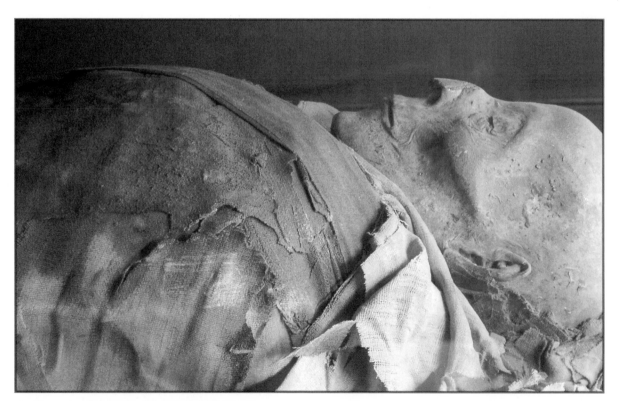

'[The ancient Egyptians'] custom of placing mummified corpses into sarcophagi of increasing refinement resulted from their belief that there are three non-physical components within the human body . . .'

The pyramids at
Giza are believed
to have been
positioned in
accordance with
corresponding
stars in the sky
above them

comparative lack of sophistication of these early societies, it is evident that they all shared a belief in spirits long before the concept of good and evil found expression in orthodox religion.

Cults of the Dead

The ancient Egyptians were so preoccupied with the prospect of an afterlife that their entire civilization was founded on the cult of the dead. Their custom of placing mummified corpses into sarcophagi of increasing refinement resulted from their belief that there are three non-physical components within the human body, (the *ka*, *ba* and *akh*) which equate with the etheric, astral or dream body of the Western esoteric tradition, the mind and the immortal soul. The etheric body is the non-physical counterpart that is effectively a blueprint for the form which our body takes on entering this material dimension.

Many believe that the pyramids may have been built not only as tombs for their pharaohs, who were venerated as living descendants of the Gods, but also as the means of initiation into the mysteries of life and death. According to this interpretation, their alignment with specific constellations was chosen to provide a path through the sky for the ascending spirit of the pharaoh to journey back to the heavens, specifically the Sirius constellation in the Milky Way whose river-like pattern of stars appeared to be a celestial reflection of the Nile. It is also feasible that the empty stone sarcophagus in the King's Chamber of the Great Pyramid at Giza was used to stimulate the conscious separation of the soul in order for the High Priests to be able to commune with the Gods. The structural shape of the pyramids was believed to have both a mystical significance and a practical purpose, focusing the Earth's magnetic energies to a specific point and to such effect that the initiate would be unable to resist the force drawing their etheric body out of its physical home. Earth energies are stronger near water which suggests one explanation of why the pyramids were built near the Nile. The theory was tested in the 1930s by English occultist Dr Paul Brunton who spent the night in the King's Chamber and there experienced an involuntary astral journey.

'. . . *all my muscles became taut, after which a paralysing lethargy began to creep over my limbs. My entire body became heavy and numb . . . The feeling developed into a kind of iciness . . . All sensation in the lower limbs was numb. I appeared next to pass into a semi-somnolent condition . . .*

I felt myself sinking inwards in consciousness to some central point within my brain, while my breathing became weaker and weaker . . . There was a final mad whirl within my brain. I had the sensation of being caught up in a tropical whirlwind and seemed to pass upwards through a narrow hole; then there was the momentary dread of being launched into infinite space . . . I had gone ghost-like out of my earthly body.'

The Egyptian belief in the three spirit elements is significant because it has its equivalent in many cultures around the world which are different in virtually every other respect. It cannot be coincidence that the Greeks wrote of the significance of the *psyche*, the *pneuma* and the *nous*; the Muslims spoke of the *sirr*, *ruh* and *nafs*; the Hindus acknowledged the *atman*, *jiva* and *pranamayakosha*; while the Jewish mystics contemplated the nature of the *neshamah*, the *ruah* and the *nefash* which the Christians assimilated and externalized in the concept of the Holy Trinity.

Belief in a spirit double which can free itself from the body during sleep and exist separate from the body also gave rise to the Roman *larva*, the Tibetan *delok*, the German *doppelgänger*, the English *fetch*, the Norwegian *vardoger* and the Scottish *taslach*.

Today belief in a spirit double is shared by cultures as diverse as the Azande in Africa, the Inuit of Alaska and the Bacairis in South America as well as the major religions and philosophies of the East. Clearly there must be a basis in fact for this shared belief. It seems unlikely that mere wishful thinking or the desire to deny our own mortality could account for the consistency of such beliefs.

Sacred Spirits

In many parts of the world, ghosts are not considered to be a creation of local folklore, but a fact of life. In China

All-night vigils amongst specially decorated graves are a popular
way of marking the Day of the Dead in South America

the dead are understood to co-exist with the living, a belief which gave rise to the practice of ancestor worship, while in South America the deceased are honoured with annual festivals known as the Day of the Dead which suggests that the material world and the spirit world might not be as distinct as we might like to believe. In the Eastern and Asiatic religions it is believed that death is not the end, but simply a transition from one state of being to another. The Hindu *Upanishads*, for example, liken each human soul to a lump of salt taken from the ocean which must ultimately return to the source.

'All the diverse elements, in the end, go back to the source and are absorbed in it, as all waters are finally absorbed in the ocean . . . A lump of salt may be produced by

The discarnate soul submits to the Buddha within

separating it from the water of the ocean. But when it is dropped into the ocean, it becomes one with the ocean and cannot be separated again.'

In Buddhism, the personality is believed to dissolve at the moment of death leaving only pure consciousness (*rupa*) to seek a new body unless the individual was an enlightened soul (*bodhisattva*) in which case it can ascend to the higher states of being and there choose when to intervene in the lives of the living as a guiding spirit. However, those individuals who are as yet unable to free themselves from earthly attachments may descend into the realm of the hungry ghosts, the Buddhist equivalent of the Christian Hell.

It is implied that the majority of discarnate souls linger in a limbo between lives, known as the *bardo*, before reincarnating. The *Tibetan Book of the Dead* was intended to act as a guidebook for the soul which found itself in this transitional state. It was to be read over the dying and the dead who, it was thought, might be disorientated by finding themselves in this unearthly environment.

'The hour has come to part with this body, composed of flesh and
    blood;
    May I know the body to be impermanent and illusory.'

Though it was written more than 1,000 years ago, its description of the three phases of death are uncannily similar to modern accounts of the near-death experience. The first stage, called *chikai bardo*, occurs when consciousness is suspended at the point of separation from the physical body. At this moment the individual is unaware that they are dead. Only when they look down on their own lifeless body do they realize that this ethereal essence is their true self.

' . . . thine intellect hath been separated from thy body.
    Because of this inability to loiter, thou oft-times wilt feel
    perturbed and vexed and panic-stricken . . . '
    The Tibetan Book of The Dead, *Evans-Wentz translation*

There then follows a detailed description of the etheric body and its capabilities.

'So Saul disguised himself, putting on other clothes, and at night he and two men went to the woman. "Consult a spirit for me," he said, "and bring up for me the one I name"'
1 Samuel 28: 8

*'Having a body [seemingly] fleshly [resembling] the
former and that to be produced, Endowed with all sense
faculties and power of unimpeded motion.'*

The following passages stress the importance of letting
go of all emotional attachments to people and places so
that the soul may ascend into the light. But some may be
unwilling, or unable, to relinquish their possessions or
may harbour regrets or resentment which will effectively
bind them to the earthly plane. Others may be literally
haunted by their own evil deeds and they will only
exorcize these memories by reliving them in a succession
of hells of their own making.

*'O now, when the Bardo of Reality upon me is dawning!
Abandoning all awe, fear, and terror of all phenomena,
May I recognise whatever appears as being my own thought-
forms,
May I know them to be apparitions in the intermediate state'*

Having faced the consequences of his actions, the
discarnate soul can then submit to the mercy of the
Buddha within, his own divine essence who determines
whether he can enter Nirvana or must reincarnate.
Assuming that most souls will need to return to the
world for further trials, the concluding prayers are
intended to guide it to re-enter under the most favourable
circumstances.

*'O procrastinating one, who thinks not of the coming of
death,
Devoting yourself to the useless doings of this life,
Improvident are you in dissipating your great
opportunity;
Mistaken, indeed, will your purpose be now if you return
empty-handed from this life'*

Spirits in the Scriptures

The oldest recorded account of an encounter with a
spirit in Western mythology can be traced back to the
appearance of the Witch of Endor in the Old Testament
who was ordered by King Saul to summon the spirit of
the prophet Samuel.

Saul, the King of Israel, had condemned all occult
practices as blasphemous, but when he heard that the
Philistines were marching on the city of Gilboa he
appealed to God for help. Receiving no answer he
disguised himself and called on the witch who used a
talisman to invoke the dead from the netherworld. The
spirit of Samuel materialized out of the earth in the form
of 'an old man . . . wrapped in a cloak' and complained
of having been disturbed. Saul begged forgiveness and
assured the spirit that he would not have disturbed him
had his kingdom not been in peril to which Samuel
replied that what is fated to befall men cannot be undone.
The spirit then departed leaving Saul to face his enemies.

The story is seen by some as a satire on the king who
is forced to acknowledge forces greater than those at his
command, and it also serves as a moral fable. Saul deceived
the witch (by coming to her in disguise), but she proved
to be the wiser. After the spirit departed she showed
compassion for the humbled ruler, killing one of her
animals to feed him. The story also underlines the Jewish
belief that the soul of the deceased hovers near its body for
12 months after death before ascending to heaven.

Communication with spirits was forbidden by the
Old Testament (Deuteronomy 18:9–14), but conscious
awareness of the higher worlds for the purpose of self-
realization or enlightenment had been practised since
biblical times by initiates of Merkabah, a forerunner of
the modern Jewish mystical teaching known as Kabbalah.

Spirits are not acknowledged explicitly in the New
Testament although their existence is clearly implied,
most notably in Luke 24:39, when Jesus tells his followers:
'Touch me and make sure that I am not a ghost, because
ghosts don't have bodies, as you see that I do!'

Elsewhere, particularly in the 'lost' Gnostic gospels
discovered at Nag Hammadi in 1947, there are several
significant references to the living spirit within every
human being and to the disciples' personal experience of
the astral world and altered states of awareness. In the
Gospel of Philip, Jesus makes a clear distinction between
'the real realm' (i.e., the material world) and 'the realm
of truth'.

*'People cannot see anything in the real realm unless they
become it. In the realm of truth it is not as [with] human*

' . . . a dream body – an etheric or spirit double composed of subatomic matter connected to our physical form by an etheric umbilical cord which is only severed upon death'

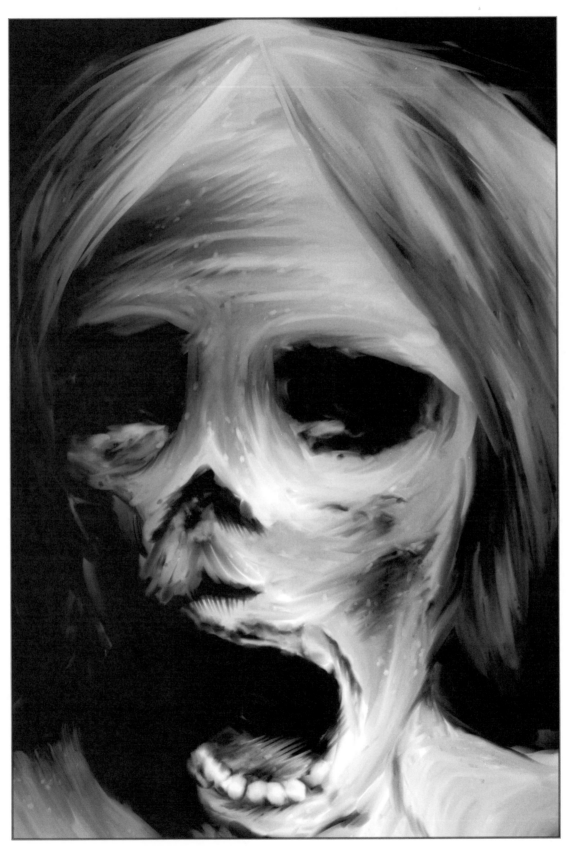

'"Watashi kirei?"
(Am I beautiful?)'
The legend of the
Kuchisake-onna
resurfaced in South
Korea as recently
as 2004
See page 23

beings in the world, who see the sun without being the sun . . . Rather, if you have seen any things there, you have become those things.'

In 1 Corinthians 15:50 and 2 Peter 1:18 it is stated that flesh and blood cannot enter the celestial kingdom; in John 3:13 it is noted that heaven is for spiritual beings and that we are all spirit in essence and will return from whence we came:

'And no man hath ascended up to heaven, but he that came down from the heaven, even the Son of man which is in heaven.'

According to the Gnostic gospels, Jesus appeared to his followers as a spirit to prove that the soul survives death, but due either to selective editing of the gospels or a mistranslation of the rich metaphorical language of the Gnostic gospels, this central teaching became literalized. St Paul attempted to clarify the idea that Jesus had risen physically from the tomb and in so doing made a distinction between our earthly form and our spirit:

'There are also celestial bodies, and bodies terrestrial: but the glory of the celestial is one, and the glory of the terrestrial is another . . . There is a natural body and there is a spiritual body.' (1 Corinthians 15:35–44).

Elsewhere, in 2 Corinthians, St Paul speaks of having attained separation of the spirit and the body at will and having ascended 'in the spirit' to the third heaven, which was a technique he may have mastered as an initiate of an aesthetic sect of Jewish mystics who practised merkabah – an advanced form of meditation which translates as 'rising in the chariot'.

Ancient Apparitions

In order to understand the nature of ghosts we need to accept the fact that we all possess what is often called a dream body – an etheric or spirit double composed of subatomic matter connected to our physical form by an etheric umbilical cord which is only severed upon death. Such a concept is central to the philosophies of the East,

but can seem too fanciful to those Westerners who have not had an out-of-body experience (OBE), or at least have no memory of the experience, for it is likely that everyone has had an OBE during the deepest stages of sleep.

So what evidence is there for the existence of this 'true self' and how might it explain the various phenomena we categorize under the broad heading of 'ghosts'? While much of the evidence is anecdotal, there are numerous cases where an apparition was witnessed by more than one person or where an individual was later able to verify details they had observed during their astral journey. There is also solid scientific evidence for the existence of the etheric double gathered from experiments conducted in the mid-1970s by Dr Karl Osis of California, USA during which the invisible presence projected by a psychic in an adjoining room was recorded either by photosensitive instruments or sensors which could detect the tiniest movements of a feather in a sealed container.

This question of evidence occupied the ancients as intensely as it continues to occupy us today. The earliest recorded discussion on the subject can be found in the writings of the Chinese philosopher, Mo Tzu (470–391 BC).

'Since we must understand whether ghosts and spirits exist or not, how can we find out? Mo Tzu said: The way to find out whether anything exists or not is to depend on the testimony of the ears and eyes of the multitude. If some have heard it or some have seen it then we have to say it exists. If no one has heard it and no one has seen it then we have to say it does not exist. So, then, why not go to some village or some district and inquire? If from antiquity to the present, and since the beginning of man, there are men who have seen the bodies of ghosts and spirits and heard their voices, how can we say that they do not exist? If none have heard them and none have seen them, then how can we say they do? But those who deny the existence of the spirits say: "Many in the world have heard and seen something of ghosts and spirits. Since they vary in testimony, who are to be accepted as really having heard and seen them? Mo Tzu said: As we are to rely on what many have jointly seen and what many have jointly heard, the case of Tu Po is to be accepted."

Lord Lyttleton was apparently visited by Mrs Amphlett at the hour of her death,
when she informed him of the hour and day that he too would die

Tu Po was minister to the Emperor Hsuan [827–783 bc] who ignored warnings that if he executed Po on false charges he would be haunted by the minister's ghost. Three years later Hsuan was killed with an arrow fired by an apparition resembling Tu Po in front of an asembly of feudal lords.'

Chapter 31, Yi-pao Mei translation

Restless Spirits

The legend of Tu Po is clearly a moral fable and was widely accepted as such. In other parts of the world such stories became the basis for local myths, especially if there was a lesson to be learned. In South America, for example, there is the legend of the Weeping Woman who is said to have committed suicide after a handsome seducer refused to marry her as he had promised to do. She is said to haunt the highways in search of her children whom she had killed in order to be free to marry him. Her tale is told to young girls entering womanhood as a warning against believing the lies of men. In Japan there is a long tradition of apocryphal ghost stories in which wronged women return from the dead to take their revenge on those who have dishonoured them. The tale of the Tofu Seller is characteristic of this type of fable. It tells of a blind tofu vendor who is tricked into removing a charm from the door of a house by a wizened old hag who claims to be the ghost of the householder's first wife. Once the charm is removed, the ghost glides inside and a horrible scream is heard from within as the old hag frightens her husband's second wife to death.

The most persistent ghost story in Japanese culture is the legend of the *Kuchisake-onna*, the spiteful spirit of a vain young girl who was the wife or concubine of a jealous samurai in the Heian period. Fearing that she had betrayed him with another man he is said to have disfigured her and then taunted her by saying: 'Who will think you're beautiful now?' Her face covered with a mask, the Kuchisake-onna wanders through the fog seeking solitary children, young men and women, whom she asks: *'Watashi kirei?'* (Am I beautiful?). If they answer 'yes' she tears off the mask and asks again. If they keep their nerve and again answer 'yes' she allows them to go on their way, but if they run screaming she pursues them, brandishing a long-bladed knife or a scythe. If she catches a man she butchers him and if she catches a girl she mutilates her, turning her into another Kuchisake-onna. The story is so deeply rooted in the Japanese psyche that as recently as 1979 there was public panic when it was rumoured that the Kuchisake-onna had been seen attacking children. In 2004, cities in South Korea were rife with similar rumours.

The earliest credible account of a spectral encounter was recorded by the Greek philosopher Athenodorus who lived during the 1st century bc. Against the advice of his friends, Athenodorus agreed to rent a room in a lodging house that was reputed to be haunted because it was cheap and he wished to prove that his actions were determined by his intellect and not his emotions. At nightfall his nerves were tested by the appearance of a gaunt-faced spirit of an old man draped in the soiled vestments of the grave. The spectre was weighed down by chains and appeared to be in anguish but was unable to communicate what it was that bound him to that place.

The philosopher kept his nerve and indicated that he was willing to follow the ghost wherever he wished to lead him. It led Athenodorus along a narrow passage and out into the garden whereupon it faded into the bushes. Athenodorus noted where the spirit had disappeared and the next morning he informed the magistrates who ordered workmen to excavate the garden. There they unearthed a skeleton weighed down by rusted chains which they assumed was that of a murder victim. They then had the skeleton reburied according to Greek funeral rites. Such stories have their counterpart in virtually every culture from ancient times to the present day.

The English ghost story tradition can be traced back to an episode involving Lord Lyttleton who, in 1779, claimed that he was tormented by the spirit of his jilted mistress, Mrs Amphlett, whose three daughters he had also seduced. She had committed suicide in despair and had returned to foretell the day and hour of his death. His friends, fearing for his sanity, thought they would try to outwit the spook by turning all the clocks forward. When the appointed hour passed without incident his lordship retired to bed much relieved and cursing himself for being a superstitious fool. But the dead are not so easily cheated and at the appointed hour Lord Lyttleton expired in his sleep from a fit.

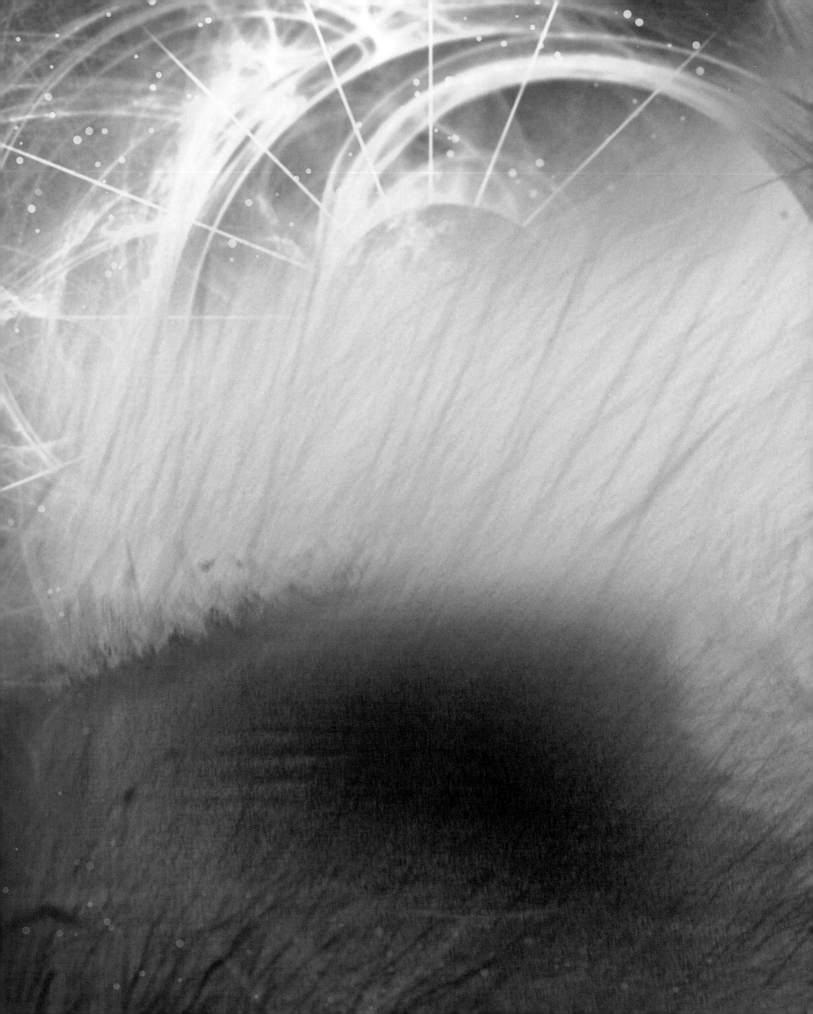

CHAPTER 2

The Night Side
of Nature

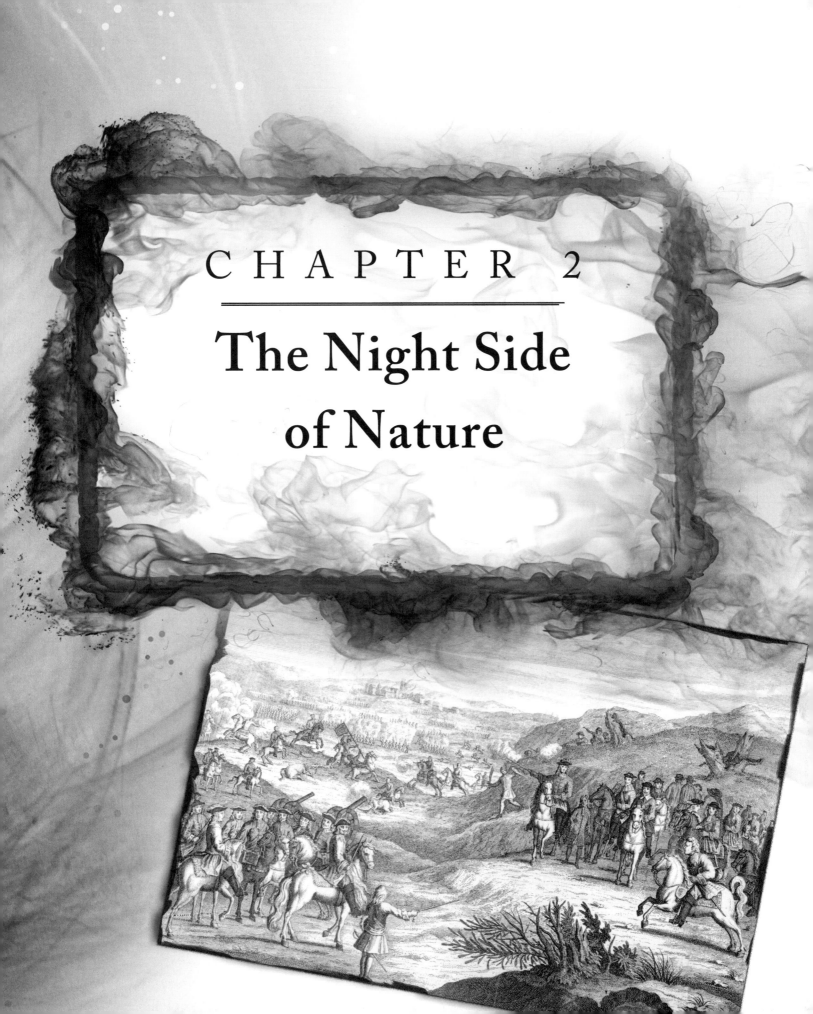

The modern obsession with the supernatural began in nineteenth-century New York State when coded communications with a restless soul gave birth to Spiritualism.

The modern preoccupation with the paranormal could be said to have begun in 1848 with the publication of *The Night Side of Nature*. The Victorians were avid readers of ghost stories, but they bought this collection in unprecedented quantities because its author, Scottish novelist Catherine Crowe, appealed both to their romanticism and their reason. Her obvious delight in describing Gothic horrors was balanced with rigorous research. Each episode was backed up by witness statements, documents and dates to reinforce the author's belief that the supernatural was as worthy of serious investigation as the natural sciences. Her view was that the scientific establishment was arrogant and presumptuous in stating that all paranormal phenomena were the result of hysteria. It was her contention that the majority of scientists 'arrange the facts to their theory, not their theory to the facts'.

Crowe's timing was opportune. The belief in the infallibility of science was beginning to be questioned, yet the literate classes were also losing their faith in religion. Neither science nor religion appeared to have all the answers, but it seemed that a commonsense approach to the supernatural – and specifically to the question of life after death – might finally reconcile the two. By insisting that at least two independent witnesses corroborate each sighting, she laid down the ground rules for conducting paranormal research which was to change little over the next 100 years.

Willington Mill

Her most thorough and intriguing investigation concerned Willington Mill, near Newcastle-upon-Tyne, England, which was a haunted mill house owned by an industrialist, Joshua Proctor, who provided a sworn statement which Mrs Crowe included as a preface to her account. The property was only 40 years old when Proctor moved in during the spring of 1840, so it did not conform to the traditional idea of a house haunted by the spirits of previous owners. Moreover, Proctor was a devout Quaker, a God-fearing Christian not given to belief in spooks. And neither was Dr Edward Drury, a hardened sceptic and amateur ghostbuster who was the first on the scene when rumours of the haunting circulated around the region. It was Dr Drury who was to bring the facts to the attention of Mrs Crowe.

In July, Drury and his trusted friend Mr Hudson inquired if they could spend the night in the mill house in order to 'unravel the mystery', implying that they expected to expose a hoax. On meeting Mr Proctor they were immediately struck by his honesty and candour and so decided that they would not need the brace of loaded pistols with which they had intended to frighten the trickster. Proctor clearly believed that something was amiss and had even sent his family away so that the investigators could have a clear field.

At 11pm on the night of 3 July 1840, Dr Drury and his companion made themselves comfortable on a third floor landing outside the haunted room and settled down for an all-night vigil. At midnight they heard the sound of bare feet running across the floor, then knocking sounds as if someone was rapping with their knuckles on the bare boards. Other noises followed in quick succession – a hollow cough and a rustling – suggesting that a presence was making itself known. By 12.45 am, Dr Drury assumed that the show was over and was planning to retire to bed leaving Mr Hudson on the landing, but before he could do so Dr Drury saw a sight that was to haunt him for the rest of his life. A closet door swung open and 'the figure of a female, attired in greyish garments, with the head inclining downwards, and one hand pressed upon the chest as if in pain', strode slowly towards him. The spectre advanced towards Mr Hudson at which point the doctor found the courage to charge at it but he passed right through the apparition, knocking over his companion. Drury confesses that he recollected nothing for three hours afterwards and was assured by Hudson and Proctor that he was 'carried down stairs in an agony of fear and terror'. The good doctor was so traumatized by his experience that he required 10 days to calm his nerves before writing his account. He ended it by stating that he had gone there as a devout disbeliever but had emerged convinced of the reality of the supernatural.

Not content with relying on Dr Drury's account and Proctor's verification, Mrs Crowe dug deeper, unearthing accounts of earlier and subsequent sightings at Willington Mill given by four other people, plus a local newspaper proprietor and a historian who discovered that ghosts had been seen in a house that had occupied the same site 200 years earlier. Mrs Crowe wrote:

'The following more recent case of an apparition seen in the window of the same house from the outside, by four credible witnesses, who had the opportunity of scrutinising it for more than ten minutes, is given on most unquestionable authority. One of these witnesses is a young lady, a near connection of the family, who for obvious reasons, did not sleep in the house; another, a respectable man . . . his daughter . . . and his wife who first saw the object and called out the others to view it. The appearance presented was that of a bare-headed man in a flowing robe like a surplice, who glided backward

At midnight they heard the sound of bare feet running across the floor, then knocking sounds as if someone was rapping with their knuckles . . .

and forward about three feet from the floor, or level with the bottom of the second story window seeming to enter the wall on each side and thus present a side view in passing. It then stood still in the window and a part of the body came through both the blind which was close down and the window, as its luminous body intercepted the framework of the window. It was semi-transparent and as bright as a star, diffusing a radiance all around. As it grew more dim it assumed a blue tinge and gradually faded away from the head downward. Had any magic lantern been used it could not possibly have escaped detection . . .'

Mrs Crowe then travelled to Willington Mill to question the witnesses herself and found them to be entirely credible.

'They spoke of the facts above detailed with the simple earnestness of people who had no doubts whatever on the subject.'

But although *The Night Side of Nature* can be credited with raising public awareness of paranormal phenomena and making a case for having the subject taken seriously, it was an event on the other side of the Atlantic which raised belief in the afterlife to such an extent that it became the foundation for a new religion – spiritualism.

The Haunting of Charles Dickens

The Victorians were very fond of ghost stories and the most popular authors of the period relished competing with one another to see who could make their readers' flesh creep the most. One of the era's best-loved storytellers was Charles Dickens, though surprisingly the author of *A Christmas Carol*, *Oliver Twist* and many supernatural short stories on ghosts was not a believer in the paranormal. In fact, Dickens was a hardened sceptic until he had a disquieting paranormal experience of his own.

Marley's ghost in *A Christmas Carol*. Contemporary fascination with the supernatural spilled over into Charles Dickens' writing

'Look at me again. You may have to take a likeness of me'

In 1861, Dickens contributed a ghost story to the popular magazine *All The Year Round* which centred on an encounter between a portrait painter and a young lady in a railway carriage. During the journey, the story goes, the pale looking lady inquired as to whether the artist could paint a portrait from memory to which he replied that he probably could. When asked the reason for her question she responded, 'Look at me again. You may have to take a likeness of me.' Shortly afterwards they parted and the painter travelled on to his destination. Two years later, an elderly gentleman by the name of Wylde called on the artist and asked if he would accept a commission to paint a portrait of his daughter from a description as she was not available to sit for the portrait in person for she had died some time earlier. Puzzled but intrigued the artist agreed and began to sketch a young lady in accordance with Mr Wylde's description. After several failed attempts to capture her likeness he was on the verge of giving up when in desperation he recalled the young woman whom he had met on the train and used her as his inspiration. 'Instantly, a bright look of recognition and pleasure lighted up the father's face,' Dickens wrote, 'and he exclaimed, "That is she!"' In the course of conversation, the artist asked when the young lady had died and was told it was two years previously on September 13 – the very date the painter had met the pale young woman on the train.

Such twists were almost clichés even in Victorian fiction, but what makes this particular story significant is that it was to have a resonance in real life. Shortly after publication, Dickens received an irate letter from a painter who claimed that the story was not fiction, but fact. It had been his own personal experience which he had written down with the intention of submitting it for publication, but had delayed and he was now convinced that Dickens had heard his story somehow and copied it – even down to the date chosen for the girl's death. The painter had told the story to his friends but had never mentioned the date until the time he wrote it all down. This is what particularly unnerved Dickens. He later wrote, 'Now my [original] story had *no date*; but seeing when I looked over the proofs the great importance of having a date, I wrote in, unconsciously, the exact date on the margin of the proof!'

Ghost Lights

Not all spirits appear in human form. Often entities will register on video film and photographs as moving lights. The following true story recorded by the Reverend Charles Jupp, warden of a Scottish orphanage, in 1878 is of great interest because it was seen by two witnesses both of whom found its presence reassuring.

As near as I can tell I fell asleep about 11 o'clock, and slept soundly for some time. I suddenly awoke without any apparent reason, and felt an impulse to turn round, my face being turned towards the wall, from the children. Before turning, I looked up and saw a soft light in the room. The gas was burning low in the hall, and the dormitory door being open, I thought it was probable that the light came from the source. It was soon evident, however, that such was not the case. I turned round, and then a wonderful vision met my gaze. Over the second bed from mine, and on the same side of the room, there was floating a small cloud of light, forming a halo the brightness of the moon on an ordinary moonlit night.

I sat upright in bed looking at this strange appearance, took up my watch and found the hands pointing at five minutes to one. Everything was quiet, and all the children sleeping soundly. In the bed, over which the light seemed to float, slept the youngest of the . . . children mentioned above.

I asked myself, "Am I dreaming?" No! I was wide awake. I was seized with a strong impulse to rise and touch the substance, or whatever it might be (for it was about five feet high), and was getting up when something seemed to hold me back. I am certain I heard nothing, yet I felt and perfectly understood the words – "No, lie down, it won't hurt you." I at once did what I felt I was told to do. I fell asleep shortly afterwards and rose at half-past five, that being my usual time.

At 6 . . . I began dressing the children beginning at the bed farthest from the one in which I slept. Presently I came to the bed over which I had seen the light hovering. I took the little boy out, placed him on my knee, and put on some of his clothes. The child had been talking with the others; suddenly he was silent. And then, looking me hard in the face with an extraordinary expression, he said, "Oh Mr Jupp, my mother came to me last night. Did you see her?" For a moment I could not answer the child. I then thought it better to pass it off, and said, "Come, we must make haste, or we shall be late for breakfast."'

The incident prayed on Jupp's mind and perhaps it was guilt at not having reassured the child that later compelled him to write an account of that night for the orphanage magazine. When the child read it his expression changed and looking up at the Reverend he said, 'Mr Jupp, that is me.' Jupp answered, 'Yes, that is what we saw.' Satisfied that he had not dreamt it the child fell into deep thought, 'evidently with pleasant remembrances, for he smiled so sweetly to himself,' recalled Jupp, 'and seemed to forget I was present.'

The Reverend Charles Jupp, outside the orphanage of which he was warden

'. . . as he sat in a circle with the medium Charles Williams, a disembodied hand materialized in mid-air'

The Ghost Club

It has been said that if two Englishmen found themselves marooned on a desert island, the first thing that they would do would be to form a club. In 1873, two eminent English academics did just that after finding themselves isolated on an island of doubt surrounded by a sea of certainty.

Professor Henry Sedgwick of Trinity College, Cambridge, had earlier resigned his fellowship because he no longer felt he could subscribe to the Thirty-Nine Articles of Faith central to the Church of England. He was later reinstated when the religious qualifications for the fellowship were rescinded, but his disillusionment was deep rooted and he no longer felt able to accept what the rest of

The SPR investigated more than 700 paranormal incidents from telepathy to out–of–body experiences which they compiled in an exhaustive 2,000 page study'

Christian society accepted in blind faith. Inevitably, his adoring students began to side with their mentor, among them Frederick Myers, the son of a clergyman.

One crisp winter's evening in 1869, Myers called on the professor and persuaded him to take a walk to discuss their reservations regarding religion. As they looked up at the stars Myers voiced his frustration with philosophy and idly asked if his companion had given any thought to the rise of spiritualism and if it might signify a breakthrough in man's understanding of the universe. Sedgwick was doubtful but a seed had been planted that was later to grow into the Society for Psychical Research (SPR), an informal collective of intellectuals and the restlessly inquisitive formed by Myers and his former mentor. Its stated aim was to investigate all forms of paranormal phenomena in a strictly scientific manner and settle the matter once and for all. Its strength was that its members included sceptics as well as believers, among them two future prime ministers – Arthur Balfour and William Gladstone – the poet Alfred Lord Tennyson, novelist Mark Twain, intellectual and critic John Ruskin and academic Charles Dodgson (better known as Lewis Carroll). The SPR investigated more than 700 paranormal incidents from telepathy to out-of-body experiences which they compiled in an exhaustive 2,000 page study published in several volumes as *Phantasms of the Living* in 1886.

Her husband recognized the intruder as his father who had died several years earlier. Shortly afterwards, Mr P fell ill and remained in a serious condition for weeks

During the four years of intense research prior to publication, Myers, who is credited with coining the term telepathy, attended several séances without success until, one evening, as he sat in a circle with the medium Charles Williams, a disembodied hand materialized in midair. Such phenomena had been faked by other psychics who had resorted to paying an assistant to appear in a darkened room dressed in black with only their hand exposed. Fearing another fake, Myers had grasped the phantom hand and felt it grow steadily smaller until it disappeared altogether like a deflating balloon, only there was nothing in his fist when he unclenched it. Myers concluded, 'Whatever else a "ghost" may be, it is probably the most complex phenomenon in nature . . . Instead of describing a "ghost" as a dead person permitted to communicating with the living let us define it as a manifestation of persistent personal energy.' It was Myers' belief that phantoms were not physical in the sense that they were solid, but occupied a physical space in a fourth dimension.

A Ghostly Intruder

The following is typical of the type of ghost stories the society investigated. It is significant because it was one of the rare occasions when a ghost was heard to speak, and also was so solid as to cast a shadow. Its appearance was witnessed by two people and supported by their signed statements along with those of another couple to whom they had told their story shortly after it had happened.

A married couple, who chose to be identified in the report as Mr and Mrs P (but whose real identity and address are on file in the SPR archives), were in bed when Mrs P was startled to see a stranger standing at the foot of the bed. He was dressed in a naval officer's uniform. She woke her husband who demanded to know what the man was doing in their bedroom at night. The officer simply spoke the husband's name as if reproving him for being so readily offended and then turned about and walked through the facing wall.

Mrs P had assumed that it prefigured some disaster for her brother who was in the navy, but her husband recognized the intruder as his father who had died several years earlier. Shortly afterwards, Mr P fell ill and remained in a serious condition for several weeks. When he recovered he confessed to his wife that he had accumulated a considerable debt and was so desperate that he had been considering going into business with a disreputable character whom he now realized might have ruined him for certain. He had taken his father's appearance and remonstration as a warning and was now determined to resolve his financial difficulties by himself.

Concern From Beyond the Grave

After the Great War, paranormal research was almost exclusively pursued by elderly academics and matronly mediums, but in February 1932 two investigators from the SPR arrived in the English village of Ramsbury, Wiltshire, to investigate a local haunting only to discover that the local vicar had beaten them to the story.

The grandchildren of chimney sweep Samuel Bull had complained that they could not sleep because they were aware of a presence outside their damp and dilapidated cottage. The case is noteworthy because the whole

Whether Ellen jumped into the sea at Brighton, or was swept to her death is immaterial. Violent or unlooked for deaths often result in the emergence of a restless spirit

family witnessed the apparition on several occasions and instinctively reacted to it without prompting from the others.

Bull had died the previous summer but on several occasions his ghost appeared in full view of the children, their mother, Mary Edwards and Samuel's invalid wife, Jane, who lived with them. They saw him walking across the living room, up the stairs and through the closed door of the bedroom where he had died. At first they were all terrified, but they gradually became used to

was his reaction to seeing them living in such squalid conditions. Shortly before the hauntings ceased Mrs Edwards received news that they were to be re-housed and thereafter the spectre of Samuel Bull appeared with a less troubled look on his face. When they moved he did not appear to them again.

Suicide Sighting

The SPR were scrupulous in their methods and, in an effort to satisfy their most hostile critics who were within their own ranks, subjected every case to the degree of scrutiny usually reserved for the natural sciences. Several of their members were distinguished physicists and guarded their reputations as staunchly as the clergy protected the sanctity of the Church. They were not interested simply in collecting ghost stories in the manner that amateur historians collected folklore. They were in search of incontrovertible evidence and that meant securing the written testimony of as many witnesses as possible. The following case is a prime example of the kind of incident they were keen to include.

One pleasant summer evening, a mother and her son were sitting in the back garden of their suburban house in Clapham, South London, when the young man exclaimed with surprise, 'Look mother, there's Ellen!' Ellen was the elder of his two sisters and had been sent to Brighton on the south coast by her parents to cool her heels after she had been forbidden to see an unsuitable suitor. The young lady was at the far end of the lawn walking toward the garden gate which led to the fields beyond. Fearing that her father might see her before she had a chance to explain her daughter's unexpected return, the mother asked her son to go after Ellen and bring her back to the house. 'I can't run after her,' he reminded her. He had sprained his ankle earlier that day. 'You'll have to send Mary.' So the mother called her younger daughter from the house and told her to run after Ellen and bring her back before her father saw her. They would send her back to Brighton in the morning without him knowing anything about it and so they would avoid an unpleasant scene.

Mary ran across the lawn and through the gate calling her sister's name, but Ellen did not respond. She

seeing the old man and were curiously reassured by his presence. He didn't look like a ghost and it was clear that he was aware of their presence. On two occasions he put his hand on Jane's head and spoke her name, but there was a sadness in his expression which the family assumed

'Read the 27th chapter of *Genesis* in my daddy's old Bible'

continued to walk down a path across the fields leading away from the house, her black cloak billowing in the breeze. 'Ellen, where are you going?' asked Mary as she finally caught up with her sister. Then, as she grasped her sister's arm, she found her hand passing right through the apparently solid figure as through a mist. When she had collected herself, she walked back in a daze to where her mother and brother were waiting and told them what she had seen and that she feared the worse. The next day the family learnt that Ellen had thrown herself into the sea and drowned at the very hour that she had appeared to them in the garden.

Last Will and Testament

One of the most famous and convincing accounts of survival after death preserved in the SPR archives described an occurrence on the other side of the Atlantic in 1885. An American farmer, Michael Conley of Chicasaw County, died of natural causes at an old people's home and was stripped of his filthy work clothes at the Dubuque County morgue. When his daughter was informed of his death she fainted, but when she recovered consciousness she claimed that her father had appeared to her and told her to recover a roll of dollar bills he had sewn into the lining of his grey shirt. Remarkably, she was able to describe the clothes he had been wearing at the time of his death, even down to the fact that he had wrapped the money in a square of red cloth torn from one of her old dresses. No one believed her, attributing her 'delusion' to grief, but to calm her down they decided to humour her by fetching the clothes from Dubuque and allowing her to examine them. In the lining of the grey shirt, wrapped in a patch of red cloth, they found the money just as the daughter had said they would.

As she grasped her sister's arm, she found her hand passing right through the apparently solid figure as through a mist. When she had collected herself, she walked back in a daze to where her mother and father were waiting and told them what she had seen

A similar incident was recorded 40 years later by the American branch of the SPR. In Davie County, North Carolina, James Chaffin, a farmer's son, dreamt that his dead father appeared at his bedside and urged the boy to look for his missing will in the pocket of the overcoat that he was wearing in the dream. When James awoke he was puzzled as the farm had been left to the elder of his three brothers, Marshall Chaffin, according to the terms of the one and only will that the family had been aware of. Besides, the old man had been dead for four years. Why had he appeared now when the matter had long been settled? His curiosity aroused, James visited his mother and asked about the coat. She told him that it had been given to his brother John. John dutifully handed it over and was witness to what happened next. James tore open the lining of the inside pocket and inside found a message in his father's handwriting. It said, 'Read the 27th chapter of Genesis in my daddy's old Bible.'

Returning to his mother's house James found the family Bible and exactly at the place indicated they found the missing will. It had been written after the one that had left the farm to Marshall and expressed the father's wish that the land be divided equally between his widow and the four boys. Initially, Marshall was inclined to contest it, but backed down when 10 witnesses testified that it was in the old man's own handwriting.

When the case came to the attention of the SPR, they hired a lawyer to investigate it and he concluded that all the facts were correct. Old man Chaffin had chosen the 27th chapter of Genesis to make a point. It described how Jacob deceived his blind father Isaac into giving him what rightly belonged to his brother Esau. Unfortunately, the family were not habitual Bible readers and so the father was forced to make a belated appearance in order to ensure his last wish was respected.

'The mast on his vessel had fallen, splitting his skull on the
very night she had seen her son standing in the doorway'

Paranormal experiences were more common than even the SPR had imagined

A Dispiriting Response

Phantasms of the Living presented a formidable accumulation of similar cases to convince many hardened sceptics. Although the general public was deterred from reading it by the mass of witness testimony and dry scholarly discussions regarding the validity of the evidence, several devout sceptics were converted. Professor James Hyslop, who was disliked by his fellow SPR members for his entrenched cynicism, felt compelled to urge other sceptics to admit defeat.

'I regard the existence of discarnate spirits as scientifically proved and I no longer refer to the sceptic as having any right to speak on the subject. Any man who does not accept the existence of discarnate spirits and the proof of it is either ignorant or a moral coward.'

Nevertheless, the scientific establishment was unimpressed. It was not that they did not accept the evidence, but rather that they lost interest in phenomena since apparitions and apports did not add to their understanding of the inner workings of nature. As the novelist Nathaniel Hawthorne observed after having compiled convincing evidence purporting to prove the existence of the paranormal:

'These soberly attested incredibilities are so numerous that I forget nine tenths of them . . . they are absolutely proved to be sober facts by evidence that would satisfy us of any other alleged realities: and yet I cannot force my mind to interest itself in them.'

And this attitude has been the bane of believers ever since. Phenomena in themselves tell us nothing about the nature of the universe or human potential. No amount of table-turning, inexplicable rapping sounds or phantom materializations add to our understanding, only to the catalogue of anomalies. In the end a person either believes in ghosts or they do not. Those who were inclined to disbelieve may have been converted by the wealth of experiential evidence, but unless they had been disillusioned with their religion and felt fired up by spiritualism they might be inclined to say, 'All right, ghosts exist, but so what? What does it all mean?'

Time-Delayed Proof

The fact that *Phantasms of the Living* was not a bestseller did not dampen SPR members' enthusiasm, nor lessen their conviction that they were on the threshold of a new world and they were braced for a radical new understanding of the universe. The first study was only 'the foundation stone', as Myers liked to call it. A second study was hastily commissioned under the title *Census of Hallucinations* and attracted an astonishing 17,000 replies from individuals as far apart as Russia and Brazil. It appeared that the SPR had breached a dam. Paranormal experiences were more common than even the SPR had imagined, but many people had felt unable to admit to having had such experiences. Now the SPR and the spiritualists made it socially acceptable to talk about such things. Again, the most persuasive evidence was the cases confirmed by several witnesses. The following incident must rank as one of the most convincing cases ever recorded.

On the night of 3 January 1856, a New Jersey housewife, Mrs Anne Collye, awoke to see her son Joseph standing in the doorway of her bedroom in a dreadful state. He had severe head injuries which had been hastily wrapped in bandages and he was wearing a soiled white nightshirt. A moment later he vanished. Her family comforted Mrs Collye as best they could, reminding her that Joseph was 1,000 miles away in command of a Mississippi steamboat and that it must have been a nightmare brought on by worry. However, Mrs Collye protested that she had been wide awake. It wasn't until two weeks later that the family learned that Joseph had been killed in a collision with another boat. The mast on his vessel had fallen, splitting his skull on the very night she had seen her son standing in the doorway. When Joseph's brother viewed the body, he found it still wrapped in the soiled white nightshirt Joseph had been wearing when called from his cabin in the middle of the night to attend to the disaster. Fortunately for the SPR, Mrs Collye had described her experience to her husband and four daughters the next morning, a full two weeks before news reached them of the tragedy.

Frauds and Fakes

Sadly, the society's efforts to bring such evidence to the attention of the scientific establishment were fatally undermined by several well-publicized scandals involving fake mediums. These occurred just prior to, and in the years immediately after, publication of *Census*

of Hallucinations and consequently public ardour towards spiritualism was dampened and the sceptics had further cause to doubt. Several SPR members were duped by hoaxers who exploited their eagerness to believe, leaving the reputation of the society irreparably damaged by the turn of the century. The episode gave rise to the saying, 'for those who believe, no proof is necessary; for those who doubt, no proof is enough.'

Though their pride had been punctured SPR members continued to pursue their investigations independently, producing some of the most significant and influential studies of the period. Sir Oliver Lodge, twice president of the SPR, recorded his communications with his dead son Raymond in a bestselling book of the same name.

Sir Oliver Joseph Lodge (1851–1940) sought to bring together the transcendental world with the physical universe

Raymond had been killed at Ypres in August 1915 and Sir Oliver required incontestable evidence that his son's spirit survived his physical death. He received it in a remarkable way.

Sir Oliver's wife, Lady Lodge, was eventually persuaded to attend a séance presided over by a medium who did not know her by name and who was unaware of her situation. During the evening the medium, Mrs Leonard, declared that she had a message from a young man named Raymond who had recently passed over and that he had met several of his father's friends including a man named Myers. Frederick Myers had died in 1901 and *Phantasms of the Living* had been published posthumously.

'Raymond' reappeared at a second séance held by a male medium, Vout Peters, during which he referred to a recent photograph in which Raymond was shown with a group of friends holding a walking stick. Raymond's parents did not possess such a photograph so Sir Oliver took the opportunity to raise the subject with Mrs Leonard on a subsequent visit. He was told that it had been taken outdoors and showed a comrade leaning on Raymond for support. A few days later a photograph arrived in the post from the mother of one of Raymond's fellow officers. She had known nothing of the séances, but had sent the photo to Lady Lodge because she had just learnt of Raymond's death. She realized that it must have been the last photo taken of her son. It showed Raymond sitting in the front row with a walking stick by his side and another officer standing behind, leaning on his shoulders.

Spectral Soldiers

During the First World War, both the Germans and the Allies reported several sightings of spectral soldiers who intervened to save the lives of their comrades. The most famous was the legendary 'Angels of Mons', which may have been the creation of the English novelist Arthur Maachen. However, the following story is generally considered to be authentic. It appeared in the August 1919 issue of the popular *Pearson's Magazine* and was credited to Captain W.E. Newcome.

'It was in September, 1916, that the 2nd Suffolks left Loos to go up into the northern sector of Albert. I accompanied them, and whilst in the front line trenches of that sector I, with others, witnessed one of the most remarkable occurrences of the war.

About the end of October, up to November 5th, we were actually holding that part of the line with very few troops. On November 1st the Germans made a very determined attack, doing their utmost to break through. I had occasion to go down to the reserve line, and during my absence the German attack began.

I hurried back to my company with all speed, and arrived in time to give a helping hand in throwing the enemy back to his own line. He never gained a footing in our trenches. The assault was sharp and short, and we had settled down to watch and wait again for his next attack.

We had not long to wait, for we soon saw Germans again coming over No Man's Land in massed waves; but before they reached our wire a white, spiritual figure of a soldier rose from a shell-hole, or out of the ground about one hundred yards on our left, just in front of our wire and between the first line of Germans and ourselves. The spectral figure then slowly walked along our front for a distance of about one thousand yards. Its outline suggested to my mind that of an old pre-war officer, for it appeared to be in a shell coat, with field-service cap on its head. It looked, first, across at the oncoming Germans, then turned its head away and commenced to walk slowly outside our wire along the sector that we were holding.

Our SOS signal had been answered by our artillery. Shells and bullets were whistling across No Man's Land . . . but none in anyway impeded the spectre's progress. It steadily marched from the left of us till it got to the extreme right of the sector, then it turned its face right full on to us. It seemed to look up and down our trench, and as each Véry light [flare] rose it stood out more prominently. After a brief survey of us it turned sharply to the right and made a bee-line for the German trenches. The Germans scattered back . . . and no more was seen of them that night.

The Angels of Mons seemed to be the first thought of the men; then some said it looked like Lord Kitchener, and others said its face, when turned full on to us, was not

'Our SOS signal had been
answered by our artillery.
Shells and bullets were
whistling across No Man's
Land . . . '

unlike Lord Roberts. I know that it gave me personally a great shock, and for some time it was the talk of the company. Its appearance can be vouched for by sergeants and men of my section.'

Later in the same article, another officer, William M. Speight, describes seeing the phantom figure in his dug-out that night. The next evening Speight invited another officer to serve as a witness in the hope that the vision might make another appearance. The dead

The Angels of Mons: that a heavenly host had been seen helping repel the German advance was a popular legend in 1914, and by 1915 was widely accepted as fact

officer duly appeared, pointed to a spot on the floor of the dug-out, then vanished. Intrigued and somewhat superstitious, Speight ordered a hole to be dug at the spot. To the amazement of Speight and the whole company, the sappers unearthed a narrow tunnel that had been excavated by the Germans, primed with mines timed to explode 13 hours later. The timers and explosives were excavated safely and destroyed.

From the numerous accounts of spectral soldiers on file it would seem that fighting men take such sightings in their stride. No doubt frayed nerves, fatigue and the proximity of death play their part in lowering the threshold of awareness which protects ordinary people from glimpsing the world beyond. In his memoirs of the First World War, the English poet Robert Graves recalled a sighting which produced only mild curiosity, rather than fear, at the time.

'I saw a ghost at Bethune. He was a man called Private Challoner who had been at Lancaster with me and again in F Company at Wrexham. When he went out with a draft to join the First Battalion, he shook my hand and said: "I'll meet you again in France, sir." He was killed at Festubert in May and in June he passed by our C Company billet where we were just having a special dinner to celebrate our safe return from Cuinchy . . . Challoner looked in at the window, saluted and passed on. There was no mistaking him or the cap badge he was wearing. There was no Royal Welch battalion billeted within miles of Bethune at the time. I jumped up and looked out of the window, but saw nothing except a fag end smoking on the pavement. Ghosts were numerous in France at the time.'

Years later Graves was asked what he thought ghosts might be and he elaborated in the same dispassionate manner.

'I think that one should accept ghosts very much as one accepts fire – a common but equally mysterious phenomenon. What is fire? It is not really an element, not a principle of motion, not a living creature – not even a disease, though a house can catch it from its neighbours. It is an event rather than a thing or a creature. Ghosts, similarly, seem to be events rather than things or creatures.'

A 'Strange Meeting'

One of the finest poets of the First World War, Wilfred Owen – who is perhaps best remembered for his atmospheric verse 'Strange Meeting' in which a German and a British soldier encounter each other in the underworld – was killed just one week before the Armistice was declared. On the day the guns finally fell silent, his brother Harold, a naval officer, was overwhelmed by a feeling of apprehension and was later 'visited' in his cabin by Wilfred's spirit. Harold's reaction to the presence of his brother contrasts with the fears of fictional characters who are confronted by unquiet spirits and for that reason his experience is strangely comforting. Harold was unaware of his brother's death at the time of their strange meeting.

'I had gone down to my cabin thinking to write some letters. I drew aside the door curtain and stepped inside and to my amazement I saw Wilfred sitting in my chair. I felt shock run through me with appalling force and with it I could feel the blood draining away from my face. I did not rush towards him but walked jerkily into the cabin – all my limbs stiff and slow to respond. I did not sit down but looking at him I spoke quietly: "Wilfred how did you get here?" He did not rise and I saw that he was involuntarily immobile, but his eyes which had never left mine were alive with the familiar look of trying to make me understand; when I spoke his whole face broke into his sweetest and endearing dark smile. I felt no fear – I had not when I first drew my door curtain and saw him there; only exquisite mental pleasure at thus beholding him. All I was conscious of was a sensation of enormous shock and profound astonishment that he should be here in my cabin. I spoke again, "Wilfred dear, how can you be here, it is just not possible . . ." But still he did not speak but only smiled his most gentle smile. This not speaking did not now as it had done at first seem strange or even unnatural; it was not only in some inexplicable way perfectly natural but radiated a quality which made his presence with me undeniably right and in no way out of the ordinary. I loved having him there: I could not and did not want to try to understand how he had got there. I was content to accept him, that he was here with me

The war poet Wilfred Owen (1893–1918), who was
killed just a few days before Armistice Day

Sir Arthur Conan Doyle (1859–1930), best known for his
creation Sherlock Holmes, was a keen follower of the
spiritualist movement

was sufficient. I could not question anything, the meeting in itself was complete and strangely perfect. He was in uniform and I remember thinking how out of place the khaki looked among the cabin furnishings. With this thought I must have turned my eyes away from him; when I looked back my cabin chair was empty . . .

I felt the blood run slowly back to my face and looseness into my limbs and with these an overpowering sense of emptiness and absolute loss . . . I wondered if I had been dreaming but looking down I saw that I was still standing. Suddenly I felt terribly tired and moving to my bunk I lay down; instantly I went into a deep and oblivious sleep. When I woke up I knew with absolute certainty that Wilfred was dead.'

> *Conan Doyle's interest in the paranormal intensified as he investigated the phenomenon and brought his conversion from agnostic to ardent believer to public attention*

The Conversion of Conan Doyle

Sir Arthur Conan Doyle, creator of the fictional detective Sherlock Holmes, became an enthusiastic advocate of spiritualism in the early days of the First World War. This was much to the dismay of his closest friends and most ardent admirers, among them King George V, Prime Minister Lloyd George and Winston Churchill. They were appalled that the man who had created the very embodiment of deductive reasoning should dabble with the specious world of spirits. They suspected it was due to his inability to cope with the death of his son Kingsley who had been killed in France, and his father, but Doyle's enthusiasm for the new fad had been awakened by a remarkable personal experience.

The author and his wife had been nursing a young lady, Lily Loder-Symonds, who was in poor health and spent much of her time practising automatic writing. Doyle was fascinated but had attributed the messages to the action of Lily's subconscious mind until one morning, in May 1915, she declared in some agitation that she had received a warning of impending disaster. 'It is terrible. Terrible. And will have a great influence on the war.' Later that day there came news that the transatlantic liner the *Lusitania* had been sunk by a German submarine with the loss of more than a 1,000 lives, 128 of them American. It was the turning point of the war. Americans were outraged and shortly after entered the war on the side of the Allies. Germany's fate was sealed.

Doyle began to take an active interest in 'spirit messages' after this and received what he considered to be incontrovertible proof of the soul's survival after death. It came in the form of a 'conversation' with his dead brother-in-law, Malcolm Leckie, who had been killed at Mons in April 1915. Doyle was stunned to witness Lily writing in Malcolm's unmistakable hand and struck up a dialogue during which he asked probing personal questions which only his brother-in-law could have known, relating to details of a private conversation which they had just before Malcolm returned to the front. Doyle had not even confided the gist of the conversation to his wife so Lily could not have learned about it from her hostess.

Doyle's interest in the paranormal intensified as he investigated the phenomenon and brought his conversion from agnostic to ardent believer to public attention. He became an active member of the Society for Psychical Research and attended many séances including one at which he heard the voice of his son and saw the revenants of his mother and nephew – an event witnessed by two independent observers. Galvanized by the experience, he embarked on a worldwide lecture tour to promote the cause to which he was now wholeheartedly committed. This was against the advice of his more sceptical friends and much to the derision of his less sympathetic readers. His own spirit photographs were pored over by fellow enthusiasts but were dismissed out of hand by critics who saw him as a credulous old fool taken in by fraudulent mediums.

The New York Ti

VOL. LXIV...NO. 20,923. ..... NEW YORK, SATURDAY, MAY 8, 1915.—TWENTY-FOUR PAGE

LUSITANIA SUNK BY A SUBMARINE, PROBA
TWICE TORPEDOED OFF IRISH COAST; SI
CAPT. TURNER SAVED, FROHMAN AND
WASHINGTON BELIEVES THAT A GRA

SHOCKS THE PRESIDENT

Washington Deeply Stirred by the Loss of American Lives.

BULLETINS AT WHITE HOUSE

Wilson Reads Them Closely, but Is Silent on the Nation's Course.

HINTS OF CONGRESS CALL

Loss of Lusitania Recalls Firm Tone of Our First Warning to Germany.

CAPITAL FULL OF RUMORS

Reports That Liner Was to be Sunk Were Heard Before Actual News Came.

Special to The New York Times.

WASHINGTON, May 7.— Never since that April day, three years ago, when word came that the Titanic had gone down, has Washington been so stirred as it is tonight over the sinking of the Lusitania. The early reports told that there had been no loss of life, but the relief that these advices caused gave way to the greatest concern late this evening when it became known that there had been many deaths. Although they are profoundly reticent, officials realize that this tragedy, involving the loss of American citizens, is likely to bring about a crisis in the international relations of the United States.

It is pointed out that the sinking of the Lusitania is the outcome of a series of incidents that have been the cause of concern to this Government in its endeavor to maintain a strictly neutral position in the great European war.

The Lost Cunard Steamship Lusitania

Cunard Office Here Besieged for News; Fate of 1,918 on Lusitania Long in Doubt

Nothing Heard from the Well-Known Passengers on Board—Story of Disaster Long Unconfirmed While Anxious Crowds Seek Details.

Official news of the sinking of the Lusitania yesterday reached New York in fragmentary reports, and several hours elapsed between the first unveri- | dently a distress call from the liner, which said: "Come at once. Big list. Position ten miles west Kinsale. A third dispatch from Queenstown

List of Saved Includes Capt. Turner; Vanderbilt and Frohman Reported Lost

LONDON, Saturday, May 8, 5:30 A. M. The Press Bureau has received from the British Admiralty at Queenstown a report that all the torpedo boats and tugs and armed trawlers, except the Heron, which went out from Queenstown to the relief of the Lusitania have returned.

These vessels have landed 595 survivors and forty dead. Fifty-two more survivors are reported aboard a steamer, while eleven others and five bodies have been landed at Kinsale, making the total number of survivors 658, besides forty-five dead. The numbers will be verified later, and it is considered possible Kinsale fishing boats may have rescued a few more.

'It is terrible. Terrible. And will have a great influence on the war'.

Doyle shared the belief at the core of the spiritualist creed that the soul is an etheric blueprint of the body and that this explained why discarnate spirits assumed human form. In *The Vital Message*, he wrote:

'The physical basis of all psychic belief, is that the soul is a complete duplicate of the body, resembling it in the smallest particular, although constructed of some far more tenuous material. In ordinary conditions these two bodies are intermingled so that the identity of the finer one is entirely obscured. At death, however, and under certain conditions in the course of life, the two can divide and be seen separately.'

In 1926, he published *The History of Spiritualism*, the result of more than 10 years' research into the subject. The book made a convincing case for the existence of psychic phenomena while acknowledging that there were many fake mediums who had no scruples about fleecing the unwary. During the latter years of his life, Doyle befriended the illusionist Harry Houdini who was incensed by the crude parlour tricks employed by fake mediums and he was intent on exposing them. He and Doyle made an odd but amiable partnership – each with his own agenda – as they attended séances around the country. Ironically, they eventually fell out over Doyle's

Escape artist Harry Houdini (1874–1926) in 1918. He tried many mediums while attempting to get in touch with his beloved mother

The Avebury circle in Wiltshire is
reputed to have been the site of
Bacchanalian rituals in pagan times

insistence on crediting Houdini's miraculous escapes to the illusionist's unconscious paranormal abilities, a theory he expounded in *The Edge of the Unknown*.

Ultimately, Doyle's credibility took a fatal blow after it was revealed that the Cottingley fairy photographs which he had publicly and enthusiastically declared to be genuine were in fact fakes, but his faith in the afterlife remained unshakable until his death in 1930.

The Phantom Fayre

In October 1916, Edith Olivier turned off the main road to Swindon in Wiltshire, in search of a public house in which she could spend the night. It was beginning to rain and she was in no hurry to reach her destination. As she peered through the darkness she saw ahead of her the imposing black monoliths which lined the road to the megalithic stone circle at Avebury. Despite the drizzle she was keen to see the site which at the time was rumoured to have been the scene of bacchanalian rituals in pagan times.

She stopped the car at the end of a long dirt road and climbed a small mound to get a better view. From here she could see a cluster of cottages in the middle of the circle and what appeared to be a village fayre in progress. From the sound of the laughter and the applause which greeted the fire eaters, acrobats and jugglers, the villagers were clearly enjoying themselves, undaunted by the weather. But then she noticed something peculiar. The fiery torches they carried were undimmed by the rain and not a single man, woman or child wore a raincoat nor carried an umbrella. It was as if they walked between the raindrops, indifferent to the drizzle which by now was becoming a steady downpour.

It was nine years before Edith visited the site again. On this occasion she was part of a guided tour and she took the first opportunity to ask the guide about the fayre. He confirmed that the villagers had held an annual fayre on the site, but the custom had stopped in 1850. It was then that Edith realized that the road approaching the mound she had stood upon was no longer there. No trace of it remained. The guide agreed that there had been a long dirt road leading to the site in former times, but it had vanished from all maps made after 1800.

Mass Materializations

While some apparitions appear to be those of earthbound spirits, this explanation cannot account for the many sightings of phantom armies or groups such as the revellers seen by Edith Oliver at Avebury. The conventional theory is that such souls are unaware that they are dead and so continue to relive the drama of their last hours as if trapped in a recurring dream. While this may be true of certain stubbornly persistent personalities, it seems unlikely that hundreds of individual souls would reconvene on the anniversary of their death to relive such an event. What would have compelled the country folk of Avebury, for example, to relive their night at the fayre if there was no tragedy that had entrapped them? It seems more likely that sightings involving a group are an echo across time which can be picked up by anyone possessing heightened perception. In short, the phantoms are not fighting their battles again, the witness is simply tuning into it in their mind and the stronger the emotional residue, the easier it is for one or more people to tune into it. If all phantom battles were genuine collective hauntings, most of Europe would echo to ghostly gunfire from dusk to dawn. Why, then, is one battlefield or village the setting for a spectral restaging and not another? Is it because the phantoms are mere ripples in the ether?

The best known example of a mass re-imagining is the phantom battle of Edgehill which was originally fought on 23 October 1642 between the Royalist Army of King Charles I and the Parliamentary Army commanded by Oliver Cromwell during the English Civil War. So violent was the clash that the ripples were seen and heard by the locals on consecutive weekends two months later.

Naturally, the king was perturbed when he heard rumours that his defeat was being replayed with the same ignominious result so he despatched three of his most loyal officers to see if there was any truth in the tales. They returned ashen faced to report that not only had they witnessed the re-enactment but that they had recognized several of their friends who had been killed on that day, as well as the king's nephew Prince Rupert who had survived.

One of the Canadian Churchill infantry tanks which penetrated the
town of Dieppe in late August, 1942, during the Dieppe Raid

It is tempting to dismiss such tales as the stuff of a more superstitious age, but such phenomena continue to be reported in more modern times. Two English women, holidaying in Dieppe, swore that they heard the sounds of a modern battle just before dawn on the morning of 4 August 1951. The sound of Stuka dive bombers, artillery shells and even the distinctive sound of landing craft hitting the beach was so loud they thought the French army were carrying out a training exercise or perhaps someone was making a war movie. But when they threw open the shutters of their hotel room they saw only empty streets. It was then that they remembered the significance of the date. On the same day nine years previously, a disastrous commando raid cost the lives of almost 1,000 Canadian soldiers.

The battle of Edgehill in Warwickshire. The battle was so fierce, ethereal shockwaves were still being felt and heard weeks later.

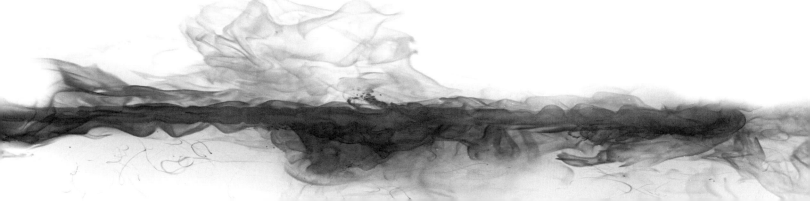

CHAPTER 3

Living
Apparitions

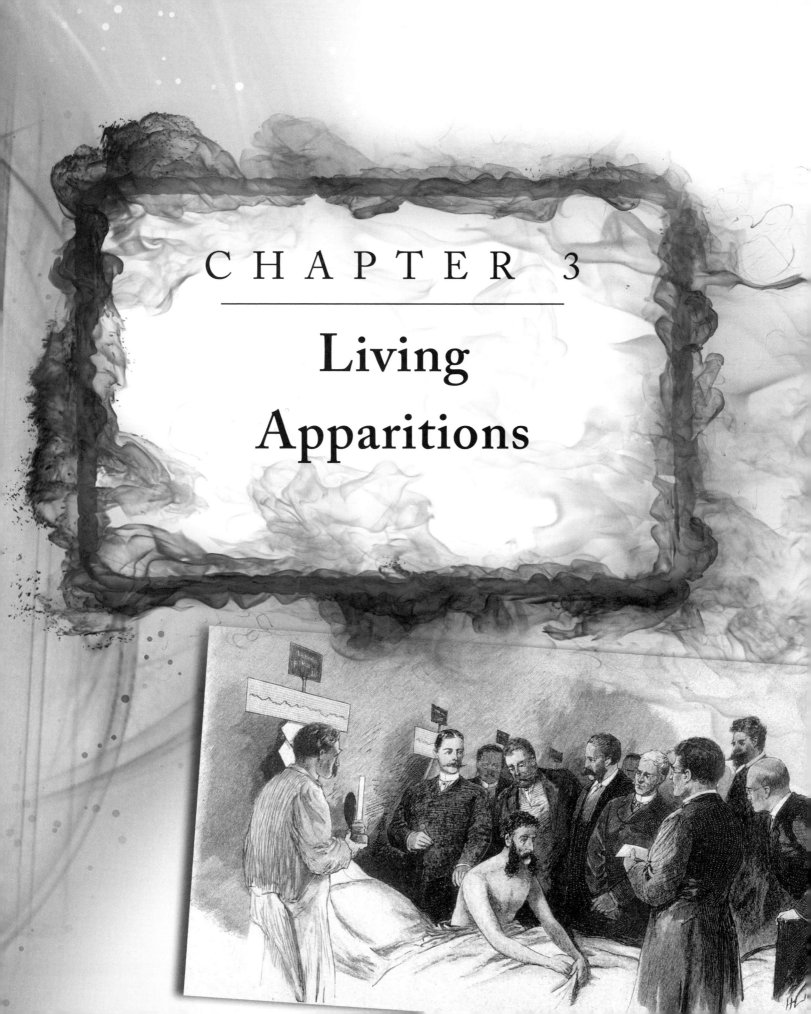

If we want to understand what a ghost is, we only need to look at living apparitions, which include out-of-body experiences, doppelgängers, crisis apparitions and other ethereal phenomena.

After devoting much of his life to paranormal research, Sir Oliver Lodge came to the conclusion that ghosts were not conscious entities but emotional energy recorded in matter. He wrote:

'Take, for example, a haunted house wherein one room is the scene of a ghostly representation of some long past tragedy . . . the original tragedy has been literally photographed on its material surroundings, nay even on the ether itself, by reason of the intensity of emotion felt by those who enacted it; and thenceforth in certain persons an hallucinatory effect is experienced corresponding to such an impression. It is this theory that is made to account for the feeling one has on entering certain rooms, that there is an alien presence therein . . .'

The Stone Tape Theory

This theory was to become known as the 'stone tape' theory, and may account for those sightings in which ghosts replay events from the most traumatic moments in their lives, exhibiting no conscious awareness of any witnesses who may be present. According to the hypothesis this type of ghost is merely an echo. But it does not explain the many incidents where apparitions of the living appear in one location while their body resides elsewhere. Neither does it explain how a living apparition can appear carrying an object, unless they have charged that object with their personal energy at the moment they are projecting their etheric body to the second location.

The SPR recorded a typical example of this in which a lady saw her uncle appear in her home carrying a roll of paper. She naturally assumed that he had decided to pay her a visit, but her uncle looked anxious as he strode across the room and out through an open door. By the time she had followed him outside he was nowhere to be seen. Later that day she received a letter from her father informing her that her uncle was gravely ill. He had died at the very same moment he had appeared in her home. As she stood by her uncle's bed, she felt an urge to look under his pillow and there she found a roll of paper on which, she assumed, he had intended to write a new will favouring her or her father.

It seems that the connection between the uncle's spirit and his body were weakening in the final moments of his life and so he was able to project his essence or his thought form to his niece's home. However, there are also well-documented cases of people who were in the best of health when they projected their image many miles away. The most famous example is that of the French school teacher Emilie Sagee.

In Two Places at Once

Miss Sagee was a popular addition to the staff at the Neuwelcke finishing school for young ladies at Livonia (now Latvia) in 1845, but there was something unsettling

' . . . the many incidents where apparitions of the living appear in
one location while their body resides elsewhere'

'The trouble was that it was not only her mind that was elsewhere. So was her *doppelgänger*, her spirit double'

about her which her pupils could not put into words. She was pretty, capable, conscientious but at the same time distracted, as if her mind was elsewhere. The trouble was that it was not only her mind that was elsewhere. So was her *doppelgänger*, her spirit double.

> *... Emilie could still be clearly seen gathering flowers, although her movements appeared to be sluggish, as if her vitality had drained away*

For weeks there had been rumours that Miss Sagee had been seen in two parts of the school at the same time. Naturally, her colleagues scoffed at the very idea and dismissed it as schoolgirl gossip, but they were soon forced to face the fact that there was more to Emilie than met the eye. One of her pupils, Antoine von Wrangel, was unusually anxious the day she prepared for a high society party. Even so, her girlish excitement cannot account for what she thought she saw when she looked over her shoulder to admire herself in the mirror. There, attending to the hem of her dress, was not one but two Mademoiselle Sagees. Not surprisingly the poor girl fainted on the spot. It became no longer a matter of rumour when a class of 13 girls saw Miss Sagee's *doppelgänger* standing next to its more solid counterpart at the blackboard one day, mimicking the movements of the 'real' Emilie.

However, no one could blame the teacher – she had done nothing improper. By now the whole school was on edge and rife with wild unfounded stories as the girls embellished their experiences for the entertainment of their friends. Eventually, these stories reached the ears of the headmistress, but there were no grounds for a reprimand, never mind a dismissal. Emilie continued to be a conscientious member of staff. The next summer, matters came to a head.

The entire school was assembled one morning in a room overlooking the garden where Miss Sagee could be seen picking flowers. But when the supervising teacher left the room another Miss Sagee appeared in her chair as if from nowhere. Outside, the 'real' Emilie could still be clearly seen gathering flowers, although her movements appeared to be sluggish, as if her vitality had drained away. Two of the more inquisitive girls took the opportunity to step forward and gingerly touch the double in the chair. To one it felt like muslin, but not entirely solid. Another girl passed right through the apparition by walking between the table and the chair. The *doppelgänger* remained still and lifeless. Moments later it faded and the girls observed that the real Emilie became herself again, moving among the flower beds with some purpose.

The girls quizzed Miss Sagee at the first opportunity, but all she could remember was that when she had seen the teacher leave the room she had wished that she could have been there to supervise the class until their teacher returned. Evidently, her thoughts had preceded her.

Unfortunately for Miss Sagee and the school this incident was not the last. Thirty fee-paying pupils were removed by their concerned parents over the following 18 months after stories about the phenomenon became the prime subject of the girls' letters home. Reluctantly, the headmistress was finally forced to let Miss Sagee go. Emilie was saddened but not surprised. It was the nineteenth position she had been forced to leave in her 16-year career.

The Absent MP

Politicians are not usually considered to be imaginative individuals and so the British newspapers made the most of an incident in 1905 in which the living apparition of British MP Sir Frederick Carne Rasch appeared in the House of Commons at the same moment that his body lay in bed suffering from influenza. Sir Frederick had been so anxious to attend the debate that he had obviously willed himself to appear, but his concentration must have weakened because he vanished before the vote was taken. When he returned to Parliament a few days later MPs delighted in prodding him to see if he was really there in the flesh.

Phantom Forerunners

Bi-location may be uncommon, but it is not inconceivable that the mind might be capable of disassociation to such a degree that it enables the essence of a person to appear elsewhere. However, the phenomenon known as the 'phantom forerunner' is far more difficult to explain. The best known example is that of businessman Erkson Gorique who visited Norway in July 1955 for the first time in his life. Or was it?

When Erkson checked into his hotel the clerk greeted him like a valued customer. 'It's good to have you back, Mr Gorique,' said the clerk. 'But I've never been here before,' Gorique replied. 'You must have mistaken me for someone else.' The clerk was certain he was not mistaken. 'But sir, don't you remember? Just a few months ago you dropped in to make a reservation and said you'd be along about this time in the summer. Your name is unusual. That's why I remembered it.' Erkson assured the clerk that this was his first visit to the country. The next day he went to introduce himself to his first potential client, a wholesaler named Olsen, and again he was greeted like a valued customer. 'Ah, Mr Gorique. I'm glad to see you again. Your last visit was much too short.' Erkson was confused and explained what had happened to him at the hotel. To his surprise, Olsen just smiled. 'This is not so unusual here in Norway,' he said. 'In fact, it happens so often we have a name for it. We call it the *vardoger*, or forerunner.'

The phantom forerunner is not exclusively a Norwegian phenomenon, but the country has such an uncommonly high occurrence of such incidents that it has given rise to the greeting, 'Is that you or your *vardoger*?'

In England such apparitions have traditionally been filed away as just another inexplicable ghost story. In 1882, Dr George Wyld reported an incident involving a close acquaintance, Miss Jackson. She had been distributing food to the poor in the neighbourhood on a bitterly cold day when she had a sudden urge to return home to warm herself by the kitchen stove. At that moment her two maids were sitting in the kitchen and observed the door knob turning and the door open revealing a very lifelike Miss Jackson. Startled at their employer's early return they jumped to their feet and watched as she walked to the stove, took off her green kid gloves and warmed her hands. Then vanished. The maids ran to Miss Jackson's mother and described what they had seen, but the old woman assured them that her daughter did not own a pair of green gloves, so they must have imagined it. Half an hour later the lady herself arrived, walked to the kitchen stove, removed her green kid gloves and warmed her hands.

Getting Ahead of Themselves

Frederick Myers' *Phantasms of the Living* includes a case of a multiple forerunner, complete with a horse and carriage.

The Reverend W. Mountford of Boston was visiting a friend when he looked out of the dining room window and saw a carriage approaching the rear of the house. 'Your guests have arrived,' said Mountford, whereupon his host joined him at the window. Both men observed the carriage turn the corner as if it was going to the entrance. But no one rang the door bell and the servants did not announce the arrival of their visitors. Instead, the host's niece entered looking rather flustered having walked all the way from her home, and informed Mountford and his host that her parents had just passed her without acknowledging her or offering her a lift. Ten minutes later the real carriage arrived with the host's brother and his wife. They denied all knowledge of having passed their daughter en route.

Such incidents are not, however, confined to the nineteenth century. As recently as 1980 an Austrian woman, Hilda Saxer, reported seeing a grey Audi belonging to her sister's fiancé, Johann Hofer, passing by at 11.30pm as she left the restaurant where she worked. She waved and the driver, whom she saw clearly and recognized as Johann, smiled and waved back. As she watched the car disappear into the distance the incident struck her as odd because Johann had left the restaurant half an hour earlier.

An hour later Johann's father heard his son's car pull into the driveway and the characteristic sound of the engine as the young man manoeuvred into his parking place. But he did not hear Johann enter the house. The next morning the father was worried

'. . . I chose for my experiment a most insignificant character: a monk short and fat, of an innocent and jolly type' (see page 62)

when his son did not join him for breakfast. The radio had reported a tunnel collapse on the route Johann had taken on his way home from the restaurant at 11.30pm that same night. The father had heard the car in the drive and assumed his son must have left early that morning. It was only days later that rescuers found the wreckage of the car and its driver, crushed beneath tons of rubble.

Thought Forms

Science is slowly and reluctantly beginning to acknowledge that the human mind has the power to project a self-image to another location or to separate spirit and body at will. But what is not generally known, even among the earlier pioneers of parapsychology, is the capacity of the human mind to create and sustain images, or thought forms, which can be empowered with a life of their own. Such forms are known as *tulpas* in the Tibetan esoteric tradition and Golem in the Jewish magical tradition where their creation is considered one of the advanced techniques which must be mastered by initiates before they can become adepts.

The only known record describing the creation of one of these man-made ghosts is the account written by the French mystic and adventurer Alexandra David-Neel (1868–1969) who became the first female lama and the only outsider to be initiated into the secret doctrine of Tibetan Buddhism.

'Besides having had the opportunities of seeing thought-forms, my habitual incredulity led me to make experiments for myself, and my efforts were attended with some success . . . I chose for my experiment a most insignificant character: a monk short and fat, of an innocent and jolly type.

I shut myself in tsams (meditative seclusion) and proceeded to perform the prescribed concentration of thought and other rites. After a few months the phantom monk was formed. His form grew gradually 'fixed' and life-like. He became a kind of guest, living in my apartment. I then broke my se-clusion and started for a tour, with my servants and tents.

The monk included himself in the party. Though I lived in the open, riding on horseback for miles each day, the illusion persisted. I saw the fat trapa (novice monk), now and then it was not necessary for me to think of him to make him appear. The phantom performed various actions of the kind that are natural to travellers and that I had not commanded. For instance, he walked, stopped, looked around him. The illusion was mostly visual, but sometimes I felt as if a robe was lightly rubbing against me and once a hand seemed to touch my shoulder.

The features which I had imagined when building my phantom, gradually underwent a change. The fat, chub-by-cheeked fellow grew leaner, his face assumed a vaguely mocking, sly malignant look. He became more troublesome and bold. In brief, he escaped my control.

Once, a herdsman who brought me a present of butter saw the tulpa in my tent and took it for a live lama. I ought to have let the phenomenon follow its course, but the presence of that unwanted companion began to prove trying to my nerves; it turned into a 'day-nightmare'. Moreover, I was . . . [going] to Lahsa . . . so I decided to dissolve the phantom. I succeeded, but only after six months of hard struggle. My mind-creature was tenacious of life.'

> *The figure appeared solid, but there was an other-worldly aspect to him and a grave expression that unnerved Bruce. When the stranger raised his head, Bruce fled, fearing disaster for all on board*

Crisis Apparitions

Sailors have always been notoriously fond of a good ghost story, but the tale told by seaman Robert Bruce to the nineteenth-century paranormal researcher Robert Dale Owen is both singular and significant as it is one of the earliest recorded examples of a crisis apparition, a phenomenon which is considerably more common than most people might imagine.

In 1828, Bruce was the first mate aboard a cargo ship ploughing through the icy waters off the Canadian coast. During the voyage he entered the captain's cabin to find a stranger bent over a slate, writing intensely and in great haste. The figure appeared solid, but there was an other-worldly aspect to him and a grave expression on his face which unnerved Bruce. When the stranger raised his head and looked at him, Bruce fled, fearing that the presence of the phantom foretold disaster for all on board. He found the skipper on deck and persuaded him to return to the cabin. 'I never was a believer in ghosts,' said Bruce as they made their way below deck, 'but if the truth must be told sir, I'd rather not face it alone.' But when they entered the cabin it was empty. However, they found the slate and on it were scrawled the words 'Steer to the nor'west.'

At first the skipper suspected that the crew were playing a practical joke, so he ordered them all to copy the message. After comparing their handwriting with the original he had to admit he could not identify the culprit. A search of the entire ship failed to find any stowaways, leaving the captain with an unusual dilemma: to ignore the message and risk having the lives of untold lost souls on his conscience, or change his course and risk being thought of as a superstitious old fool in the eyes of the crew. He chose to change course.

Fortunately, he had made the right decision. Within hours they came upon a stricken vessel that had been

'Within hours they came upon a stricken
vessel that had been critically damaged
by an iceberg'

critically damaged by an iceberg. There were only minutes to save the passengers and crew before it sank beneath the waves. Bruce watched with grim satisfaction and relief as the survivors were brought aboard, but then he saw something which haunted him to his dying day. He came face to face with the stranger he had seen scrawling the message earlier that day in the captain's cabin.

After the man had recovered sufficiently to be questioned, Bruce and the captain asked him to copy the message on the slate. They compared the two sets of handwriting. There was no question about it – they were identical. Initially, the 'stranger' couldn't account for his early presence on the ship until he recalled a dream that he had had about the same time that Bruce had seen his 'ghost' in the captain's cabin.

After falling asleep from exhaustion he had dreamt that he was aboard a ship that was coming to rescue him and his fellow survivors. He told the others of his dream to reassure them that help was on its way and he even described the rescue ship, all of which proved correct in every detail. The captain of the wrecked ship confirmed his story. 'He described her appearance and rig,' he told their rescuers, 'and to our utter astonishment, when your vessel hove in sight, she corresponded exactly to his description of her.'

Escaping Worldly Bonds

One of the most revealing examples of an out-of-body experience happens to be one of the first to be published in a respected medical journal, the *St Louis Medical and Surgical Journal*, in February 1890. It is also of great interest because the subject was a doctor who understood what was happening to him and was able to observe his own 'death' with clinical detachment.

Dr A.S. Wiltse of Kansas contracted typhoid fever in the summer of 1889. After saying his last goodbyes to his family, he lapsed into unconsciousness. But although his body exhibited no signs of life – neither pulse nor heartbeat – inside his own dead body Dr Wiltse was fully conscious and observing the grieving around him with a curious detachment. It was as if he had reverted to pure consciousness, acutely alert but unemotional. 'I learned that the epidermis [skin] was the outside boundary of the ultimate tissues, so to speak, of the soul.' He then felt a gentle swaying and a separation which he compared to the snapping of tiny cords. In another moment he was looking out from his skull . 'As I emerged from the head I floated up and down . . . like a soap bubble . . . until I at last broke loose from the body and fell lightly to the

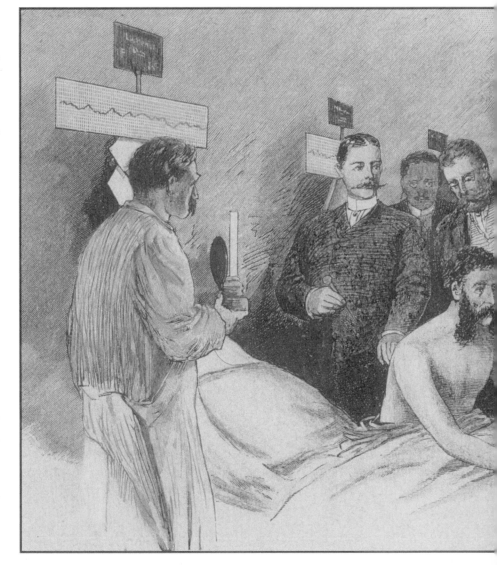

floor, where I slowly rose and expanded into the full stature of a man.' At this point he felt embarrassed to discover that there were two women in the room, but then he realized that he was not naked but clothed – merely by wishing to be so.

Here, perhaps, is a crucial clue as to why ghosts appear in the form that they do, often younger and in better health than when their physical shell expired. Dr Wiltse had left his body as a

As I emerged from the head I floated up and down . . . like a soap bubble . . . until I at last broke loose from the body and fell lightly to the floor . . .

' . . . Dr Wiltse had been clinically dead for four hours, but had suffered no permanent brain damage or otherill effects, contrary to the laws of medical science'

shapeless, colourless bubble of etheric energy, but as soon as he became aware of his surroundings he was able to assume a more acceptable form and projected his own self-image which would have been his ideal self. It was then that he passed straight through another man in the room before he realized what he was doing. He saw the funny side of the situation, which may have been partly due to the relief in finding himself very much alive in this new reality. He intuitively 'knew' that this was his natural state, his true self. His personality was the same after death as it had been in life, but he had left behind his fears and his sense of identity. He no longer identified with the body on the bed. He was no longer concerned with what happened to it. That was the part of him that felt pain, disappointment, regrets. This 'greater self' was beyond those petty, worldly concerns. If this was 'death', it was nothing more than slipping off a worn out coat or walking through an open door into the world outside.

He was becoming accustomed to his new 'body' and was eager to explore. As he passed through the door he looked back and saw a thin elasticated web-like cord connecting him to the lifeless body on the bed, the etheric equivalent of the umbilical cord. So long as he remained attached by this cord he knew he could return to his body at will. He was not dead, as he had originally thought, but merely temporarily detached – a living ghost. He walked along a road idly wondering where the other 'dead' people might be and if this is all there

'But I was now infinitely more beautiful. My
face appeared as if it were chiselled out of the
finest alabaster and it seemed transparent ...'

was to being dead. Suddenly he lost consciousness and when he next became aware of where he was he found himself in an unfamiliar landscape over which hung a black cloud. Ahead he saw three enormous rocks which an inner voice informed him was the boundary to the 'eternal world'. At this point he intuitively knew that this was as far as he would be permitted to go on this occasion and with that realization he woke up – much to the surprise of his doctor. Dr Wiltse had been clinically dead for four hours, but had suffered no permanent brain damage or other ill effects, contrary to the laws of medical science. A religious man might call this a miracle, but in the years that followed it became increasingly evident that such out-of-body experiences have been shared by hundreds of thousands of people around the world and that they are neither miraculous nor supernatural. They are perfectly natural.

The next thing I knew was that I . . . was standing on the floor beside my bed looking down attentively on my own physical body lying in it

A Ghost in the Mirror

Vermont housewife Caroline Larsen considered herself an unremarkable person, preoccupied with social conventions, her standing in the community and her obligations as the dutiful middle-class wife of an amateur musician. But, one autumn evening in 1910, she discovered her true self as she went one step further than Dr Wiltse had done during a strikingly similar out-of-body experience.

As Mrs Larsen lay in bed listening to her husband and his friends practising a Beethoven string quartet she began to feel a creeping sense of foreboding. No matter how hard she tried to focus on the soothing strains of the music she was unable to relax and throw off her apprehension.

'The overpowering oppression deepened and soon numbness crept over me until every muscle became

paralyzed . . . finally everything became a blank. The next thing I knew was that I, I myself, was standing on the floor beside my bed looking down attentively on my own physical body lying in it.'

She observed that her room was unchanged. But after proceeding down the hall into the bathroom she instinctively reached for the light switch and was surprised that she couldn't connect with it. It was then that she noticed that the room was illuminated by a softer light emanating from her own body.

'Looking in to the mirror I became aware for the first time of the astonishing transformation I had undergone. Instead of seeing a middle-aged woman, I beheld the figure of a girl about 18 years of age. I recognised the form and features of my girlhood. But I was now infinitely more beautiful. My face appeared as if it were chiselled out of the finest alabaster and it seemed transparent, as did my arms and hands when I raised them to touch my hair . . . But they were not entirely translucent for in the centre of the arms and hands and fingers there was a darker, more compact substance, as in x-ray photographs. My eyes, quite strong in the physical body, were piercingly keen now . . . my hair, no longer grey, was now, as in my youth, dark brown and it fell in waves over my shoulders and down my back. And, to my delight, I was dressed in the loveliest white shining garment imaginable – a sleeveless one-piece dress, cut low at the neck and reaching almost to the ankles.'

She then had the idea to walk down the stairs and surprise her husband and his friends in her new youthful form.

'Turning away from the mirror I walked out into the hall, enjoying in anticipation the success of my plan, I stepped on gaily. I revelled in the feeling of bodily

lightness . . . I moved with the freedom of thought.

'[But] just as I came to the little platform which divides the stairway into two flights I saw, standing before me, a woman spirit in shining clothes with arms outstretched and with forefinger pointing upwards . . . she spoke to me sternly, "Where are you going? Go back to your body!" . . . I knew instinctively – that from this spirit's command and authority there was no appeal.'

Returning to her room she found her body on the bed, just as 'still and lifeless' as she had left it.

'I viewed it with feelings of loathing and disappointment. I knew that I would soon have to enter it again, no matter how ugly it seemed to me or how much I shrank from it. In another instant I had again joined with my physical form. With a gasp and a start, I woke up in it.'

The image she describes may sound like an aging person's fantasy, but the deceased often appear as their younger selves. In effect, they are so used to having a physical body that they cannot imagine themselves without one and so manifest as their ideal self-image.

Projecting His Own Ghost

Most of the hundreds of thousands of out-of-body experiences and near-death experiences that have been recorded involve the involuntary separation of the spirit from the body at a moment of crisis or physical danger or during an altered state of consciousness. But there are a surprising number of incidents in which the astral traveller has consciously projected their spirit double to another location.

Sylvan Joseph Muldoon, the son of a spiritualist in Clinton, Iowa, claimed to have acquired the ability to leave his body at will. He had enjoyed dozens of liberating out-of-body experiences since the age of 12, but it was not until 10 years later, in 1925, that he had

Sylvan Joseph Muldoon, the son of a spiritualist in Clinton, Iowa, claimed to have acquired the ability to leave his body at will

the confirmation that what he was experiencing was more than a lucid dream.

During this excursion he found himself propelled at incredible speed to an unfamiliar farmhouse somewhere in the same rural region where he lived. There he observed four people passing a pleasant evening, including an attractive young girl who was engaged in sewing a black dress. They seemed unaware of his presence so he wandered around the room noting the furnishings and ornaments until it occurred to him that he had no business being there. With that thought he returned to his body. It was more than a month later that Muldoon happened to see the same girl in town and asked her where she lived. She thought he was prying or being 'fresh' and told him to mind his own business, but when he described her home in astonishing detail and told her how he knew this, she confirmed everything that he had seen.

The Astral Visit

To obtain a truly objective result in this experiment you will need the co-operation of a friend whom you can trust to take the exercise seriously. The object of the exercise is to obtain conclusive proof of your ability to visit them at will in your etheric body.

To do this ask your friend to put a book of their choice on a chair in their bedroom with the cover face up. They must not tell you what they are going to place there and they should not decide which book to use until shortly beforehand, otherwise it is possible that you will obtain the answer by telepathy instead. Decide on a specific time for the experiment so that your partner can note any changes that may occur in the atmosphere and can be alert at the allotted time.

Again, be patient. It may take several attempts to make the breakthrough.

'During this excursion he found himself propelled at incredible speed to an unfamiliar farmhouse somewhere in the same rural region where he lived'

Inducing an Out-Of-Body Experience

If you wish to prove the existence of the etheric body for yourself, this exercise can be used to trigger an OBE. Although such experiences occur naturally and should never be forced, this safe and simple technique for the gradual separation of spirit and body has been practised by mystics through the centuries. However, it needs to be stressed that such techniques should never be attempted while under the influence of alcohol or drugs of any kind. Nor should they be attempted by anyone who has, or is currently suffering from, any form of psychological disturbance, abnormal grief or trauma. If in doubt you should seek medical advice before attempting any of these techniques.

1 Lie on your back on the floor, an exercise mat or bed and ensure you support your neck with a small pillow or cushion. Your arms should be loose by your side and not crossed over on your chest or stomach. Your legs must be straight.

2 Establish a steady rhythm of breathing and, as you dissolve deeper into relaxation, repeat a phrase that relaxes you and induces a sense of security, such as 'calm and centred' or 'I am perfect and at peace'.

3 After a few minutes you may sense a warming of the solar plexus centre beneath your navel. Visualize a soft pulsing light in your abdomen as this energy centre softens, loosening the silver umbilical cord of etheric energy which connects your spirit double to your physical shell. Feel it unwinding as you sink deeper and deeper into a detached state. As you do so you will begin to lose the sense of the weight and solidity of your body. You become lighter with every breath.

4 Now visualize your breath forming a cushion of air under your back until you feel that you can float away like a cloud on the breeze. Feel yourself rising a few inches above your body and then being drawn back by the silver cord as you enjoy exercising control over your new found ability. You are safe and in control at all times. You only have to wish to return to your body and you will do so in an instant.

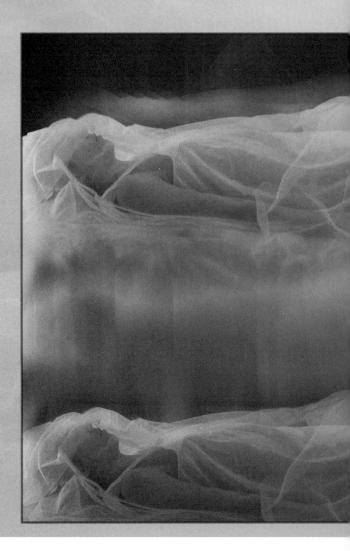

5 Transfer your awareness to this 'real you' by visualizing the room from a new perspective as if you were standing and walking around. Then imagine yourself looking down on your physical body from the ceiling – you may find you have 'popped out' and are now free to explore. If not, visualize yourself exploring the room in your spirit body and your awareness will be transferred to it. Until you are comfortable being outside your body it would be advisable to stay within the confines of your own home, but as soon as you feel confident you can begin to explore the neighbourhood and beyond.

• Be patient and persistent. It may take several attempts to make the breakthrough. You will know that you are out of the body and not dreaming because you will experience a euphoria as you realize you have liberated the real you. If you want to obtain absolute proof of this you can try the following experiment. However, if you do so, make sure your partner will treat it seriously or you risk having your confidence undermined.

• **Remember:** You are under no obligation to try this exercise. Out-of-body experiences are a natural phenomenon and should never be forced. If you feel uncomfortable for any reason do not attempt this exercise or you risk instilling fear in your self which may inhibit your development.

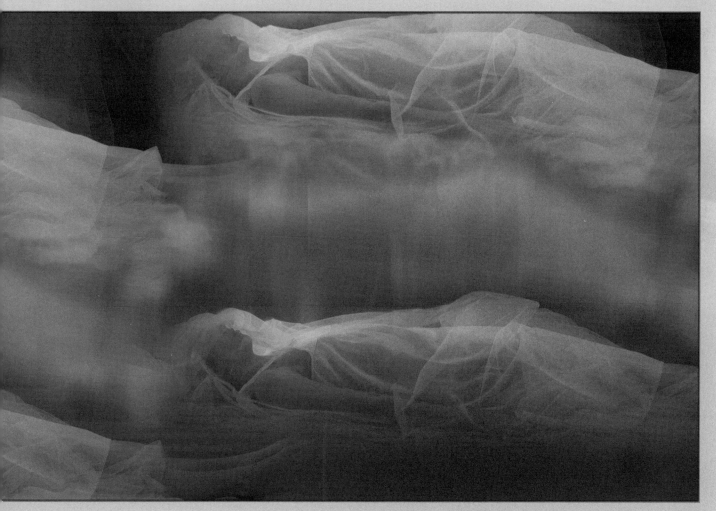

A Message From the Other Side

Near-death experiences typically involve an individual leaving their body, passing through a tunnel of light into a more vibrant reality and then returning to their body with a renewed appetite for life. But the experience of Dr Karl Novotny was different in one significant respect. He did not return. Instead he described the process of dying from the other side using the services of a medium. Such anecdotal evidence usually has the sceptics shrieking with derision, but the case of Dr Novotny is notable for several reasons.

Two days prior to his death in Easter 1965, Novotny's friend, Grete Schroeder, dreamt that he appeared before her to announce his death. Neither Schroeder nor Novotny were interested in psychic phenomena – in fact quite the reverse. Novotny was a pupil of the celebrated psychologist Arthur Adler and was inclined to explain every phenomenon in terms of the untapped powers of the unconscious. When Novotny died as 'he' had predicted, Grete felt compelled to consult a medium rather than risk becoming prey to doubts for the rest of her life. She evidently chose a reputable psychic because not only did the details of his death – as relayed by the medium – tally with the facts, she also transcribed what he told her in a script which Grete recognized as Novotny's own handwriting even though the medium had never met him. The description of his dying moments is uncannily similar to that related by thousands of other individuals from around the world who have had a near-death experience and it is worth quoting for comparison.

'I turned back to my companions and found myself looking down at my own body on the ground. My friends were in despair, calling for a doctor, and trying to get a car to take me home. But I was well and felt no pains. I couldn't understand what had happened. I bent down and felt the heart of the body lying on the ground. Yes – it had ceased to beat – I was dead. But I was still alive! I spoke to my friends, but they neither saw me nor answered me . . .

And then there was my dog, who kept whining pitifully, unable to decide to which of me he should go, for he saw me in two places at once, standing up and lying down on the ground.

'Near-death experiences typically involve an individual leaving their body, passing through a tunnel of light into a more vibrant reality and then returning to their body with a renewed appetite for life'

Novotny was a pupil of the celebrated psychologist Arthur Adler and was inclined to explain every phenomenon in terms of the untapped powers of the unconscious

When all the formalities were concluded and my body had been put in a coffin, I realised that I must be dead. But I wouldn't acknowledge the fact; for, like my teacher Arthur Adler, I did not believe in after-life.'

Novotny then visited his friend Grete and found her sitting alone and immersed in grief, but again his attempts to communicate were fruitless. She did not seem aware of his presence and did not respond when he spoke to her.

'It was no use. I had to recognise the truth. When finally I did so I saw my dear mother coming to meet me with open arms, telling me that I had passed into the next world – not in words, of course, since these only belong to the earth. Even so, I couldn't credit her statement and thought I must be dreaming. This belief continued for a long time. I fought against the truth and was most unhappy . . .'

The Psychologist and the Spirit

Dutch psychologist Elleke Van Kraalingen was a pragmatic, scientifically-minded woman who prided herself on having a healthy scepticism towards the supernatural. The demands of her professional life meant that she was totally grounded in the here and now and had no desire to probe the secrets of life and death. That was until she witnessed the sudden and violent death of her fiancé, Hermod, in a hit and run accident. In her autobiography, *Beyond the Boundary of Life and Death*, Elleke describes how she was awoken to the reality of the soul's survival after death as she knelt over his body

'She then "saw" his soul leave his body as a mist'

and sensed a 'tearing apart' of the subtle bond between them, as it was severed. She then 'saw' his soul leave his body as a mist and sensed his presence standing behind her during her desperate efforts to revive him. While the emotional part of her was in turmoil, the intellectual aspect of her being calmly reassured her that he was well. After the ambulance had taken his body, Elleke walked back to their hotel, all the while sensing that Hermod was beside her holding her hand.

That evening he materialized in their room, sitting on the edge of her bed as solid as he had been 24 hours earlier. Having been trained to dismiss everything connected with the paranormal as irrational and the creation of a troubled mind, Elleke instinctively denied what she was seeing as a hallucination brought on by grief. She covered her eyes and affirmed that she was imagining it, but when she looked again he was still there, as large as life. It was at this point that she heard him speak inside her head in a quiet consoling tone that was quite distinct from her own thoughts. 'I'm still here,' he told her. 'There is no death, there is no time, there's only reality.'

He was not the only discarnate spirit in the room. Elleke sensed the presence of others that she felt were there to help his transition from this world to the next. When he and his companions had gone she wrote everything down so that she could analyze her thought processes at a later date when she was not so emotionally involved. She hoped this would help her discover the cause of her delusion. Even at this point Elleke was convinced that what she had seen was a projection of her own internal turmoil. Perhaps this was a replay of her memories of Hermod triggered automatically as a result of an emotional crisis, like a drowning person who sees their life replayed in their mind like a film.

But the next day Hermod reappeared again, as solid as he was when he was alive. Elleke was the only person who could see him, presumably because she perceived him with the eyes of the spirit – the inner eye or third eye

After the ambulance had taken his body, Elleke walked back to their hotel, all the while sensing that Hermod was beside her holding her hand

of psychic sight. That day he remained with her as she sleepwalked through the traumatic process of identifying his body and dealing with the police. It was only after the funeral that she sensed him withdraw, leaving her to cope with life alone.

And then an extraordinary thing happened. Several days later, while Elleke was meditating in an attempt to calm and centre herself, he reappeared and drew her out of her body. In this state she was able to look down at her physical self sitting cross-legged on the floor and view the world with a detachment she could not have attained while in her body. She described this state as liberating and more vibrantly real than what she had previously considered to be reality. When they embraced she felt totally absorbed in the core of his being, not merely comforted or connected as she had done when they were in their physical bodies. She sensed that it was only when they were out of body that they could truly know each other. Soon she felt drained and snapped back into her physical shell – either the effort of remaining out of the body for a long period was too much for her, or perhaps he was unintentionally draining her of her life force in order to remain at this level.

Over the following months, Hermod materialized and took her on an astral tour of other realms or realities where discarnate beings communicated with them by thought alone. In these realms the dead created their own heaven and hell according to their expectations and beliefs. Those who could not accept their own death remained earthbound, reliving the most significant experiences of their lives as if in a recurring dream and visible to the living as ghosts.

Psychology and the Paranormal

Mainstream science and orthodox religion are considered custodians of good sense by those who believe in the infallibility of science or the absolute truth of the Bible.

In his youth Jung witnessed at first hand phenomena during séances held by his 15-year-old cousin, Helene Preiswerk, who had developed mediumistic powers

But both fields have their share of individualists who are not as rigid in their thinking as one might suspect.

Carl Jung (1875–1961), the founding father of analytical psychology, was fiercely proud of his reputation as a pioneer of the new science, but in private he continually wrestled to reconcile psychology and the paranormal. He wrote:

'In the end the only events in my life worth telling are those when the imperishable world irrupted into this transitory one. That is why I speak chiefly of inner experiences, among which I include my dreams and visions. These form the prima materia of my scientific work. They were the fiery magma out of which the stone that had to be worked was crystallised.'

Jung's maternal grandfather was the vicar of Kesswil, Switzerland, and was said to be blessed with 'second sight'. His family blithely accepted that he conversed with the dead in defiance of church edicts. As Jung wrote:

'My mother often told me how she had to sit behind him while he wrote his sermons because he could not bear [to have] ghosts pass behind him while he was studying. The presence of a living human being at his back frightened them away!'

His own home life was equally unconventional. As a child Jung was constantly aware of the presence of spirits.

'From the door to my mother's room came a frightening influence. At night Mother was strange and mysterious.

One night I saw coming from her door a faintly luminous indefinite figure whose head detached itself from the neck and floated along in front of it, in the air like a little moon.'

In his youth Jung witnessed at first hand phenomena during séances held by his 15-year-old cousin, Helene Preiswerk, who had developed mediumistic powers. Helene channelled a number of dead relatives who spoke in their own distinctive voices and passed on personal details which the young 'Helly' could not have known about. Jung was particularly struck by the change in his cousin's manner when she went into a trance. She exhibited a maturity and breadth of knowledge that was at odds with her provincial frivolous nature. But although Jung was initially convinced that her abilities were genuine, he later felt obliged to find a rational explanation when writing up the case for his inaugural dissertation. It was a classic example of multiple personality, he concluded, brought on by hysteria and sexual repression. Although such a diagnosis might account for a good number of fraudulent mediums, Jung also knew that he risked being discredited as a serious man of science if he subscribed to the spiritualist creed. Privately, however, he remained a firm believer in the paranormal and was intolerant of those, like Freud, who scoffed at such things on principle.

'I wondered at the sureness with which they could assert that things like ghosts and table turning were impossible and therefore fraudulent, and on the other hand, at the evidently anxious nature of their defensiveness. For myself I found such possibilities extremely interesting and attractive. They added another dimension to my life; the world gained depth and background.'

In his autobiography, *Memories, Dreams, Reflections,* Jung describes his own paranormal experiences including the plague of poltergeist activity with which his home was besieged in the summer of 1916.

'The house was filled as if it was crammed full of spirits and the air was so thick it was scarcely possible to breathe ... My eldest daughter saw a white figure pass through

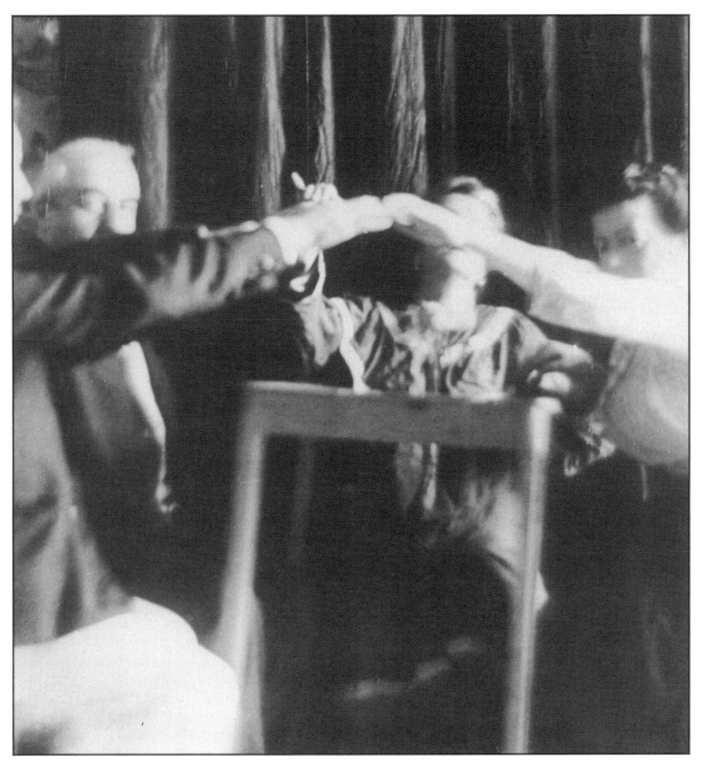

Table tilting or turning in Geneva, 1906

her room. My second daughter, independently . . . related that twice in the night her blanket had been snatched away . . .'

Over three successive evenings he channelled a series of messages from discarnate spirits which formed the basis of Seven Sermons From The Dead, a series of Hermetic discourses on the nature of God, and Good and Evil in a contrived archaic style. It was only when he had completed this task that the spirits withdrew and the 'haunting' ceased. Jung dismissed the attendant poltergeist activity as 'exteriorization phenomena', meaning that he interpreted it as his own unconscious demanding his attention to the coming task.

'It has taken me virtually forty-five years to distil within the vessel of my scientific work the things I experienced and wrote down at that time . . .

The years when I was pursuing my inner images were the most important in my life – in them everything essential was decided. It all began then; the later details are only supplements and clarifications of the material that burst forth from the unconscious, and at first swamped me. It was the prima materia *for a lifetime's work.'*

In 1919, Jung wrote a paper for the SPR entitled 'The Psychological Foundation of Belief in Spirits' in which he stated that such phenomena can be dismissed as projections of the unconscious mind

The Haunted Cottage

Despite a lifetime of witnessing paranormal phenomena at first hand, Jung still felt the need to hedge his bets. In 1919, he wrote a paper for the SPR entitled 'The Psychological Foundation of Belief in Spirits' in which he stated that such phenomena can be dismissed as projections of the unconscious mind. The following year the spirits had their revenge.

In 1920, Jung arrived in Britain on a lecture tour and stayed in a country cottage so that he could be alone. The rent was nominal, but either Jung did not suspect that this might be because the place was haunted, or he didn't

attach any importance to it. On the first weekend he was disturbed by a rancid odour permeating the bedroom, although there was no obvious source of the smell. The following weekend, the smell returned accompanied by a rustling noise as if an animal was exploring the room, or perhaps a woman in a crinoline dress was brushing against the walls. On the third weekend, his work was interrupted by inexplicable rapping sounds. Again, there was no obvious source for these noises. On the fifth weekend, he was startled to wake up next to the ghost of an old woman, her face partly dissolved as if pressed into a pillow.

The locals subsequently confirmed that the cottage was inhabited by a malevolent spirit and that is why they refused to stay there after dusk. But Jung was not so easily disturbed. He invited the friend who had rented the cottage for him to spend the night, and the man was so terrified when he heard phantom footsteps that he abandoned his bed after just a few hours and spent the rest of the night sleeping in the garden with a shotgun by his side. Jung recollected, 'It gave me considerable satisfaction after my colleague had laughed so loudly at my fear of ghosts.'

His own attitude to such phenomena remained ambiguous despite his extraordinary experiences. He was clearly impressed with the 'performance' of respected medium Rudi Schneider (whose talents were detailed in Thomas Mann's essay 'An Experience With The Occult') although he could not bring himself to credit his cousin Helly with the same abilities. For all his insights into the human mind, Jung was forced to admit that he did not have an explanation for these phenomena. 'Either there are physical processes which cause psychic happenings, or there is a pre-existent psyche which organises matter.'

If he expected his mentor Sigmund Freud to resolve the question he was to be cruelly disappointed. In one particularly memorable episode, Jung and Freud were

'He invited the friend who had rented the cottage for him to spend the night, and the man was so terrified when he heard phantom footsteps that he abandoned his bed after just a few hours . . .'

arguing about the existence of poltergeists when a loud report shook a nearby bookcase. Freud insisted it was merely the furniture settling, even though the weather was mild and could not have caused the wood to contract or expand. But Jung had felt heat building up in his solar plexus from his frustration at being treated like a wilful student of the great man and he was certain that he himself was the source of the kinetic activity. 'There will be another report in a moment,' he predicted and, sure enough, there was.

Out of This World

Paranormal phenomena and psychic experiences pursued Jung all through his life. Then, in April 1944, at the age of 68, he had an out-of-body experience that was to have a profound effect on his perception of the world and which turned his concept of reality on its head. The extracts below are from his autobiography, *Memories, Dreams, Reflections* (1961):

'It seemed to me that I was high up in space. Far below I saw the globe of the earth, bathed in a gloriously blue light. I saw the deep blue sea and the continents. Far below my feet lay Ceylon, and in the distance ahead of me the subcontinent of India. My field of vision did not include the whole earth, but its global shape was plainly distinguishable and its outlines shone with a silvery gleam through that wonderful blue light . . . I knew that I was on the point of departing from the earth.

Later I discovered how high in space one would have to be to have so extensive a view – approximately a thousand miles! The sight of the earth from this height was the most glorious thing I had ever seen . . . I myself was floating in space.'

At this point Jung felt that he was stripped down to the essence of his being.

' . . . everything I aimed at or wished for or thought, the whole phantasmagoria of earthly existence, fell away or was stripped from me – an extremely painful process. Nevertheless something remained; it was as if I now carried along with me everything I had ever experienced

or done, everything that had happened around me . . . This experience gave me a feeling of extreme poverty, but at the same time of great fullness. There was no longer anything I wanted or desired. I existed in an objective form; I was what I had been and lived. At first the sense of annihilation predominated, of having been stripped or pillaged; but suddenly that became of no consequence. Everything seemed to be past.'

While he was contemplating the significance of this greater reality he became aware of another presence, that of his doctor who appeared before Jung in his 'primal form'.

' . . . a mute exchange of thought took place between us. The doctor had been delegated by the earth to deliver a message to me, to tell me that there was a protest against my going away. I had no right to leave the earth and must return. The moment I heard that, the vision ceased.

I was profoundly disappointed, for now it all seemed to have been for nothing. The painful process of defoliation had been in vain . . . Life and the whole world struck me as a prison, and it bothered me beyond measure that I should again be finding all that quite in order. I had been so glad to shed it all . . . I felt violent resistance to my doctor because he had brought me back to life. At the same time, I was worried about him. "His life is in danger, for heaven's sake! He has appeared to me in his primal form! When anybody attains this form it means he is going to die, for already he belongs to the 'greater company'." Suddenly the terrifying thought came to me that the doctor would have to die in my stead. I tried my best to talk to him about it, but he did not understand me. Then I became angry with him.

In actual fact I was his last patient. On April 4, 1944 . . . I was allowed to sit up on the edge of my bed for the first time since the beginning of my illness, and on this same day the doctor took to his bed and did not leave it again. I heard that he was having intermittent attacks of fever. Soon afterward he died of septicemia . . .

It was not a product of imagination. The visions and experiences were utterly real; there was nothing subjective about them; they all had a quality of absolute objectivity.'

C. S. Lewis (1898–1963) in his usual 'well-worn' tweeds

In *Synchronicity* (1952), Jung cites the case of a woman patient who left her body during childbirth and observed the medical procedures used to revive her which she described to her nurse after recovering consciousness. She was correct in every detail. The most astonishing part was her discovery that while in her astral body she possessed perceptions independent of her physical senses. At the same moment that she was watching the frantic efforts of the medical staff, she was also aware of a vivid pastoral landscape 'behind' her which she knew to be the 'other world'. By a conscious effort of will she remained focused on the doctors and nurses for fear that she might be tempted by the bliss of the other world to drift into it and not return.

Crisis of Faith

Eminent theological scholar Canon J.B. Phillips regarded himself as a conscientious servant of the Church of the England with an unshakable belief in the articles of his faith. These denied the existence of apparitions other than the Holy Ghost, yet Canon Phillips was convinced that he had had a visitation from C.S. Lewis, the recently deceased Christian philosopher and author of the *Narnia* novels, in late November 1963. He confided the details of his encounter in his journal.

'Let me say at once that I am incredulous by nature and as unsuperstitious as they come. I have never bothered about . . . any of the current superstitions which may occupy the human heart in the absence of faith . . . But the late C.S. Lewis, whom I did not know very well and had only seen in the flesh once, but with whom I had corresponded a fair amount, gave me an unusual experience. A few days after his death, while I was watching television, he 'appeared' sitting in a chair a few feet from me, and spoke a few words which were particularly relevant to the

He was ruddier in complexion than ever, grinning all over his face, and, as the saying has it, positively glowing with health

difficult circumstances through which I was passing. He was ruddier in complexion than ever, grinning all over his face, and, as the saying has it, positively glowing with health. The interesting thing to me was that I had not been thinking about him at all . . . A week later, this time when I was in bed reading before going to sleep, he appeared again, even more rosily radiant than before, and repeated to me the same message, which was very important to me at the time. I was a little puzzled by this and mentioned it to a certain saintly bishop who was then living in retirement in Dorset. His reply was, 'My dear J. this sort of thing is happening all the time.'

Canon Phillips' experience is noteworthy for several reasons. The first being that he was not a believer in spirits – in fact he was effectively under orders to deny their existence and had much to lose by admitting to what he had seen. Secondly, he saw the same apparition on two separate occasions which would seem to rule out the possibility that they were hypnagogic hallucinations (the hypnagogic state is that state between being awake and falling asleep), or waking dreams caused by fatigue or stress. Thirdly, Lewis' 'ghost' spoke and the advice he gave was relevant to Canon Phillips' situation. Furthermore, on the one occasion when Phillips had met Lewis during the latter's lifetime, Lewis was dressed in clerical robes and not the 'well-worn tweeds' in which he appeared after death and which was his customary mode of dress. It was only after Phillips had reported his encounter with the author's ghost that he learnt that Lewis dressed in tweeds. And, lastly, the bishop had evidently heard of such things in the course of his ministrations and took it all in his stride. If it was not a genuine encounter there is only one other explanation, that the apparition was a projection of Canon Phillips' subconscious which took the form of a friend he admired and whose advice he would heed. And that is no less remarkable a phenomenon.

Thomas Edison (1847–1931) in 1928. In 1892, he received a patent for his invention of a two-way telegraph machine, going on to think of designs for a device to contact the dead (see page 84)

The first serious hint that audible communication with the departed may be feasible occurred in June 1959 when Swedish ornithologist Friedrich Jurgenson replayed a recording of birdsong and heard a faint Norwegian voice discussing the habits of nocturnal birds

Voices From Beyond

In the 1920s, Thomas Edison, the prolific American inventor of the phonograph, the electric lamp, the microphone and the kinetoscope (a forerunner of the movie projector), to name but a few of his creations, admitted to working on a device for contacting the dead. He told *Scientific American* magazine that he believed it was perfectly possible 'to construct an apparatus which will be so delicate that if there are personalities in another existence or sphere who wish to get in touch with us in this existence or sphere, this apparatus will at least give them a better opportunity to express themselves than the tilting tables and raps and Ouija boards and mediums and the other crude methods now purported to be the only means of communication.' Unfortunately, Edison passed over before he could build the contraption, but it now seems that his dream may be closer to being realized than ever before.

The first serious hint that audible communication with the departed may be feasible occurred in June 1959 when Swedish ornithologist Friedrich Jurgenson replayed a recording of birdsong and heard a faint Norwegian voice discussing the habits of nocturnal birds. At first he thought it must be interference from a local broadcaster or amateur radio enthusiast, but there was no transmitter in the area. Intrigued, he decided to make test recordings at his home to determine whether or not the tape recorder was faulty, but when he listened to the recordings he caught something which chilled him to the marrow. There were voices on the tape that he had not heard when he was recording. They mentioned Jurgenson and his dog by name and correctly predicted an incoming phone call and the name of the caller. In subsequent recording sessions, Jurgenson merely had to turn on the tape for an unspecified length of time and then play it back to hear a babble of faint voices talking among themselves, commenting on him and the other people whom he had invited to be present as witnesses.

As Jurgenson researched the subject he discovered that EVP (Electronic Voice Phenomena) were only one aspect of a wider range of phenomena known collectively as Instrumental Transcommunication (ITC) covering spirit communication through all manner of electronic equipment including radios, telephones, television sets and even computers. Although the more common forms of ITC are indistinct disembodied voices, there have been incidents where the face of the deceased has been seen and positively identified by their relatives breaking through a regular broadcast on a television screen.

Recording EVP

If you want to experiment with EVP all you need is a digital recording device such as a mini-disc, DAT recorder or computer and an analogue radio. Cassette recorders are unsuitable as they produce excessive hiss at low volume and also mechanical noise which can cloak the signal. The radio needs to be tuned to a frequency between stations so that a background of white noise is audible for the voices to print through. You will have to be objective when analyzing what you have recorded as it is possible to interpret random interference, 'print-through' from previous recordings, digital 'artefacts' and signals bleeding from adjacent stations as being significant.

The potential for misinterpretation is so common that a medical term has been coined to describe it – auditory pareidolia. Consequently, it is necessary to remain detached and foster a healthy scepticism, otherwise you are at risk of reading something significant into what is really only random interference.

Pope Pius XII at the age of 75, in 1951 (see page 86)

The Pope's Parapsychologists

In 1952, two Italian Catholic priests, Father Ernetti and Father Gemelli, were playing back a tape recording they had made of Gregorian chants when they heard an inaudible whispering in the silence when the singing had stopped. At first they thought it might be radio interference or 'print through', the echo of an earlier recording which occurs when the tape has not been properly erased or the playback heads are misaligned. But when they turned up the volume Father Gemelli recognized the whispering as the voice of his father who had died many years earlier. It was calling Gemelli by his childhood nickname. 'Zucchini, it is clear, don't you know it is I?'

Contact with the dead is forbidden by the Catholic church, but there was no denying what they had heard. So the priests dutifully asked for an audience with Pope Pius XII in Rome and put the problem before him. The Pope's verdict was later published in the Italian Journal *Astra*.

> 'Dear Father Gemelli, you really need not worry about this. The existence of this voice is strictly a scientific fact and has nothing to do with spiritism. The recorder is totally objective. It receives and records only sound waves from wherever they come. This experiment may perhaps become the cornerstone for a building for scientific studies which will strengthen people's faith in a hereafter.'

The nonchalant reply stunned the priests, but evidently such phenomena were not news to the Vatican. It later transpired that the Pope's cousin, the Rev Professor Dr Gebhard Frei, co-founder of the Jung Institute, was the President of the International Society for Catholic Parapsychologists and had collaborated with an early pioneer of EVP, Dr Konstantin Raudive, of Germany.

Before his death in October 1967, Frei had gone on record as a staunch advocate of investigating EVP. 'All that I have read and heard forces me to believe that the voices come from transcendental, individual entities. Whether it suits me or not, I have no right to doubt the reality of the voices.' Ironically, as if to validate his own life's work, just a month after his death, the voice of Dr Frei was caught on tape and identified by Professor Peter Hohenwarter of the University of Vienna.

Pope Paul VI, successor to Pope Pius XII, continued the good work, giving his blessing to researches carried out by Swedish film producer Friedrich Jurgenson, who confided to a British voice researcher in the 1960s, 'I have found a sympathetic ear for the Voice Phenomenon in the Vatican. I have won many wonderful friends among the leading figures in the Holy City. Today "the bridge" stands firmly on its foundations.' Presumably, 'the bridge' referred to the work which would reconcile the Church with what it insisted on calling spiritism.

It is believed that the Vatican even agreed to novice priests attending a course in parapsychology under the auspices of Father Andreas Resch. The Church's interest in these phenomena was hardly a secret although it was certainly not widely known. In 1970, the International Society of Catholic Parapsychologists convened in Austria and openly discussed such phenomena as EVP.

Perhaps the Church's most active involvement with such matters was the Pye Recording Studio sessions which took place in England in 1972, funded by the *Sunday Mirror*. The sessions were conducted by theologian Dr Peter Bander, a senior lecturer in Religious and Moral Education at the Cambridge Institute of Education, who was initially hostile to the whole notion of communicating with the dead by any means. Prior to the experiment, Bander declared that it was 'not only far-fetched but outrageous' to even consider the possibility of recording spirit voices. He invited four senior members of the Catholic hierarchy to witness the proceedings in expectation that they would put the matter to rest once and for all. But during the recordings, which were held in a soundproof studio to eliminate the possibility of external interference, it was claimed that the participants heard the voice of a naval officer who had committed suicide two years earlier, a voice that had been recorded by Dr Raudive at an earlier session. The studio's chief engineer, Ken Attwood, conceded, 'I have done everything in my power to break the mystery of the voices without success; the same applies to other experts. I suppose we must learn to accept them.'

When the *Sunday Mirror* refused to publish Bander's conclusions, he published them himself the following

Dr. Konstantin
Raudive with
apparatus
for receiving
messages from
the dead

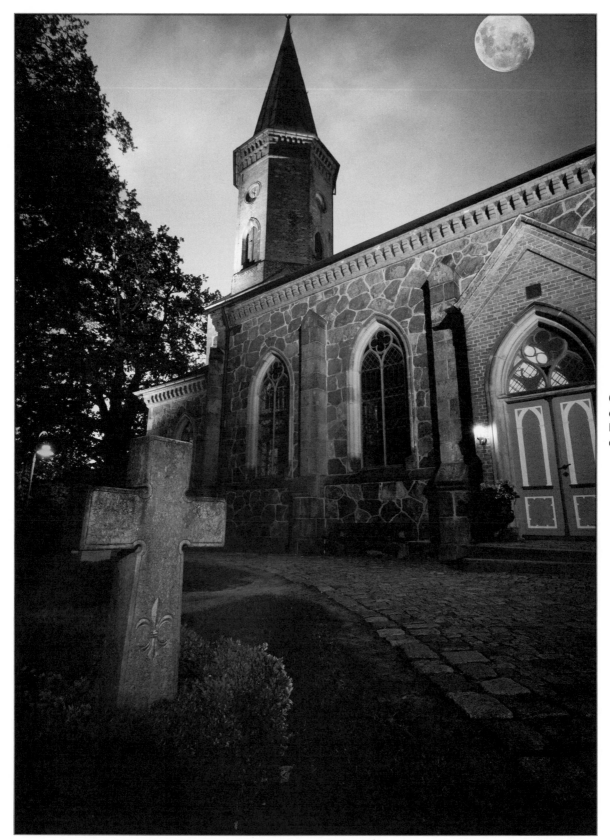

Contact with the dead is forbidden by the Catholic church

year in a book entitled *Breakthrough*. Father Pistone, Superior of the Society of St Paul in England, gave Bander's experiment and his book what sounded like a positive endorsement.

'I do not see anything against the teaching of the Catholic Church in the Voices, they are something extra-ordinary but there is no reason to fear them, nor can I see any danger. The Church realizes that she cannot control the evolution of science. Here we are dealing with a scientific phenomenon; this is progress and the Church is progressive. I am happy to see that representatives of most Churches have adopted the same attitude as we have: we recognize that the subject of the Voice Phenomena stirs the imagination even of those who have always maintained that there could never be any proof or basis for discussion on the question of life after death. This book and the subsequent experiments raise serious doubts, even in the minds of atheists. This alone is a good reason for the Church supporting the experiments. A second reason may be found in the greater flexibility of the Church since Vatican II; we are willing to keep an open mind on all matters which do not contradict Christ's teaching.'

Bander also managed to convert Archbishop H.E. Cardinale, Apostolic Nuncio to Belgium, who remarked, 'Naturally it is all very mysterious, but we know the voices are there for all to hear them'. The Right Reverend Monsignor, Professor C. Pfleger added, 'Facts have made us realize that between death and resurrection, there is another realm of post-mortal existence. Christian theology has little to say about this realm.'

Following the publicity surrounding the Pye sessions, the Vatican commissioned Swiss theologian Father Leo Schmid to embark on further research. Schmid went on to amass over 10,000 recordings which were transcribed and edited in his posthumously published book *When the Dead Speak* (1976). More recently, Vatican spokesman Father Gino Concetti told the papal newspaper *Osservatore Romano*:

'According to the modern catechism, God allows our dear departed persons who live in an ultra-terrestrial dimension, to send messages to guide us in certain difficult moments of our lives. The Church has decided not to forbid any more the dialogue with the deceased with the condition that these contacts are carried out with a serious religious and scientific purpose.'

It would appear that the Church has made its peace with the dead.

CHAPTER 4

Talking to the Dead

The most convincing evidence of the soul's survival after death comes from psychic mediums who act as a channel between the living and the dead.

Most people have never seen a ghost, but that does not mean that ghosts do not exist. There is considerable experiential evidence that discarnate spirits do exist, but in an alternate reality to our own. This is a non-physical dimension of which we are not conscious because our perception of this greater reality is limited by our five physical senses.

Science and the Spirit World

We operate at the lowest frequency of existence on the densest level, the physical plane. Naturally, we tend to believe that what we perceive is real and that anything that we cannot touch, taste, see, smell or hear does not exist. Our world appears solid but, as science has recently discovered, this is an illusion created by the comparatively low processing power of the human brain which cannot see the spaces that exist between matter at the subatomic level. It is comparable to looking at a photograph in a newspaper. We do not see the millions of dots that make up the image and the white spaces in between unless we look at it through a magnifying glass. Nevertheless, the dots are there. The same is true of moving images. Movie film is composed of hundreds of thousands of individual frames passing through a projector gate at the rate of 24 frames per second giving the illusion of continuous movement. We do not see the individual frames, only fluid action. Although our apparently solid, physical world is an illusion, it is a reality to us while we remain within our physical bodies, but there is another world of finer matter operating at a higher frequency in the spaces in between our own.

Quantum physicists now theorize that subatomic particles, known as 'dark matter', combine to produce the illusion of solidity in the same way that tones and overtones combine to create identifiable sounds. In a similar way, ghosts may be a transitory image indicative of a real presence, or a vibration in the ether created by residual personal energy but having no more physical substance than a sound wave created by a musical note. And like a note this residual energy will pass away echoing presumably into eternity but imperceptible to human beings. Consequently, we cannot afford to dismiss the existence of ghosts and other paranormal phenomena as unscientific and irrational simply because we are not aware of their presence. In fact, we can alter our perception to become aware of these other realities and we most often do so involuntarily when we are not so intensely focused on material matters.

Our Sixth Sense

We have all experienced an involuntary shift in consciousness such as when we intuitively 'know' that someone will phone us moments before they do so, or when we meet someone who we had been thinking about the day before. Carl Jung, the Swiss analytical psychologist, whose own mystical experiences and insights formed the basis of today's modern psychotherapy, coined the useful term 'synchronicity' for these seeming coincidences.

'So strong is our need to believe that our physical world is the only reality that more significant experiences such as the lucid dream in which we sense ourselves floating or flying are rarely accepted for what they are . . .'

So strong is our need to believe that our physical world is the only reality that more significant experiences such as the lucid dream in which we sense ourselves floating or flying are rarely accepted for what they are (genuine out-of-body experiences) and what they reveal about our true nature. However, we all possess an innate sixth sense which is merely an acute sensitivity to the more subtle forces and presences around us and not something abnormal or supernatural.

There are some people who are not only aware that they possess this heightened sensitivity but who have developed it to a remarkable degree. We call them psychics and attribute all manner of paranormal powers to them such as precognition (foreseeing future events), psychometry (picking up impressions from personal objects) and remote viewing (projecting consciousness to another location). Those psychics who claim to be able to communicate with the dead are known as mediums and are either regarded as gifted by those who have received comfort and closure from having been given compelling evidence of their loved ones' survival after death, or as charlatans by those who remain sceptical.

When the dead try to communicate with us we tend to block them out, either because we fear that acknowledging their presence will disturb our sense of reality or because we need to be grounded in the material world. Many of us have been conditioned to dismiss their influence on our lives as coincidences or as figments of our imagination. However, if we continue to ignore their presence they may intensify their efforts, moving small objects around and contriving to arrange uncanny coincidences. To this end, mediums are able to facilitate a meeting of minds between this world and the next, until we are willing and able to do this for ourselves.

There are those who are sceptical of mediums on principle and they accuse their 'gullible' clients of unconsciously colluding with the medium and of being highly selective in what they choose to remember from a

When the dead try to communicate with us we tend to block them out . . . because we fear that acknowledging their presence will disturb our sense of reality . . .

session. Sceptics frequently charge psychics with 'fishing' for information, but they disregard the many thousands of mediums who offer personal information that the client could not possibly have known – consciously or otherwise. Although, no doubt, it does occur, many mediums do not tease clues from their clients or trick them into revealing information, then take credit for having 'channelled' those facts from the dead. In fact, they explicitly instruct their clients not to tell them anything until after the session has finished so that they will not be unduly influenced. Also, many refuse to accept money for themselves, agreeing only to accept a modest donation for their chosen charity.

Convincing Evidence

Karin Page, founder of the Star of the East spiritual healing centre in Kent, England, had been seeing ghosts since the age of six, but it took a message from the 'other side' to finally convince her.

'One day my elderly mother-in-law promised me that she would come back after her death so that I would have proof of the survival of the soul. I didn't take it seriously at the time, but two months after her passing all the clocks in the house starting behaving strangely. They all showed a different time and a travelling alarm clock rolled off the shelf and crashed at my feet just as I was telling my daughter about how oddly they were all behaving. Another day the phone jumped off its holder on the wall and started swinging from side to side. Then the electric blanket and toaster switched themselves on. Each time I felt a chill in the air. It was Mary trying to tell me that she was with me.

The final proof came when I went to a spiritualist meeting and was told by a medium, who I'd never met before, that my husband's mother was trying to communicate, that her name was Mary and that she had died of cancer, both of which were true. She just wanted to say thank you for all the time I had looked after her. Then the medium said that Mary sent her love to my husband, my son and his girlfriend and she named them all which left me speechless. The only thing I couldn't understand was when she said, 'I'm with Emma now', because I didn't know of an Emma in the family. Mary had never mentioned her. Afterwards I learnt that Emma had been Mary's sister who had died 11 years earlier. Since then I have smelt Mary's talcum powder on many occasions and I know then that she is watching over me.'

Positive Benefits

English medium Jill Nash believes that the job of a psychic is to provide evidence of survival on the other side to give comfort to those left behind, not to impress clients with manifestations of ectoplasm and moving objects.

'Initially I talk to spirit in my mind and ask for their help. I feel their presence and can sense if they are male or female, but I never see them. I'm not communicating with the dead because nobody ever dies. They are the same personalities that they were in life. They are simply discarnate. I ask them to give me names and details that only the client will know which helps the client to relax and open up. Then I close my eyes and visualise drawing that person closer so that I am absorbed into their aura. When I make the connection I get excited. It's like having a present that you can't wait to open. At that point I usually feel a warmth and I might see a colour or a letter, or a combination of letters. If, for example I see them surrounded by blue I will know it is a communication issue and I'll ask them if they know of anyone whose name begins with the letter I've seen or a place beginning with that letter that has a significance for them. That's the starting point. It's an entirely intuitive, automatic process. It's like picking at a strand in a ball of wool. It unravels slowly. When spirit has something to add it impresses itself in my mind. I only receive what spirit wants me to have at that time. It wouldn't help me or the client to know all the answers. We would stop working things out for ourselves and would only put an effort into something that would guarantee to reward our efforts.

Unfortunately I couldn't tell my parents about my psychic experiences when I was young because they were very religious and were frightened of anything which challenged their faith. It made them uncomfortable. I used to sense a presence occasionally and my mother would shut me up by shouting, "I don't want to hear about dead people." But I was never scared because I know nothing really dies. Energy can't die. It can only be transformed.'

Jill sees a medium's role as helping the bereaved attain closure by facilitating a reunion with their loved ones.

'On one particularly memorable occasion I opened the door expecting to see a little elderly lady and instead saw her and her late husband. He walked in behind her. She was, of course, unaware that he was with her but I could see him plain as day, although he was fainter than a living person, almost transparent and there was nothing to see below the knee. He was tall and slim and when she sat down he stood behind her with a satisfied grin on his face as if he was thinking, 'At last, now I can tell her what I have been trying to say to her for months'.

As soon as we were settled he communicated to me telepathically, mind to mind, that he wanted me to tell her about a rose. Of course I didn't know what he meant, I hadn't met this lady before. But she did. He had apparently been trying to create a new type of rose by grafting and it hadn't taken while he was alive but he wanted her to keep the plant alive because he knew it was going to work. I described the plant and the type of pot it was in and the fact that it was underneath the front window of their bungalow. Of course I had never seen their house but I could see it in my mind as he transferred his thoughts to mine.

He wanted her to know that he was alright and that he was with her if she wanted to say anything or share her feelings. He told me to tell her that he often stood behind her when she sat in her armchair in the evenings and that if she felt something like a cobweb brushing against her cheek or a gentle pat on the head that it was only him reassuring her that he was still around. And as soon as I said that, she admitted that she had felt these things and had wondered if it was him, although she couldn't trust her own feelings or believe that he was really there.'

'I described the plant and the type of pot it was in and the fact
that it was underneath the front window of their bungalow'

Jill's experiences have convinced her that the dead remain the same personalities they were on this side of life and recalls an incident with her father's ghost which revealed that he had not lost his mischievous sense of humour when he passed over.

'I went to an open day at Stanstead College which is popularly known as England's "psychic school". Some of the best mediums in the country were giving readings in various rooms and my friends and I began our "tour" in the main hall which was filled to capacity with several hundred people. We were standing at the back when the medium said that he had to interrupt his demonstration because he was being literally nagged by a spirit who was insisting he be allowed to come through. It was an elderly man by the name of Percy who had passed over 20 years ago. The medium described Percy and his habits including his compulsive need to pat his hair and the fact that one of his fingers was missing. And it was my dad! He had lost a finger in a factory accident when he was a young man. He just wanted to tell me that he was fine and that I had been right about what I told him would be waiting for him on the other side.

But the funniest thing was that when I went on to watch a demonstration of direct voice mediumship in the next room my dad's spirit followed me and said "hello" again through that medium. The medium actually spoke in his voice which I recognised immediately. And if that wasn't enough he did it again in the next room through another medium, so then I had to tell him to stop and give someone else a turn!'

Betty Shine

Some people are born with an acute psychic sensitivity or 'sixth sense' which enables them to see and communicate with discarnate spirits while others seem to develop this ability as the result of a traumatic event. Celebrity psychic Betty Shine, dubbed 'the World's number one healer' by the British popular press, was evidently blessed with more than her share of mediumistic gifts but was initially reluctant to develop them.

At the outbreak of the Second World War she was evacuated to the comparative safety of the English

. . . she thought that everyone shared the same clairvoyant gifts until a friend assured her that seeing dead people was unusual . . .

countryside with thousands of other children whose parents were desperate to save them from the dangers of the London Blitz. One night a stray bomb landed near the house in which she was staying, blowing in all the windows and sending a large shard of glass into the headboard just an inch above her head. The shock appears to have stimulated her psychic sensitivity because the following night Betty began to see 'misty people' passing through her bedroom door, across the room and through the opposite wall. Even though they seemed oblivious to her she found their presence oddly reassuring and accepted her extraordinary psychic experiences as entirely natural. At the time she thought that everyone shared the same clairvoyant gifts until a friend assured her that seeing dead people was unusual to say the least.

While the traditional view is that ghosts are discarnate spirits haunting our world, Betty had a more rational interpretation for the visitations – she believed she was looking into another dimension in which the discarnate spirits were going about their normal activities. That would explain why many ghosts appear unaware of the living – they are not intruding into our world but we are peering into theirs.

At first Betty was reluctant to pursue her calling as a medium and healer, but by the time she had reached adulthood the build-up of suppressed psychic energy was making her physically ill. When she finally opened up to the power within she was overwhelmed by self-generated phenomena such as moving objects and disturbances which are commonly associated with poltergeist activity. 'I was seeing spirit faces everywhere – on the walls, in the carpet, everywhere and I would hear voices too as if I was suddenly able to hear people talking in the next room, only they weren't in this world but the next.'

Thousands of children were evacuated from London during the Second
World War. For Betty Shine, it was to prove a life-changing experience.

She claims to have seen spirits in airports, on buses, in pubs and all manner of public places, perhaps proving that our world and theirs are simply different facets of a greater, multi-dimensional reality and that there is no need to create a special atmosphere with candles and paranormal paraphernalia in order to communicate with our loved ones.

Most spirits are evidently content to co-exist with the living in a parallel plane, but according to Betty the dead can refuse to pass into their own world and instead linger in the presence of the living if they have 'unfinished business' to resolve.

On one occasion she sensed a dark entity overshadowing a female patient and heard its voice in her own head saying; 'I will never leave her, she's mine.' As soon as she began praying for protection, Betty saw a bright white light appear around the entity putting it into silhouette. It was a man and as he was pulled away by some unseen force into the light he screamed. At the same moment, the woman instinctively covered her ears, though she later told Betty that she hadn't actually heard anything. After the session the woman told Betty that she had once been married to a possessive, sadistic man who had pursued her for years after she had left him before finally suffering a fatal heart attack on her doorstep. After his death she remarried but still felt his suffocating overbearing presence and had become chronically depressed. A few weeks after the exorcism the woman returned to Betty's healing centre radiant and relieved, finally free of the black cloud she felt had been smothering her for years.

Betty's experiences have given her a unique insight into the true nature of ghosts – or spirits as she prefers to call them. It is her understanding that we are not purely physical beings but possess an energy counterpart which animates the body and which can be seen by psychics as an aura of vital energy which radiates from each living person. It may be this residual energy which lingers in the atmosphere after death and is mistaken for a ghost while our spirit moves onto the next world.

The Psychic Cleric

It is believed by some that everyone attends their own funeral in spirit, if only to see who has turned out to say goodbye. It is not uncommon for family members to see the deceased who often appear bemused at what they perceive as the fuss being made over their empty shell. Catholic sacristan Tina Hamilton often senses the presence of discarnate spirits during the funeral services at which she presides at St Thomas Church, Canterbury, England.

'I rarely see them, but I hear them and sense the force of their personality which has survived the death of the physical body. Sometimes I may even feel an arm around my shoulder. If it is a particularly strong presence they might try to communicate in which case I will hear them as another voice in my head. These are not my own thoughts. The tone of voice is quite distinct from my own. They tell me that they feel more alive than they did in life and will express frustration at not being able to be seen by their friends and family. Many express surprise at the number of people who have come to pay their respects while others seem amused at seeing a relative who didn't like them but who has reluctantly turned up out of a sense of duty. Curiously, it's usually their sense of humour that touches me most strongly. I suspect it stems from the relief of having been unburdened of their earthly responsibilities and fears and the sense that they are now free from the constraints of the physical body.

I have been presiding over funeral services for more than 50 years and can truly say that I have never sensed a spirit that appeared disturbed, although I once conducted the funeral service for a teenage suicide who came through to say how sorry she was for having brought her parents so much pain. She asked me to tell them that it wasn't their fault. She had been suffering from depression and other problems which her family later confirmed to have contributed to her death.

Unfortunately being 'open' or receptive means that I attract lost souls like a moth to a flame. A psychic is like a lighthouse in a storm for those spirits who are disorientated after a fatal accident or sudden, unexpected death. Occasionally, when I am walking in the town I will hear someone calling my name and it is only when I turn round and find that there is no one there that I'll realize that it is a spirit. So I'll ask who it is in my mind and what they want with me. If I have a name it helps me to establish an empathy and later I can find out who it was that I was helping. If they were unprepared for death they may be confused and even anxious as they can see us but most people can't see or hear them. So I tell them to remain calm and go into the light which is the threshold to the next dimension and moments later I will sense the presence fade and a feeling of peace or relief overwhelming me. A typical incident was that involving a young man who had just been killed on the dual carriageway while travelling down from Scotland. He couldn't understand how he could be in the town as he couldn't remember the end of the journey. He kept reliving the accident like a bad dream and couldn't accept that he had not survived the crash which had killed him. He identified himself by name so I was able to verify later. But even he wasn't distressed, simply confused. My experience leads me to believe that the soul does not suffer even a violent death, but is simply separated from the physical body by the event.'

The Soul Rescuer

Exorcisms are rarely performed these days. The most common method of clearing a haunted house of earthbound spirits today is a technique known as 'soul rescuing'.

British psychic Pamela Redwood typifies the new breed of 'sensitives' who can sense spirits – malign or otherwise – and work quietly to rid homeowners of their uninvited guests, bringing both parties peace of mind. She explains:

'What is sad is when someone cannot return to the light after their death because they are so attached to their life. I have cleared several houses where there have been disturbances or where the owner complains that they cannot live there because a certain room is cold even in the summer. They call me in and the first thing I pick up on is a thickness in the atmosphere as if it is charged with an invisible presence. Sometimes my spirit guides will give me different colours and I will see that soul taken up through the ray of colour by my guides into the light and then the atmosphere will clear as if the room has been aired. I used to take the spirit up through my own body as I thought that I had to act as a channel for its return to

the light but now the guides do it for me. Which is just as well as it could be very exhausting to be a host to someone else's spirit even for a few minutes. I would feel as if I'd absorbed their essence into my own being but occasionally if they were reluctant to go I would still have them with me when I went home. My daughter is very psychic and she would see me hobbling down the garden path, bent double like an old hag with a spirit on my shoulder and calmly say to her dad, "Mum's back and she's brought a ghost home."

I don't feel any fear when I do soul rescuing otherwise I couldn't do it. I know my guides are assisting me and it is work that needs to be done. Unfortunately people are too eager to build anywhere these days and most of my work comes from people who have bought new houses built on the site of old burial grounds.

Who knows who else is at the funeral of a loved one?
The loved one themselves?

You have to treat earth bound spirits as if they were still alive as they are the same personalities that they were in life. I once had to persuade the spirit of a pipe-smoking stubborn old man to pass over by promising him that he would have all the tobacco he could smoke if he went over to the other side!'

John Edward

The young American medium John Edward (whose hugely popular TV show *Crossing Over* has been syndicated around the world) is one of a new generation of 'celebrity psychics'. His affability and commonsense approach have dispelled the suffocating gloom of Victorian spiritualism that gave mediumship a bad name with its candlelit séances, Ouija boards and obsession with ectoplasm. His extraordinary experiences demonstrate that spirits are not an unsettling paranormal phenomena but simply discarnate individuals who initiate contact with the living because they wish to assure their grieving loved ones that they are fine and to encourage them to move on with their own lives. John's experiences offer more insights into the true nature of the spirit world than were ever revealed by the mediums of the spiritualism movement. This suggests that we might now be ready to accept the existence of a wider reality. Perhaps we are even being prepared by being drip fed insights into the mysteries of the universe as an aid to our understanding, and evolution of our beliefs. John Edward was tested and his abilities verified under rigorous laboratory conditions by Gary Schwarz, professor of Psychology at the University of Arizona.

The first hint that he possessed an unusual talent came at an early age when he casually commented on events in his family history. These were events which he shouldn't have known about as they had occurred before he was born, yet he assured his parents that he remembered being there at the time. By the age of five he had informed his teachers that he could see a radiance around them. It was only much later that he learnt that not everyone could see these coloured auras. The first flowering of his psychic gifts began with visions of his maternal grandfather who had died in 1962, seven years before John was born. He saw the old man sitting at the dinner table next to his grandmother who took John's announcement that the old man was present as a comfort, even though she couldn't see her husband herself. John soon graduated to premonitions that relatives would drop by unexpectedly – a talent his mother soon learnt to take seriously and be grateful for.

John's particular ability for communicating with the departed developed in fits and starts during his adolescence. At first, the connection was tentative and difficult to decipher like receiving a weak signal from a distant radio station. There was considerable static obscuring the communications, but over time he learnt how to 'tune in' and filter out the interference. By the time he was 16, John was giving readings using tarot cards at psychic fairs, but then he began to receive

Tarot cards from the Rider Waite tarot deck

John Edward, in a publicity shot for his show
Crossing Over with John Edward

messages for his clients in the form of intrusive thoughts which evidently did not originate in his own unconscious. To begin with they were simply names of dead people who were obviously attempting to communicate with his clients, but John felt uncomfortable being 'used' in this way. He resented the distraction as he was trying to concentrate on the cards. Predicting the future was fine as far as he was concerned, but talking to the dead spooked him. It also didn't sit well with his Catholic faith. Eventually, John began to trust these inner voices which became increasingly louder and more insistent. Subsequently, the names evolved into messages which he passed on to the delight of the living. The relief on the faces of anxious or grieving loved ones convinced him that what he was doing could not be a sin, but was instead a blessing.

Then one day, while he was still in his teens, he witnessed his first significant materialization. His aunt Anna had teased him into reading the tarot cards which she regarded

John Edward hosts his television show, popular with celebrities – Deborah Gibson (right) – and the public alike

as little more than a child's magic trick. But when John looked up from the cards he saw a woman standing behind his aunt. She was a stout lady in her sixties, wearing a black dress and a flower-shaped brooch and she appeared to have only one leg. John's description gave Aunt Anna a start. She immediately identified the mystery woman as her mother-in-law who had lost her leg through diabetes. Aunt Anna had never met her and neither had John because the old lady had died before he was born. But that was only the beginning. As John looked past his aunt, the old woman vanished and another figure appeared in her place. It was an impeccably dressed man in a pinstripe suit carrying a pocket watch. He was tall and slender with grey hair. This time Aunt Anna didn't recognize him from John's description so John opened up a dialogue with the man in his head. 'Show me something so that she will know who you are,' he said and was rewarded with a vision of the man lifting a large comb from his pocket and then pointing to a clock surrounded by flowers. The time on the clock read ten past two. The vision faded leaving John and his aunt none the wiser.

One week later, John's Uncle Carmine died unexpectedly of a heart attack. Only it wasn't such a shock to John because he had seen his uncle dying before his eyes in a particularly vivid vision three months earlier. It was so strong in fact that John had insisted that his uncle see a doctor, but the physicians gave the old man a clean bill of health. Three months later at his uncle's wake, John stood before the coffin staring at a clock surrounded by roses. The time on the clock was ten minutes past two, the moment of his uncle's death. It was a family tradition to mark the time of death in this way. That same day John learnt the identity of the man with the comb. A cousin recognized the description as that of Uncle Carmine's father who had been a barber. From that moment, John's psychic sensitivity went into overdrive.

Consulting the Ouija board. 'Ouija' comes from the French and German for 'yes'

Interpreting the Spirits

The number of readings he was asked to give put enormous demands on his time, but the most taxing aspect was the sheer intellectual effort he had to make in order to interpret the subtle signs the spirits were showing him. Often they would use obscure references because they couldn't communicate directly, but on one occasion John learnt that there was a danger in trying too hard. During a reading for a recently bereaved lady, her dead husband kept showing John a bell. The reading had been going well up to that point and she had been able to verify everything John had passed on to her. But he was puzzled by the bell. He asked if she or her husband had had any connection with Philadelphia or Ben Franklin. Did they know of anyone called Ben or Franklin? It was only when John said that he kept seeing the image of a bell but couldn't think of another association for that image that the woman understood and became tearful. On the morning of his death her husband had given her a souvenir bell he had picked up on a business trip. 'If you ever need me, ring this and I'll be there,' he had said. Then he kissed his wife goodbye and went to work. He was killed in a car accident later that day. Sometimes a bell just means a bell.

As his fame spread, first by word of mouth and then through his TV show, John found his appointments diary filled to overflowing and the spirits crowding in, jostling for his attention in their eagerness to have their messages passed on to their loved ones. They would pull him to one side of the room and home him in on a particular member of the audience, then tease him with tantalizing clues. The atmosphere was good-natured, although often emotional, as friends and family members recognized a pet name or a half-forgotten incident which the spirit recalled to validate the evidence of their survival. Occasionally, the experience was dramatic. A victim of a car accident came through to give her version of events, offering unknown evidence implicating another vehicle's involvement which was subsequently verified by the police. And several murder victims described the guilty party which the family recognized as fitting the description of a suspect the police had had under observation but could not arrest for lack of evidence.

More often, though, spirits speak of mundane matters which sceptics argue is proof that mediumship is a dangerous delusion. If it was a genuine communication from the afterlife, they argue, then surely the spirit would have something profound to say about life after death. Instead, they usually talk of routine family matters. John Edward contends that such minor personal details are more important for the grieving family as what they really need is proof that they are talking to their loved ones.

The Ouija Board is the second highest-selling board game with 25 million sold in Europe and the USA to date and it continues to be available in toyshops and novelty stores around the world despite its dubious reputation

The Ouija Board

The Ouija (which is said to take its name from a combination of the French and German words for 'yes') was re-invented as a parlour game in 1898 at the height of the spiritualism craze by the Fuld brothers of Baltimore. It is the second highest-selling board game with 25 million sold in Europe and the USA to date and it continues to be available in toyshops and novelty stores around the world despite its dubious reputation.

The brothers may have been inspired by a similar technique used by the ancient Egyptians to contact their ancestors. The Egyptians used a ring suspended by a thread which they held over a board inscribed with mystic symbols. The inquirer then asked their questions and noted which symbols the ring indicated. The Ouija board works in a similar way. Participants place a finger on a pointer called a *planchette* (named after its creator) which moves on casters or felt with the slightest movement

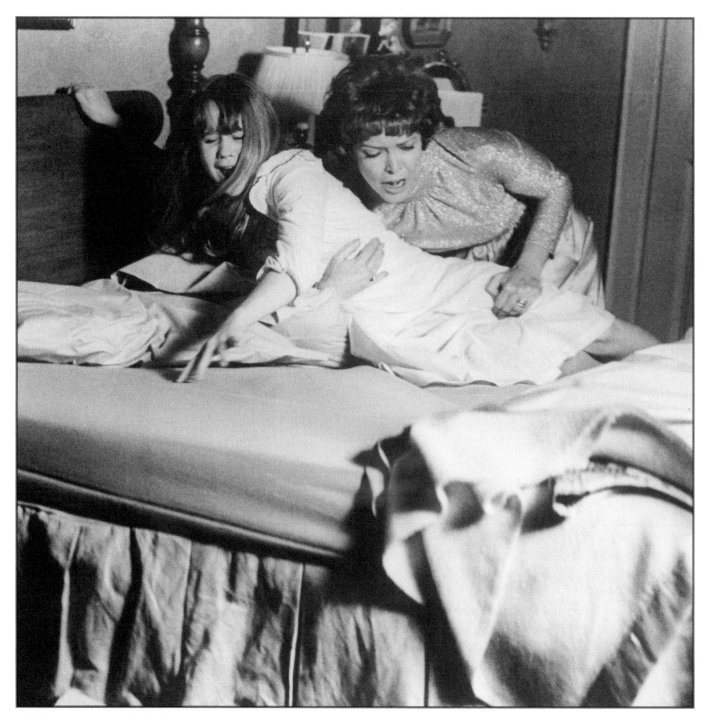

Ellen Burstyn and Linda Blair (l) in a scene from the
1973 movie *The Exorcist*

of the wrist, supposedly manipulated by the spirits, to spell out words using the alphabet printed on the board. Detractors argue that the 'spirit messages' originate in the participants' unconscious and that the imperceptible movements in the hand are caused by involuntary muscle contractions known as ideomotor actions. Whatever the source, there is no doubt that messages – many of them predicting death – have been recorded using this method.

Horror film fans will recall that it is through the use of the Ouija board that the little girl in *The Exorcist* becomes possessed, but in real life too there have been an alarming number of satanic-style murders and teenage suicides involving unstable and impressionable individuals who claim to have been acting on the instructions of demonic forces contacted through the board. It is marketed as a 'fun' game in which the 'players' consult the 'Mystifying Oracle', but the evidence suggests that in the wrong hands it can become dangerously addictive and can be profoundly disturbing to those who are psychologically unsound.

It is comparable to punching in a random phone number and hoping to connect with a family member, old friend or guru. Your call is far more likely to be picked up by a stranger who may find the temptation to tease or torment too good to resist. Even if the discarnate spirits who are attracted by this activity are not malevolent or intent on mischief, they may nevertheless influence how the players interpret their 'messages' simply by the fact that they are earthbound and therefore must be distressed or addictive personalities. This would account for the predominance of negative messages. Benign spirits are presumably beyond the influence of the board, enjoying their eternal rest.

The board itself may not be intrinsically bad, but it attracts the irresponsible and the immature who are not able to handle what they receive. If you have natural mediumistic ability, you won't need the board or any other focus object to induce the light trance state which will make you receptive to spirit communication.

However you view it, the Ouija board spells danger.

CHAPTER 5

Haunted Houses

Ghosts do not only haunt crumbling castles, but have been sighted in the homes of celebrities, hotels, aircraft, restaurants and even a Toys "R" Us store.

If any site deserves its formidable reputation for spectral sightings it is the Tower of London whose weathered stones are soaked in the blood of countless executed martyrs and traitors. It is said that the walls still echo with the screams of those who were tortured there during the most violent chapters of English history and with the muffled sobbing of those innocents who were put to death for displeasing the monarchy. It is a place of pain where the unquiet souls of those who were imprisoned relive their suffering seemingly for eternity with no prospect of finding peace.

Among the Tower's most illustrious residents were the young princes Edward and Richard who were declared illegitimate and imprisoned in the so-called Bloody Tower by their ambitious uncle the Duke of Gloucester

The Bloody Tower

Its long and bloody history began almost 1,000 years ago in 1078 when William the Conqueror built the White Tower in a strategically significant location on the River Thames. Over the next 500 years, the 18-acre site was developed into a formidable fortress within which a succession of kings exercised their divine right over the lives and deaths of their subjects; former friends, wives and enemies alike.

By the dawn of the seventeenth century, English royalty had moved to more palatial quarters and the Tower became a soldier's garrison and prison. On the morning of their execution, condemned prisoners were ceremoniously paraded past jeering crowds to the scaffold erected on nearby Tower Hill where they would be beheaded, or hung, drawn and quartered, and then their bodies would be brought back for burial within the walls of the Tower. These processions of sombre figures have been seen in modern times by sentries who were able to describe accurately the uniforms worn by the burial party.

Among the Tower's most illustrious residents were the young princes Edward and Richard who were declared illegitimate and imprisoned in the so-called Bloody Tower by their ambitious uncle the Duke of Gloucester. It is believed by some that he ordered their murder so that he could be crowned King Richard III. The princes have been sighted several times walking hand in hand through the chilly corridors after dusk, possibly in search of their murderous uncle. Their alleged murderer has not been seen skulking around the scene of his

The White Tower
was the first
structure to be
built on the site
of the Tower of
London and has
a long history of
hauntings

Lady Margaret Pole, found guilty of treason, refused to
kneel for the executioner and was hacked to pieces in a
bloody chase around Tower Green

hideous crimes which may suggest that his conscience was clear. Given the murdered princes' sense of injustice or revenge, ghosts appear to be an emotional residue rather than a conscious presence.

This is borne out by the nature of the other ghosts which haunt the Tower – they are all victims, not the perpetrators, of the many crimes which took place there. Edward IV, father to the murdered princes, ordered the death of his Lancastrian rival Henry VI on 21 May 1471 at the end of the War of the Roses, but it is not Edward who haunts the oratory in the Wakefield Tower where the killing took place, but Henry who has been seen seated outside the oratory praying that his soul might find peace.

The second wife of Henry VIII is said to still walk in the Tower Chapel where she made her peace with her God before she was despatched to his heavenly kingdom in 1536. She is reported to have been seen leading a spectral procession through the chapel both with and without her head.

One of the most gruesome episodes in the Tower's history was the botched execution of Margaret Pole, Countess of Salisbury. Margaret was 70 years old when she was condemned to death in 1541 by Henry VIII, even though she posed no threat to his dynasty. Standing resolutely regal on the scaffold, she refused to submit to the hooded executioner who waited for her to rest her head on the block, but instead she commanded him to sever her head from her neck where she stood. When he refused she fled, forcing him to pursue her around Tower Green swinging the axe like a serial killer in a modern splatter movie. Within minutes the hideous spectacle was at an end; the last female Plantagenet had been hacked to pieces. If you find that too gruesome to be true, you only have to ask permission to remain in the Tower after dark on 27 May, the anniversary of her execution, to see the scene re-enacted by the principal players themselves as Margaret's ghost tries once again to outrun her executioner.

Other apparitions are less active. The headless ghost of James Crofts Scott, the illegitimate son of King Charles II, for example, is said to do little more than walk the battlements connecting the Bell and Beauchamp Towers dressed in cavalier attire. Apparently, James was not satisfied with being made Duke of Monmouth as compensation for losing the crown to his uncle, James II, in 1685, and chose to assert his claim by force of arms. His rebellion was short lived and he paid for his disloyalty by forfeiting his head.

One of the most gruesome episodes in the Tower's history was the botched execution of Margaret Pole, Countess of Salisbury

Arguably the most tragic figure to haunt the site of her untimely death is Lady Jane Grey who was a pawn in the Duke of Northumberland's stratagem to usurp the English crown from the rightful heir, Mary Tudor. Lady Jane, who was only 15, ruled for less than two weeks before she was arrested and condemned to death together with her young husband and his father in February 1554. Her grieving ghost has been sighted by reliable witnesses on several occasions. In 1957, two sentries swore they witnessed the apparition of the young queen form from a ball of light on the roof of the Salt Tower while others have reported seeing the spirit of the Duke sobbing at the window of the Beauchamp Tower as he had done on the morning of his execution.

One would imagine that a spell in the Tower would be sufficient to bring even the most rebellious subjects to their senses, but Sir Walter Raleigh incurred the monarch's displeasure more than once. In 1592, Queen Elizabeth I ordered him to be thrown into the Tower, but upon his release he continued to bait the Queen in the belief that he was too popular to be executed. After Elizabeth's death, James I lost patience with Raleigh's preening and boasting and had him convicted on a trumped up charge of treason. He was eventually freed in 1616 on condition that he journeyed to the New World in search of gold to fill the royal coffers, but he ignored the King's express orders not to plunder from England's

Lady Jane Grey was put on the throne by scheming guardians in an audacious move that
saw her executed by Mary Tudor when she successfully claimed – then lost – the throne

Spanish allies and was beheaded on his return. His ghost still walks the battlements near what were once his apartments in the Bloody Tower.

Not all of the Tower's non-corporeal residents have returned because they cannot rest or because they desire revenge. The ghost of Henry Percy, 9th Earl of Northumberland, has been sighted strolling amiably on the roof of the Martin Tower where he enjoyed walks during his enforced incarceration which began in 1605. Percy, who had been implicated in the Gunpowder Plot, was one of the few prisoners to have been allowed to keep his head and he whiled away the days debating the latest advances in science and other subjects with other educated nobles until his release 16 years later. Percy owed his release to his willingness to pay a fine of £30,000. Since he is clearly reluctant to leave the Tower centuries after his death, perhaps he feels he hasn't had his money's worth.

The Ghosts of Glamis

If the typical collection of 'true' ghost stories is to be believed, every castle in the British Isles has its own resident ghost. Whether there is any truth in that or not, Glamis Castle in Scotland certainly has more than its share.

Glamis is the oldest inhabited castle north of the border and is renowned for being both the setting for the tragedy of Macbeth and also the ancestral home of the late Queen Mother, Elizabeth Bowes-Lyon. It also has an unenviable reputation as the most haunted castle in the world. Not all the ghosts are tortured souls. In the Queen Mother's sitting room the ghost of a cheeky negro servant boy has been sighted playing hide and seek. There is no doubt that the legends of Glamis provide more gruesome thrills than an old-fashioned Gothic thriller. However, fact and fiction are so creatively intertwined that it is now impossible to know which is which.

The forbidding exterior of Glamis Castle

Several visitors and guests have been distressed by the apparition of a pale and frightened young girl who has been seen pleading in mute terror at a barred window. Legend has it that she was imprisoned after having had her tongue cut out to keep her from betraying a family secret – but what that secret might be remains a mystery. In the 1920s, a workman was said to have accidentally uncovered a hidden passage and to have been driven to the edge of insanity by what he found there. Allegedly, the family bought his silence by paying for his passage to another country. There are also tales of a hideously deformed heir who was locked in the attic and an ancient family curse of which the 15th Earl is reputed to have said: 'If you could only guess the nature of the secret, you would go down on your knees and thank God that it was not yours.'

The family's troubles are believed to date from 1537 when the widow of the 6th Lord Glamis was accused of witchcraft and burned at the stake. From that day to this her ghost has been seen on the anniversary of her death on the roof of the clock tower, bathed in a smouldering red glow. Several of the castle's 90 rooms have a dark and bloody history. King Malcolm II of Scotland was murdered in one of them and the floor was boarded because the bloodstains could not be scrubbed clean. It is thought that this may have been the inspiration for the murder of King Duncan, Thane of Glamis, in Shakespeare's play *Macbeth*.

During the years of inter-clan warfare, the castle acquired an entire chamber of vengeful spirits when men from the Ogilvy clan were given refuge from their enemies in the dungeon, but were then betrayed by their host who walled them up alive. When the wall was torn down a century later, it is said that their skeletons were found in positions which suggested that they had been gnawing on their own flesh. The Scottish novelist Sir Walter Scott, who considered himself a hardy adventurer, braved a night there in 1793 and lived to regret it: 'I must own, that when I heard door after door shut, after my conductor had retired, I began to consider myself as too far from the living, and somewhat too near the dead.' In his classic survey of supernatural stories, *The Ghost Book* (1936), Lord Halifax recounts the unnerving experience of a Mrs Monro who was the guest of the new owners Lord and Lady Strathmore in November 1869, a story later verified by Lady Strathmore herself.

'In the middle of the night, Mrs Monro awoke with a sensation as though someone was bending over her; indeed, I have heard that she felt a beard brush her face. The night-light having gone out, she called her husband to get up and find the matches. In the pale glimmer of the winter moon she saw a figure pass into the dressing room. Creeping to the end of the bed she felt for and found the matchbox and struck a light, calling out loudly, "Cam, Cam I've found the matches."

To her surprise she saw that he had not moved from her side. Very sleepily he grumbled, "What are you bothering about?"

At that moment they heard a shriek of terror from the child in the dressing room. Rushing in, they found him in great alarm, declaring that he had seen a giant. They took him into their own room, and while they were quieting him off to sleep they heard a fearful crash as if a heavy piece of furniture had fallen.

At that moment the big clock had struck four.

Nothing more happened, and the next morning Mr Monro extracted a reluctant promise from his wife to say nothing about her fright, as the subject was known to be distasteful to their host. However, when breakfast was half over, [another guest] Fanny Trevanion, came down, yawning and rubbing her eyes and complaining of a disturbed night. She always slept with a night-light and had her little dog with her on her bed. The dog, she said, had awakened her by howling. The night-light had gone out, and while she and her husband were hunting for matches they heard a tremendous crash, followed by the clock striking four. They were so frightened they could not sleep again.

Of course, this was too much for Mrs Monro, who burst out with her story. No explanation was offered and the three couples agreed on the following night to watch in their respective rooms. Nothing was seen, but they all heard the same loud crash and rushed out onto the landing. As they stood there with scared faces the clock again struck four. That was all; and the noise was not heard again.'

Lord Halifax (1881–1959), ambassador to the US 1941–46, and witness of a ghost

Pursued by Dreams

So far this follows the customary ghost story tradition, but then it becomes even more intriguing. On the night of 28 September, Lord Halifax was staying at Tullyallan Castle, a modern comfortable home with no hint of a ghost when he dreamt that he was back at Glamis, which had once been his late brother-in-law's home. It was a fearful dream in which he was pursued by a huge man with a long beard. In a desperate effort to keep the ghost at bay – for in his dream Lord Halifax knew the man was dead – he offered him broken chains which a maid had found hidden in the hollow space below the grate in his room. His story continues:

'"You have lifted a great weight off me," sighed the ghost. "Those irons have been weighing me down ever since ..." "Ever since when?" asked his Lordship.

"Ever since 1486," replied the ghost.'

The next moment Halifax awoke.

In itself the dream would not be significant, but on the very same night the daughter of Lord Castletown was staying at Glamis unaware of the ghosts who were said to haunt several of its rooms. According to Lord Halifax:

'During the night she awoke with the feeling that someone was in the room and sitting up in bed she saw, seated in front of the fire, a huge old man with a long flowing beard. He turned his head and gazed fixedly at her and then she saw that although his beard rose and fell as he breathed the face was that of a dead man ... after a few minutes he faded away and she went to sleep again.'

Some years later, Lord Halifax had the chance to relate his dream to Lady Strathmore who remarked on the uncanny 'coincidence' and she gave a start when he mentioned the year of the ghost's death. Apparently Glamis' most infamous ghost, Earl Beardie, was murdered in 1486.

Thirteen Guests

The Winchester Mansion in San Jose, California is unique among haunted houses. It was built by ghosts. Haunted houses are usually host to the restless spirits of their previous occupants, but in the case of the Winchester Mystery House, as it is known locally, its ghosts were not only invited to make themselves at home, they even directed the owner as to how they wanted the house built.

In 1884, Mrs Winchester was grieving for the loss of both her son and her husband who had made his fortune manufacturing the famous Winchester repeating rifle – 'The gun that won the West'. In her grief Mrs Winchester became convinced that the restless spirits of those killed by her husband's weapons would torment her unless she devoted the rest of her life to extending the mansion according to their wishes so that they could while away eternity in comfort.

Every evening she presided over a spooky supper at a long dining table laid for 13, herself and 12 invisible guests. The servants indulged her eccentricities as they were allowed to

' . . . a pair of paranormal investigators stayed overnight in the house and were aroused
by music from a ghostly organ which, on examination, proved to be disconnected'

partake of the leftovers. After dinner the widow conducted a private séance to hear the spirits' latest plans which she would interpret for the workmen the next morning. Either the spirits had a sense of mischievous humour or else Mrs Winchester may have been deliberately trying to disorientate her guests. The house features a number of staircases leading up to the ceiling and doors which open onto a brick wall or a sheer drop. In one particular room there is a single entrance but three exits on the facing wall, one of which leads to an 8 ft drop into the kitchen on the floor below and another into a windowless room. The door to this room has no handle on the other side, perhaps to entrap a curious ghost or because Mrs Winchester believed it wouldn't need a door knob as a ghost could supposedly float through the door!

The ghosts seem to have had an obsession with the number 13. They demanded that every new staircase should have 13 steps and new rooms must have 13 windows. The chandeliers should boast 13 bulbs and the same number of coat hooks should be available in case they needed to hang up their spectral raincoats. There were even 13 fan lights in the greenhouse in case the spirits fancied a spell of hot house horticulture.

By the time Mrs Winchester passed away on 5 September 1922 at the age of 82, she had devoted the last 38 years of her life to extending the mansion which by then had grown to 160 rooms.

In the 1990s, a pair of paranormal investigators stayed overnight in the house and were aroused by music from a ghostly organ which, on examination, proved to be disconnected. Moments later they were unnerved by a violent disturbance as the house was shaken to its foundations. In the morning they asked the tour guides if any damage had been caused by the earthquake and were dumbfounded to learn that no tremors had been reported in the area, although in 1906 the destructive San Francisco earthquake had struck at the very same time and severely damaged part of the house.

Not surprisingly, perhaps, the mansion has become a popular tourist attraction, and in case any visitor sneers at the idea of a house being built for ghosts the guides are ready to assure them that at least three spirits walk the house – a young female servant, a carpenter who had died at the site and the indomitable Mrs Winchester, whom staff have seen in Victorian dress, sitting at a table. When they asked their colleagues why they needed someone dressed up as Mrs Winchester they were told that no one was employed to dress up and play the part.

'The house features a number of staircases leading up to the ceiling and doors which open onto a brick wall or a sheer drop'

Borley Rectory

During the 1930s and 1940s, Borley Rectory acquired a sinister reputation as 'The Most Haunted House in England'. This unimposing vicarage near Sudbury, Essex, was built in 1863 on the site of a Benedictine monastery which had a dark and unholy history. It was said that a Borley monk had seduced a local nun and the pair had planned to elope. They were caught and the monk was executed and the nun was walled up alive in the cellar.

The first incumbent of the new rectory was the Reverend Bull who built a summerhouse overlooking a path known as the Nun's Walk. From there he sometimes observed the materializations of the weeping woman as she wandered the gardens searching for her murdered lover. Bull often invited guests to join him on his ghost watch but few stayed long enough to share his vigil. Once they had caught the nun peering in through their ground floor bedroom window they made their excuses and cut their visit short. Bull's four daughters and his son Harry resigned themselves to regular sightings of the forlorn spirit drifting across the lawn in broad daylight, but when it was joined by a spectral coach and horses galloping up the drive, the surviving Bull children decided to move on. Their father had died in the Blue Room in 1892 and his son Harry in the same room in 1927.

At the end of the 1920s, the Reverend Eric Smith and his wife took up residence, shrugging off stories of phantom carriages and sobbing nuns. They had barely had time to unpack their belongings before a burst of

Bones were found in the cellar of the rectory and, in an effort to quieten the ghost, given a decent burial in Liston churchyard in 1945, attended by the Rev A.C. Henning, two local residents and Harry Price

Borley Rectory ablaze, in 1939

poltergeist activity encouraged them to sell up and move out. However, during their two-year tenure they took the unusual step of calling in the man who was to ensure Borley a place in paranormal history – ghost hunter extraordinaire Harry Price.

Price was a notorious self-publicist and one-time music hall conjurer who had hoped to make a name for himself by exposing fake mediums and debunking the whole spiritualist movement as mere charlatanism. The more he saw at first hand, however, the more convinced he became that some of it was genuine. Eventually, he came to the conclusion that he was more likely to fulfil his ambition of getting into *Debrett's* (a directory of the

rich and famous) if he could find proof of life after death than if he merely unmasked a few fraudulent mediums.

At the invitation of the Reverend Smith, and later with the encouragement of the next tenants Mr and Mrs Foyster, Price recorded incidents involving phantom footsteps, flying objects and even physical attacks: on one notable occasion Mrs Foyster was even turned out of bed by an invisible assailant. She was also the subject of unintelligible messages scrawled on the walls. Her husband had the house exorcized but the spirits persisted. The servants' bells rang of their own accord and music could be heard coming from the chapel even though no one was in the building. The Foysters admitted defeat

The ruins of Borley Rectory at the start of its demolition. A brick (circled) flies through the air at the time of the photograph. A paranormal event? Or a staged trick?

and left the spooks in peace. Subsequent owners fared little better. Eventually, the house burned down in a mysterious fire in 1939 as predicted by a spirit 11 months earlier during a séance conducted on the site by Price. Witnesses stated that they saw phantoms moving among the flames and the face of a nun staring from a window.

The Ghost-Hunter's Book

Price published his findings in 1940 under the title *The Most Haunted House in England*, boasting that it presented 'the best authenticated case of haunting in the annals of psychical research'. The book was an instant bestseller providing as it did some escapism in the first anxious months of the Second World War and quickly established a non-fiction genre of its own – the haunted house mystery. Its success generated a slew of similar books by self-proclaimed experts and sufficient interest in Price to spawn several (highly critical) biographies. Price revelled in his new found fame, but it was short-lived. He died in 1948 having spent the last 40 years of his life providing what he believed to be irrefutable evidence of the paranormal. But he was not allowed to rest in peace. In the decade after his death there were spiteful personal attacks on his reputation by rival ghost hunters alleging that Price had faked certain phenomena. Mrs Smith wrote to the *Church Times* denying that she and her husband had claimed that the rectory was haunted, although it is thought that she may have done this to ingratiate herself with the Church authorities who had been embarrassed by the whole affair. An investigation by the SPR, conducted by members who were openly hostile to Harry Price, concluded that he had manipulated certain facts to substantiate his claims and that other incidents probably had a 'natural explanation'. Price's reputation was seriously undermined, but the fact remains that the Reverend Bull and his family had said that they had seen spirits before Price arrived on the scene. (Miss Ethel Bull had reported seeing a phantom figure at the end of her bed and of sensing another sitting on the end of the bed on more than one occasion.) Also Mrs Foyster appears to have provoked an outbreak of genuine poltergeist activity. Price himself suspected that she augmented it with some phenomena of her own creation, perhaps because she craved attention, or

at least so as not to disappoint his expectations.

Either way, questions remain. If Price had faked phenomena, why did he rent the rectory for a year after Mrs Foyster moved out, only to admit that there was nothing anomalous to report? He would have had more than enough time and opportunity to stage something truly astounding to substantiate his claims. The inactivity during that period suggests that the spirits might have been attracted by the presence of the Reverend Bull and Mrs Foyster who perhaps possessed mediumistic abilities.

A subsequent investigation by the SPR under R.J. Hastings unearthed previously unpublished letters from the Reverend Smith and his wife to Price, written in 1929, in which Smith states emphatically that 'Borley is undoubtedly haunted'. This discovery forced the SPR to revise its earlier findings. Price had been vindicated. Whatever short cuts Price may have taken to enhance his reputation as Britain's foremost ghost hunter it cannot be denied that there was something out of the ordinary occurring at Borley.

A footnote to the Borley investigation was added in the 1950s by the novelist Dennis Wheatley, author of *The Devil Rides Out* and dozens of occult thrillers:

'Kenneth Allsop, the book reviewer of the Daily Mail, told me that when Borley was in the news he was sent down to do an article on it, and with him he took a photographer. Borley was then being 'debunked' so that had to be the tone of the article. But when the photographer developed his photos the figure of a nun could be quite clearly seen on one of them. He took it to Allsop, who took it to his editor, but the editor said, "No, I just daren't print it."'

A curious postscript to the Borley saga occurred on 28 August 1977 when ley line expert Stephen Jenkins visited the area with a view to seeing if there was anything to the theory that the 'curious manifestations' might be linked to a spider's web of ley line alignments.

'The time was precisely 12.52 pm and we were driving south-west along the minor road which marks the north end of the hall ground, when on the road in front in the

act of turning left into a hedge (I mean our left across the path of the car), instantaneously appeared four men in black – I thought them hooded and cloaked – carrying a black, old fashioned coffin, ornately trimmed with silver. The impression made on both of us was one of absolute physical presence, of complete material reality. Thelma and I at once agreed to make separate notes without comparing impressions. We did so and the descriptions tallied exactly, except that she noted the near left bearer turned his face towards her. I did not see this as I was abruptly braking at the time. What I had seen as a hood, she described as a soft tall hat with a kind of scarf falling to the left shoulder, thrown across the cloak body to the right. The face was that of a skull.

'The next day we returned to the spot at precisely the same time and took a picture. It is a Kodak colour slide. In the hedge near the gap where the 'funeral party' vanished (there's a path there leading to Belchamp Walter churchyard) is a short figure apparently cloaked, his face lowered with a skull-like dome to the head . . . I hazard a guess that the dress of the coffin bearer is that of the late 14th century. There seems to be no local legend of a phantom funeral.'

A cake of soap on the washstand was lifted and thrown heavily onto a china jug standing on the floor with such force that the soap was deeply marked

Weird Night in a Haunted House

While Harry Price was accused of having falsified some of the 'evidence' and having made fraudulent claims in order to boost his reputation as Britain's foremost ghost hunter, the following article from the *Daily Mirror* of 14 June 1929 suggests that Harry's first visit to Borley was lively enough without the need for artificial aids or exaggeration:

'Weird Night In "Haunted" House'
from our Special Correspondent
There can no longer be any doubt that Borley Rectory, near here, is the scene of some remarkable incidents.

Last night Mr Harry Price, Director of the National Laboratory For Psychical Research, his secretary Miss Lucy Kaye, the Reverend G.F. Smith, Rector of Borley, Mrs Smith and myself were witnesses to a series of remarkable happenings. All these things occurred without the assistance of a medium or any kind of apparatus. And Mr Price, who is a research expert only and not a spiritualist, expressed himself puzzled and astonished at the results. To give the phenomena a thorough test however, he is arranging for a séance to be held in the rectory with the aid of a prominent London medium.

The first remarkable happening was the dark figure that I saw in the garden. We were standing in the Summer House at dusk watching the lawn when I saw the 'apparition' which so many claim to have seen, but owing to the deep shadows it was impossible for one to discern any definite shape or attire. But something certainly moved along the path on the other side of the lawn and although I quickly ran across to investigate it had vanished when I reached the spot.

Then as we strolled towards the rectory discussing the figure there came a terrific crash and a pane of glass from the roof of a porch hurtled to the ground. We ran inside and upstairs to inspect the room immediately over the porch but found nobody. A few seconds later we were descending the stairs, Miss Kaye leading, and Mr Price behind me when something flew past my head, hit an iron stove in the hall and shattered. With our flash lamps we inspected the broken pieces and found them to be sections of a red vase which, with its companion, had been standing on the mantelpiece of what is known as the Blue Room which we had just searched. Mr Price was the only person behind me and he could not have thrown the vase at such an angle as to pass my head and hit the stove below.

We sat on the stairs in darkness for a few minutes and just as I turned to Mr Price to ask him whether we had waited long enough something hit my hand. This turned out to be a common moth ball and had apparently dropped *from the same place as the vase. I laughed at the idea of a spirit throwing moth balls about, but Mr Price said that such methods of attracting attention were not unfamiliar to investigators.*

Finally came the most astonishing event of the night. From one o'clock till nearly four this morning all of us, including the rector and his wife, actually questioned the spirit or whoever it was and received at times the most emphatic answers. A cake of soap on the washstand was lifted and thrown heavily onto a china jug standing on the floor with such force that the soap was deeply marked. All of us were at the other side of the room when this happened. Our questions which we asked out loud were answered by raps apparently made on the back of a mirror

in the room and it must be remembered though that no medium or spiritualist was present.

The White House

When the tour guides in Washington, DC, talk of the White House being haunted by the ghosts of former US presidents they are not speaking metaphorically, neither are they being melodramatic. It is known that Eleanor Roosevelt held séances in the White House during the Second World War and she claimed to be in contact with the spirit of Abraham Lincoln. During the Roosevelt residency their guest Queen Wilhelmina of the Netherlands was awoken in the night by a knock

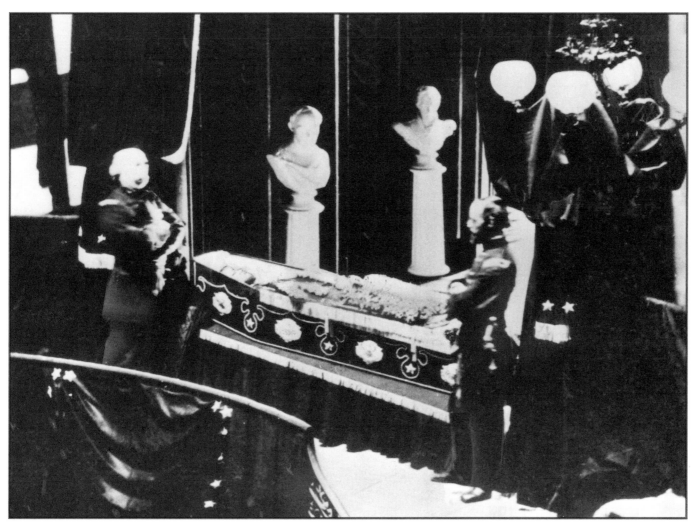

Lying in state but not, apparently, resting. The ghost of Abraham Lincoln is a reassuring presence at the White House

' . . . Native Americans warned the US army not to build a fortress on 'The Rock' as it was the dwelling place of evil spirits'

on her bedroom door. Thinking that it might be Eleanor Roosevelt she got out of bed, put on her nightgown and opened the door. There, framed in the doorway and looking as large as life, was the ghost of Abe Lincoln. Queen Wilhelmina's reaction is not recorded.

Winston Churchill was a frequent visitor to the White House during the Second World War and he often indulged in a hot bath, together with a cigar and a glass of whisky. One evening he climbed out of the bath and went into the adjoining bedroom to look for a towel when he noticed a man standing by the fireplace. It was Abraham Lincoln. Unperturbed, Churchill apologized for his state of undress: 'Good evening, Mr. President. You seem to have me at a disadvantage.' Lincoln is said to have smiled and tactfully withdrawn.

The wife of President Calvin Coolidge entertained guests to the White House with her recollections of the day she entered the Oval Office and saw Lincoln looking out across the Potomac with his hands clasped behind his back – a habit he acquired during the Civil War. Lincoln himself was a firm believer in the afterlife and enthusiastically participated in séances during his tenure in office prior to his assassination in 1865. He confided to his wife that he had a premonition of his own death. He dreamt that he was walking through the White House when he heard the sound of weeping coming from the East Room. When he entered he saw an open coffin surrounded by mourners and guarded by a detachment of Union soldiers. He asked one of the guards who it was who lay in the coffin, to be told, 'The President. He was killed by an assassin.' Lincoln then approached the coffin and saw his own corpse.

President Harry Truman often complained that he was prevented from working by Lincoln's ghost who would repeatedly knock on his door when he was attempting to draft an important speech. Truman wasn't known for his sense of humour and no one would have thought of playing practical jokes during his tenure in the Oval Office so it is assumed he was in earnest.

In the 1960s, Jacqueline Kennedy admitted that she had sensed Lincoln's presence on more than one occasion and 'took great comfort in it'. It is thought that Lincoln's ghost might be drawn to the White House because his son Willie died there and it is reported that the son has himself been seen wandering the corridors in search of his father.

Alcatraz

Long before Alcatraz Island in San Francisco Bay was converted into a prison to house America's most notorious criminals, the Native Americans warned the US army not to build a fortress on 'The Rock' as it was the dwelling place of evil spirits. Needless to say, their warnings were ignored. When the fortress was converted into a military prison in 1912, several soldiers were said to have been driven insane by mysterious noises in the night, by cold spots which turned their breath to mist even on warm summer evenings and by the sight of two burning red eyes which appeared in the cells on the lower level.

By 1934, the spirits had company when the Rock re-opened for business to house the most notorious gangsters of the prohibition era including 'Scarface' Al Capone and Machine Gun Kelly. But even the most hardened inmates feared being thrown into 'the hole', the windowless cells of D Block where the red-eyed demon was said to be waiting to consume lost souls.

On one memorable night during the 1940s a prisoner was hurled screaming into solitary in 14D and continued yelling until early the next morning. When the guards finally opened his cell, they found him dead with distinctive marks around his throat. An autopsy was conducted and the official cause of death was determined to be 'non self-inflicted strangulation'. The story gets more extraordinary when, according to the sworn statement of an eyewitness, the prisoners were lined up for roll-call the next morning and the number didn't tally. There was one extra prisoner in the line. So a guard walked along the line looking at each face to see if one of the inmates was playing a trick on him. He came face to face with the dead man who had been strangled in the night and who promptly vanished before his eyes. The guard later related this story to others and swore on the life of his children that it was true.

Despite the Warden's boast that the prison was escape-proof, several inmates tried to break out and died in the attempt. Their ghosts are said to haunt the hospital block where their bodies were taken. Other parts of the prison are host to the unquiet spirits of the five suicides and eight murders which took place before the prison was closed in 1963.

Since the Rock opened to tourists, visitors have claimed to have seen cell doors closing by themselves and to have heard the sound of sobbing, moaning and phantom footsteps, the screams of prisoners being beaten as well as the delirious cries of those made ill or driven insane by their confinement. Others have spoken of seeing phantom soldiers and prisoners pass along the corridors and out through solid walls, and many have complained of being watched even though the corridors and cells were empty.

'Other parts of the prison are host to the unquiet spirits of the five suicides and eight murders which took place before the prison was closed in 1963'

Those brave enough to try out one of the bunks for size have found themselves pinned down by a weight on their chest as the previous occupant made his presence known and showed his resentment at having his privacy invaded. In the lower cells, 12 and 14 in particular, even the least sensitive tourists have admitted to picking up feelings of despair, panic and pain, and they have excused themselves to catch a breath of fresh air. Whenever a thermometer has been placed in cell 14D it has consistently measured between 20–30 degrees colder than the other cells in that block.

And what of the Rock's most notorious inmate, 'Scarface' Capone? Well, Capone may have been a 'big shot' on the outside but in the 'big house' he was apparently a model prisoner who sat quietly on his bunk in cell B206 learning to play the banjo. It is said that if you sit quietly in that cell you can hear the ghostly strains of Capone whiling away eternity playing popular tunes of the Roaring 20s.

The Edgar Allan Poe House

The spirit of Edgar Allan Poe, author of *The Fall of the House of Usher* and other tales of terror, haunts both American fiction and the house in Baltimore where he lived as a young man in the 1830s. The narrow two and a half-storey brick house at 203 North Amity Street in an impoverished area is said to be so spooky that even local gangs are scared to break in. When the police arrived to investigate a reported burglary in 1968 they saw a phantom light in the ground floor window floating up to reappear on the second floor and then in the attic, but when they entered the property there was no one to be seen.

Even in daylight the house is unsettling. An eerie portrait of Poe's wife, painted as she lay in her coffin, hangs in one room, her melancholic gaze following visitors around the room. Local residents have also reported seeing a shadowy figure working at a desk at a second floor window, although Poe, whose morbid

'. . . there did stand the enshrouded figure of the lady Madeline . . . there was blood upon her white robes, and the evidence of some bitter struggle upon every portion of her emaciated frame. For a moment she remained trembling and reeling to and fro upon the threshold, then with a low moaning cry, fell heavily inward upon . . . her brother, and in her violent and now final death agonies, bore him to the floor a corpse . . .'

From *Fall of the House of Usher* by Edgar Allan Poe

obsession with premature burial led to his incarceration in an asylum, worked in the attic.

The curator has recorded many incidents of poltergeist activity and this appears to originate in the bedroom that belonged to Poe's grandmother. Here, doors and windows have opened and closed by themselves, visitors have been tapped on the shoulder and disembodied voices have been heard. Psychic investigators have also reported seeing a stout, grey-haired old woman dressed in clothing of the period gliding through the rooms.

In a twist of which the master of the macabre might have been perversely proud, local parents still use the spectre of the horror writer to terrify their children into doing what they are told. Poe has become the bogeyman of Baltimore.

Toys "R" Us

It is a common misconception that ghosts only inhabit crumbling castles and mouldering mansions. The modern Toys "R" Us superstore in Sunnyvale, California occupies a substantial plot on what had been a ranch and an apple orchard back in the nineteenth century. It is assumed that the poltergeist activity that has been witnessed there is connected with the previous owner John Murphy who, it appears, disliked children, as well as the commercial development of his former home.

Each morning, employees arrive to find stock scattered across the floor and items placed on the wrong shelves. Turnover in staff increased when sensitive staff members heard a voice calling their name and were then touched by invisible hands. The fragrant scent of fresh flowers has unsettled several employees, but it was the unwanted attentions of a phantom who assaulted female staff in the ladies' washroom which brought the matter to the attention of the local press and ghost buffs around the globe in 1978.

As a result, local journalist Antoinette May and psychic Sylvia Brown camped out in the store overnight with a photographer and a number of ghost catchers.

Once the staff had left for the night and the lights were dimmed, Sylvia began to sense a male presence approaching the group. In her mind's eye she 'saw' a tall, thin man striding down the aisle towards her with his hands in his pockets. In her head she heard him speak with a Swedish accent, identifying himself as Johnny Johnson and warning her that she would get wet if she stayed where she was. It later emerged that a well had existed on that spot. Sylvia established such a strong connection with Johnson that she was able to draw out his life history. He had come to California in the mid-1800s from Pennsylvania where he had worked as a preacher before succumbing to an inflammation of the brain which affected his behaviour. This appears to account for his antics in the aisles and the ladies' washroom, as well as the nickname 'Crazy Johnny', given to him by locals at the time.

Johnny lived out his later years working as a ranch hand for John Murphy, pining for a woman named Elizabeth Tafee who broke his heart when she left him to marry a lawyer. Johnny was 80 when he died from loss of blood after an accident with an axe while chopping wood.

Infra-red photographs taken for Arthur Myers' book on the haunting, *The Ghostly Register*, appear to show the figure of a man in the aisles of the store. Surprisingly, the publicity surrounding the haunting hasn't put off the customers, and it has allayed the fears of the employees who are no longer upset by the disturbances – they now know it's only 'Crazy Johnny'.

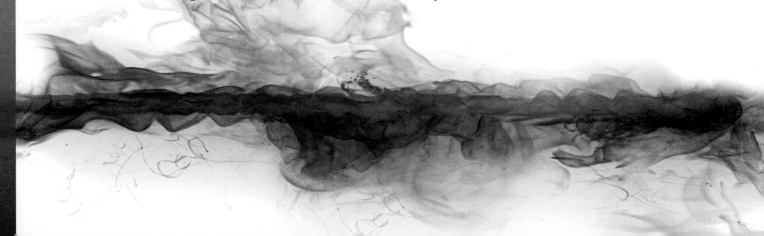

'Each morning, employees arrive to find stock scattered across the
floor and items placed on the wrong shelves'

CHAPTER 6

Spooky Sites

Unquiet spirits rarely linger in graveyards as they do not wish to be reminded of how they died. Some may even be unaware that they are dead.

Dead soldiers lie on the battlefield of Gettysburg, July 1863

In three days of fighting at the battle of Gettysburg in July 1863, a battle that was to mark the turning point in the American Civil War, 53,000 men lost their lives. The scale of the slaughter surpassed even that of the bloodiest days on the Somme during the First World War. No wonder then that visitors to the site have sworn that they have seen spectral soldiers wandering the battlefield as disorientated as the day they were killed. Some say it is the most haunted place in America.

Haunted Hotel

On the first day of the battle rebel snipers were able to pick off retreating Union soldiers from their vantage point in the Farnsworth House on Baltimore Pike. The house, still pockmarked with bullet holes, is now a small hotel where guests have awoken in the night to find an indistinct figure at the end of their bed. Odder still was the occasion when a local radio station set up an outside broadcast from the Farnsworth House only to have the power and telephone lines cut out. A local psychic, who was on site to give impressions to the listeners, heard disembodied voices warning their comrades that 'traitors' were around and he suddenly realized that the sound engineers were dressed in blue shirts and blue jeans – the same colour as the Union uniforms of the Civil War.

Several tourists have approached the park rangers over the years to ask the identity of a ragged, barefooted man dressed in a butternut shirt and trousers with a large floppy hat who appears at the rock formation known as

Confederate General Lewis Armistead at Pickett's Charge at the battle of Gettysburg. His forces were virtually annihilated

the Devil's Den. He always says the same thing, 'What you're looking for is over there,' while pointing north-east towards the Plum Run, then promptly vanishes. The description fits that of the Texans who were a rag-bag unit feared for their fighting spirit.

At the wooded end of the Triangular Field, site of Colonel Chamberlain's heroic bayonet charge which drove Confederate troops off the hill known as Little Round Top, visitors have documented chaotic paranormal activity including phantom musket fire and drum rolls. Shadowy rebel sharpshooters have been seen taking cover among the trees, but whenever the ghost hunters enter the field to record these phantom figures their cameras malfunction. There appears to be some form of electromagnetic disturbance hanging like a pall over the field; even photographs of the area taken from the outside looking in are either fogged or fail to develop. One possible explanation is that it is a mass of residual personal energy discharged into the atmosphere following the violent death of so many soldiers.

Several visitors have regaled their fellow travellers with tales of having heard musket fire from Little Round Top and even having smelt acrid clouds of cordite and cannon smoke. In fact, it is known that on the third day of the battle the sound of the massed cannons was so loud that it could be heard in Washington, 80 miles away. But the most unearthly episode must have been that experienced by a group of volunteer re-enactors who worked as extras on the epic recreation of the battle for the movie *Gettysburg* in 1993. During a break in the filming the group were admiring the sunset from Little Round Top when a grizzled old man approached them in the uniform of a Union private. He smelt of sulphur which was used in gunpowder of the period and his uniform was threadbare and scorched, unlike those of the extras. The man handed out spare rounds and commented on the fury of the battle. It was only later when they showed the rounds to the armourer that they learnt these were authentic musket rounds from the period.

The battle was finally decided by a single suicidal assault, the infamous attack known as Pickett's Charge, in which 12,000 Confederate infantry marched shoulder to shoulder across an open field only to be massacred by massed cannons and musket fire. In that single, fatal hour

Tombstone, 1885.
The town suffered two major fires in 1881 and 1882. Those, with the decline in the silver mines, meant that by the mid-1880s the place was virtually abandoned

10,000 were killed and with them died General Robert E. Lee's hopes of victory. Park rangers have witnessed many apparitions in the field after visiting hours including an unidentified mounted officer and another who was the image of General Lee. Local residents have maintained that on warm summer evenings they have encountered cold spots while out walking which transformed their breath to mist.

The Town Too Tough To Die

They called Tombstone, Arizona, 'The Town Too Tough To Die' and it appears that certain of its most notorious inhabitants are equally reluctant to go quietly. The town is now preserved as a national museum with many of the old buildings lovingly restored to their former rickety glory and stocked with original artefacts from its violent past including the hearse that transported bodies to Boot Hill, the hangman's noose and the honky-tonk piano which accompanied many a barroom brawl. Some say that if you stay after closing time you can hear the piano playing 'Red River Valley', the cowboys' favourite tune and hear the echo of their raucous laughter.

Some of the meanest gunfighters of the old West did their hardest drinking and gambling in the town's notorious Bird Cage Theatre which took its name from the 14 cribs suspended from the ceiling in which 'painted ladies', dressed in exotic feathers, would swing. The Bird Cage also served as a saloon where the cowboys and card sharps took their pleasure with women who could out-drink and out-cuss the best of them. Arguments were settled with a six gun and the loser was buried on Boot Hill, so named because many of its residents died with their boots on.

The streets of Tombstone were the setting for numerous showdowns, the most famous being the gunfight at the OK Corral when Marshall Wyatt Earp, his brothers and their consumptive trigger-happy friend Doc Holliday faced down the Clanton and McLaury gang, three of whom were killed. In the aftermath, the surviving Clantons and their friends took their bloody revenge. Virgil Earp was shot in the back while playing pool in the Bird Cage and his dying words are said to echo there after dark.

The tour guides are fond of telling visitors that as many as 31 ghosts are thought to haunt the saloon which was the site of 26 killings – a fact borne out by the 140 bullet holes that can be seen peppering the ceiling. The spook most frequently seen in the saloon is a stage hand dressed in black striped trousers, wearing a card dealer's visor and carrying a clipboard. He is said to appear from nowhere, walk across the stage and exit through the facing wall. Tourists have also reported seeing the ghost of a young boy who had died of yellow fever in 1882 and heard an unidentified woman sighing plaintively as if pining for her lost love. Others have commented on how impressed they have been by the authenticity of the actors' clothes in the gambling parlour and the dancehall, only to be told that the museum doesn't employ actors, nor does it ask its staff to dress in period costumes.

Since it is a museum, no one is allowed to smoke inside the buildings but nevertheless visitors will often remark on the strong smell of cigar smoke which lingers round the card tables and some have spoken of the delicate scent of lilac perfume in the backstage bathroom. Equally odd is the $100 poker chip which mysteriously appeared

Virgil Earp's last words echo down the ages; the Bird Cage Theatre in 1946

works in the gift shop on the ground floor of the Bird Cage Theatre swears she once saw on a security monitor a lady in a white dress walking through the cellar at closing time when all the visitors had left.

Residents and tourists have also reported seeing a man in a black frock coat who starts walking across the street but never appears on the other side

on the poker table one day then promptly vanished after being locked away in a desk before turning up in a filing cabinet some days later. And this is not the only object which appears and disappears to the bewilderment of the museum staff. The ghosts seem to enjoy playing hide and seek with small but significant items which they know the staff will notice if they are missing or out of place. Furniture has moved by itself and one member of the museum staff was physically attacked by a mischievous spirit who hit the tour guide on the back of the knee causing him to fall to the floor. Anyone who doubts that there is a physical presence in the old saloon only has to put his hand in the notorious 'cold spot' and feel the contrast with the warm air surrounding it to sense a distinct chill in the atmosphere.

Over the years several ghost hunters have attempted to capture the ghosts on film, but their cameras have malfunctioned as if triggered by an influx of energy as ghosts appear. Unattended still cameras have fired off exposures by themselves and have altered focus in the middle of shooting before resetting themselves correctly. However, it seems the ghosts can register on electrical equipment if their emission is strong enough. Small balls of light have been captured on film floating up from the floor and a face has been seen in the large painting which hangs behind the bar. One female member of staff who

Tombstone's Spooky Sites

Other haunted sites in Tombstone include Nellie Cashman's Restaurant, where customers and employees have reported seeing dishes crash to the floor, and Schiefflin Hall where rowdy town council meetings were held in the 1880s. At the Wells Fargo stage stop ghostly drivers and phantom passengers have been seen alighting from a spectral stagecoach on their way to the Grand Hotel – renamed Big Nose Kate's after its most famous owner, a prostitute who enjoyed a volatile relationship with its most famous resident, Doc Holliday, who lived in room 201. Residents and tourists have also reported seeing a man in a black frock coat who starts walking across the street but never appears on the other side and traffic often stops for a woman in white who committed suicide after her child died of fever in the 1880s.

The town's tour guides thought they had heard and seen it all until recently when they were shown photographs taken by visitors on two separate occasions. Both were taken at the same spot on Boot Hill and at first sight they appeared to be typical snapshots of their relatives standing in front of the gravestones, but on closer inspection the first subject was shadowed by the faint but unmistakable image of a cowboy in period costume.

However, there was nothing discernible of this phantom figure below the knee. In the second shot, taken by someone unconnected with the first tourist, their friend or family member smiled from the photo unaware that behind them could be seen a ghostly pair of cowboy boots and the lower part of their owner in precisely the spot where the legless cowboy had been seen in the first photograph. It may be that the film or exposure setting on the first camera was less sensitive to residual personal energy and so captured the cowboy's upper half which would be the stronger emanation, while the second camera captured the fainter portion only.

A Glimpse Into the Past

For over a century, tourists have been allowed access to enjoy the elegant palace and gardens of Versailles, near Paris, where Louis XVI and his queen Marie Antoinette lived in splendour just prior to the French Revolution. However, few can have seen as much of the palace's past glories as Eleanor Jourdain and Anne Moberly did in the summer of 1901.

Miss Moberly, aged 55, was the head of a women's residential hall at Oxford University and 35-year-old Miss Jourdain had been offered a post as her assistant. It had been Miss Jourdain's idea to invite Miss Moberley to spend part of the summer vacation touring France with her in the hope of becoming better acquainted while she considered the offer. Both were the daughters of Anglican clerics and not given to a belief in the supernatural, but what they saw on their visit to Versailles on 10 August shook their faith and forced them to question their beliefs.

They began with a tour of the main palace and then decided to walk to the Petit Trianon, one of two smaller palatial buildings in the grounds where the ill-fated Marie Antoinette retreated to escape the formalities of the court. It was a pleasantly warm day with barely a cloud in the sky, cooled by a soft freshening breeze – ideal walking weather, in fact – but after strolling through a large formal garden and a glade the ladies lost their way. Perhaps they had been distracted in the course of conversation, or had misread their guidebook, but whatever the reason, they now found themselves at the Grand Trianon, the palace built for Louis XIV.

Unperturbed, they consulted their Baedeker guide, which offered an alternative route to the smaller building by way of a lane which lay ahead of them. Neither lady remarked on the fact that they appeared to be the only visitors in this part of the grounds, although it struck them both as very strange considering how popular

They were overcome by a profound sense of melancholy and a detachment from reality as if they were sleepwalking through a particularly lucid dream

Versailles was with tourists at that time of the season. But Miss Jourdain *did* think it odd when her companion did not take the opportunity to ask directions from a domestic servant who was leaning out of the window of a building shaking the dust from a bed sheet. It later transpired that the older woman had not seen the servant. In fact, when they compared notes some months later they discovered that their shared experience differed in small but significant details.

The end of the lane divided into three paths and it was here that the English visitors came upon two men dressed in green coats and three-cornered hats whom they assumed were gardeners. One of the men offered directions in such a gruff, offhand manner that Miss Jourdain felt the need to ask again, but she received the same response. Looking around for a more civil guide she caught sight of a woman and a young girl standing in the doorway of a cottage and thought it odd that they should be dressed in such old-fashioned clothes. She later learnt that Miss Moberly had not commented on it because she hadn't seen the women – nor, for that matter, had she seen the cottage.

It was at this point that both women began to sense a change in the atmosphere. They were overcome by a profound sense of melancholy and a detachment from reality as if they were sleepwalking through a particularly lucid dream. Miss Moberly was later to describe the atmosphere as 'unnatural' and distinctly 'unpleasant': ' . . . even the trees behind the building seemed to have become flat and lifeless, like a wood worked in tapestry. There were no effects of light and shade, and no wind stirred the trees. It was all intensely still.'

The atmosphere was unusually oppressive as they came to the edge of a wood in front of which was a pillared kiosk, intended perhaps for tired visitors who wished to sit and shield themselves from the sun. But neither lady felt disposed to do so when they caught sight of the

The entrance to the palace of Versailles

A cottage built for Queen Marie Antoinette in the vast gardens
of Versailles, as part of the rustic village, or 'petit hameau'

face of a man in a cloak who was seated nearby. Both women sensed a shiver of repulsion as they looked on the swarthy, malevolent features. But was he looking at them or through them? Neither said a word, but instead debated whether to take the left or right-hand path. While they were considering what to do a handsome looking young man, his face framed in black ringlets, appeared in period costume complete with buckle shoes, a cloak and wide-brimmed hat and he advised them to take the path to the right through the wood. An instant later he was gone, but his directions had proven correct. As they emerged from the trees they saw the Petit Trianon in the clearing and approached it with a palpable sense of relief. It was then that Miss Moberly spotted a rather pretty fair-haired young woman in period costume sketching near the terrace. She was attired in a low cut white dress with a full skirt, a light coloured scarf around her shoulders and a wide-brimmed hat to shield her pale skin from the sun. There was something about this artist that predisposed Miss Moberly to dislike the woman, but she couldn't put her feelings into words. Curiously, her companion made no comment as they passed and it was only weeks later that Miss Jourdain admitted that she hadn't seen anyone sketching in the garden. The oppressive stillness returned as they toured the outside of the house but swiftly evaporated when they encountered a French wedding party in modern dress near the entrance whom they joined for a tour of the rooms.

Sense of Foreboding

Neither lady spoke of their experience until a week later when Miss Moberly was overcome with the same stifling sense of foreboding that she had sensed at the kiosk while recalling her experiences in a letter to her sister. At this she turned to Miss Jourdain and asked if the younger woman thought that the palace might be haunted. 'Yes I do,' replied Miss Jourdain. The two women then shared their recollections of that day. It was only later that they learnt that 10 August had been a significant day in French history for it was the day that revolutionaries marched on Versailles and seized the royal family. Had the two women unconsciously tapped into a residual memory of that pivotal day in the minds of those who had been present and sensed the approaching threat? And could it have been Marie Antoinette herself that Miss Moberly had seen sketching in the garden of the Petit Trianon? Miss Jourdain determined that another visit to Versailles was called for. Her second outing proved no less remarkable.

On a chilly damp day in January 1902 she returned

It was only later that they learnt that 10 August had been a significant day in French history for it was the day that revolutionaries marched on Versailles and seized the royal family

to Versailles and immediately set off in search of the Hameau, a model peasant village where Marie Antoinette had amused herself play-acting an idyllic rustic life with her friends. As she neared the site Miss Jourdain was again overcome with a sense of unreality, as if she was sleepwalking through someone else's dream. When she came in sight of the Hameau she passed two labourers in hooded cloaks who were gathering lopped branches and loading them into a cart. When she turned to observe them more closely they had gone. In the model village she was overwhelmed by an oppressive atmosphere and was tempted to turn back, but decided to press on as she suspected this might be her last opportunity to get to the bottom of the mystery. Eventually she emerged into a wooded park where she wandered a labyrinth of paths screened by dense hedges. The only person she saw there was an elderly gardener, but she heard the rustle of silk dresses which she thought impractical in wet weather and overheard the excited chatter of women

Did the tension of the days leading up to the imprisonment and subsequent guillotining of Marie Antoinette imprint themselves on the grounds of Versaille, so that over one hundred years later two friends 'saw' what happened there in a spectral re-enactment?

speaking French. Occasionally she thought she could hear faint strains of chamber music although there were no musicians in sight. On returning to the main palace she asked the tour guides if there were any actors on the grounds in historical costume, or musicians, and was informed that there were neither.

Determined to verify what they had seen, Miss

> *They also found proof that there had been a pillared kiosk at the spot where they had observed the malevolent looking man who answered the description of the Comte de Vaudreuil*

Jourdain and Miss Moberly embarked on a thorough examination of all the documents they could find relating to the palace during the period immediately prior to the Revolution. What they found appeared to validate their experiences. They traced a plan of the grounds which showed a cottage precisely where Miss Jourdain had said she had seen it, although nothing remained by 1901. They also found proof that there had been a pillared kiosk at the spot where they had observed the malevolent looking man who answered the description of the Comte de Vaudreuil. He had betrayed the queen by fooling her into permitting the staging of an anti-royalist play which had incited disaffected elements within the court to join the revolutionaries. As for the costumed figures, they identified the men in the three-cornered hats and green coats as Swiss Guards and the young man with black curls who had offered directions near the kiosk as the messenger who had hurried to warn the queen of a mob marching on the palace. This incident occurred on 5 October 1789, the same day that a cart had been hired to carry firewood from the park near the Hameau. If Miss Moberly and Miss Jourdain had indeed tuned in to this particular day it would explain why all the men

they had seen on that hot day in August were dressed in autumnal clothes and why the two women had been oppressed by a sense of foreboding.

Published, and Damned

Convinced that they had experienced a genuine glimpse into the past – a phenomenon known as retrocognition – the two ladies decided to publish their story. The resulting account, modestly titled *An Adventure* (1911), became an instant sensation and has remained a hotly debated issue ever since. Sceptics have argued that the women had mistaken actors in period costume for genuine spectres and in evidence of this offer Phillipe Jullian's biography of turn of the century poet Robert de Montesquiou. Jullian notes that de Montesquiou and his friends often amused themselves by dressing in period costume and rehearsing historical plays in the grounds of Versailles and that Marie Antoinette was a prominent character. Although a perfectly rational scenario, this does not explain why Miss Jourdain did not see the domestic servant shaking a cloth from the window or the lady sketching in the garden, both of whom were observed by Miss Moberly. Neither does it explain the appearance of the woman and girl at the doorway of the cottage which had long been demolished, nor does it account for the kiosk which had also gone by 1901. Miss Moberly and Miss Jourdain were equally adamant that the handsome young messenger and the men collecting fallen branches had vanished within moments of being seen and could not have had time to move on in so short a time.

Unfortunately both women naively willed the copyright to a sceptical friend, art historian Dame Joan Evans, who subscribed to Phillipe Jullian's rational explanation of events. Consequently, Dame Joan Evans refused to allow the book to be reprinted after the authors' death, but a century later their story continues to be cited as one of the most compelling cases of retrocognition.

Such episodes are very rare, but perhaps they are not as uncommon as one might imagine. In 1926, two English ladies shared a similar experience. They took a walking tour of the villages near their new home to familiarize themselves with the area when they came upon a large Georgian house in substantial grounds surrounded by a

wall. But when they made enquiries as to the owner and its history none of the locals knew which house they were talking about. Intrigued, on their next outing the ladies retraced their steps but found only a vacant plot with no sign of the house.

The Ghosts of Glastonbury

Glastonbury is one of the most sacred and mysterious sites in Britain, and of great spiritual significance to mystically minded Christians and pagans alike. Legend has it that King Arthur and Queen Guinevere are buried within the ruins of Glastonbury Abbey and that the Holy Grail, the chalice from which Jesus is said to have drunk on the night before his crucifixion, is hidden nearby. But of all the legends associated with Glastonbury the most extraordinary and controversial is that concerning the discovery of the ruins of the abbey itself.

In 1907, architect and archaeologist Frederick Bligh Bond (1864–1945) was appointed director of excavations by the Church of England and charged with the task of unearthing the abbey ruins which several previous

The ruins of
Glastonbury Abbey

incumbents had spent their lives searching for in vain. The work was unpaid, but Bligh had a thriving architectural practice in Bristol and he viewed the search for the abbey as an almost mystical mission. He was confident that he would succeed where the others had failed for he believed that he had an uncommon advantage over his predecessors.

His interest in paranormal phenomena had led him to join the Society for Psychical Research through which he had met Captain John Allen Bartlett, an eager advocate of automatic writing. Together the two men took up

pen and paper in the hope of pinpointing the location of the ruins by tapping into what Jung had called the Collective Unconscious. The quality of the messages they received swiftly persuaded them that they were in communication with separate discarnate personalities, quite possibly the ghosts of long dead monks who had lived in the monastery.

At the first session, which took place in November 1907, the two men sat opposite each other across an empty table in reverent expectation. Bartlett took the part of the medium and Bond the 'sitter'. This involved

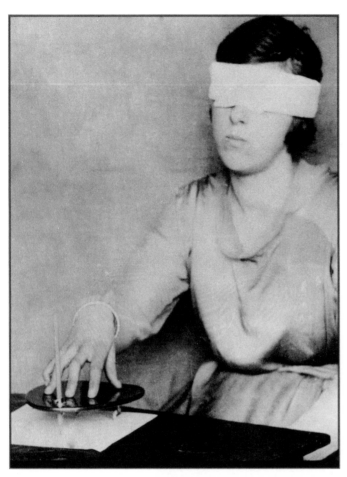

A girl using a planchette – a wheeled platform with a pencil attached – another 'automatic' way of receiving messages from spirits

Bond asking the questions while placing two fingers on the back of Bartlett's hand to make a connection with the spirits.

'Can you tell us anything about Glastonbury,' asked the architect, to which an invisible force answered in a legible scrawl by animating Bartlett's hand: 'All knowledge is eternal and is available to mental sympathy.'

The connection had been made and information as to the location of the chapels and other buried structures was freely given in a mixture of Latin and English by a disembodied spirit who identified himself as a fifteenth-century monk named Brother William (possibly William of Malmesbury).

To Bond and Bartlett's delight the 'monk' and his companions, known as 'The Watchers', supplied very detailed information regarding the location of the abbey's foundations. When the excavations started, often the workmen would simply have to dig a few feet down to hit the precise spot, after which the archaeologists would move in and begin sifting the soil for artefacts. Needless to say, Bond's benefactors were beside themselves and the full extent of the ancient site was revealed over dozens of sessions during the next five years.

By 1917, Bond felt justly proud in having uncovered one of Britain's most sacred sites and decided to tell his story in print. But when *The Gates of Remembrance* was published in 1918, the Church condemned it and strenuously denied that anything other than conventional methods had been used to unearth the abbey. In an effort to distance themselves from Bond they terminated his employment, banned him from ever setting foot within the grounds again and ordered that his guidebook to Glastonbury be removed from the shelves of the gift shop.

Since that time the occult significance of the abbey's location has been argued over by scholars who believe that it was intentionally built on an ancient pagan site to conform to an alignment of stars. Bond's communications with 'Brother William' appear to confirm this.

'. . . our Abbey was a message in ye stones. In ye foundations and ye distances be a mystery – the mystery of our faith, which ye have forgotten and we also in ye latter days.

All ye measurements were marked plain on ye slabbes in Mary's Chappel, and ye have destroyed them. So it was recorded, as they who builded and they who came after knew aforehand where they should build. But these things are overpast and of no value now. The spirit was lost and with the loss of the spirit the body decayed and was of no use to (us).

There was the Body of Christ, and round him would have been the Four Ways. Two were builded and no more. In ye floor of ye Mary Chappel was ye Zodiac, that all might see and understand the mystery. In ye midst of ye chappel he was laid; and the Cross of Hym who was our Example and Exemplar.'

Ghosts of the London Underground

The London Underground, or the Tube as it is known to the commuters who use it, shuts down not long after midnight, which is a likely relief to its many late-night workers. Many employees fear they will meet more than muggers, drug addicts and drunks if they work the 'graveyard shift'.

When the original underground tunnels were excavated during the Victorian era several historic graveyards were destroyed to make way for the network, and it is believed that their inhabitants were none too pleased at having their eternal rest disturbed. Other historic sites including gaols, pauper's graves and, most significantly, seventeenth-century plague pits were wilfully destroyed in the name of progress.

During the construction of St Pancras Station the church complained that the reburying of caskets at the site of an old cemetery was being carried out in haste and with disrespect for the dead. As recently as the 1960s the construction of the new Victoria line had to be delayed when a boring machine tore through a plague pit unearthing the corpses and traumatizing several brawny navvies.

If you add to this the number of poor souls who have committed suicide by throwing themselves under trains and those who have perished in disasters, you have a real-life ghost train experience waiting for the unwary traveller.

Aldwych

This station was built on the site of the Royal Strand Theatre and was said to be haunted by the ghost of an actress who hungers for applause. Closed in 1994, Aldwych had a higher than average turnover of cleaning and maintenance staff as dozens refused to work there

London Underground workers building the Piccadilly Line extension, 1930

Merchant seaman and tea planter turned actor, William Terriss or 'Breezy Bill' as he was known, was stabbed to death by a deranged and out-of-work actor in December, 1897

years until her death, outside the bank where he had worked.

Covent Garden

Staff at Covent Garden demanded a transfer to another station in the 1950s after a tall Edwardian gentleman in a frock coat, top hat and wearing opera gloves appeared unannounced in their rest room. It is thought that he might be the actor William Terriss who was stabbed to death outside the Adelphi Theatre in the Strand in 1897. The station was built on the site of a bakery which the actor patronized en route to rehearsals.

Elephant & Castle

After closing time, when the station falls silent, the night staff have reported hearing phantom steps, inexplicable rapping sounds and doors banging shut. It is believed the platforms are haunted by the ghost of a traveller who was in such haste that he tripped and fell under an oncoming train.

Farringdon

Of all the London Underground stations, Farringdon is the one to avoid if you are travelling alone. It is the haunt of the 'Screaming Spectre', a vengeful young apprentice hat maker who was murdered in 1758 by her master and his daughter.

after being confronted by a 'figure' which suddenly appeared on the tracks inside one of the approach tunnels without warning.

Bank

When Bank station was built, workmen are said to have disturbed the restless spirit of Sarah Whitehead, known locally as the 'Black Nun'. In life she was the sister of a bank cashier who had been executed for forgery in 1811. She acquired her nickname from the commuters who saw her dressed in black waiting, every evening for 40

Highgate

Highgate underground station is in the vicinity of the famous cemetery of the same name, a place that guarantees some serious spectral activity. Contrary to popular belief, ghosts do not linger around their graves as they do not want to be reminded that they are dead or how they met their end. Instead they 'commute' to where they can relive their routine lives and for many recently deceased Londoners this means their home, office and the Tube network. And you thought the trains were overcrowded with the living!

Curiously, local residents claim to be able to hear the

sound of trains running through an abandoned and overgrown cutting that was intended to connect with the Northern line when the station was extended in 1941.

South Kensington

The only reported sighting of a ghost train was made by a passenger in December 1928. The commuter claimed to have heard the screech of its brakes and to have seen a phantom figure dressed in an Edwardian smoking jacket and peaked cap clinging to the side of the engine just moments before it was swallowed up in the darkness of the tunnel.

Ghost Flight

Executives of American carrier Eastern Airlines were literally haunted by their past when they decided to reuse parts salvaged from a crashed Tristar Lockheed L-1011 to repair other planes in their fleet. Their troubles began in December 1972 when Flight 401 fell out of the sky over the Florida Everglades claiming more than 100 lives including the pilot, Bob Loft, and flight engineer, Don Repo.

Within months of the crash, members of the cabin crew were reporting sightings of both men on their flights and these were augmented by sightings from passengers who had been disturbed by faint but full-length figures, subsequently identified as Loft and Repo from their photographs. One female passenger became hysterical when she saw the man in the seat next to her disappear. He had looked so pale and listless that she had called an attendant to see if he was ill. The attendant arrived just in time to see the man disappear before her eyes. He had been dressed in an Eastern Airlines uniform and was later identified from photographs as Don Repo.

On several occasions the pair have taken an active interest in the flight. A flight engineer was half way through a pre-flight check when Repo appeared and assured him that the inspection had already been carried out. One particularly persuasive account was recorded by a vice president of Eastern Airlines who had been enjoying a conversation with the captain of his Miami-bound flight from JFK until he recognized the man as Bob Loft. Needless to say, the apparitions played havoc with the schedules. When the captain and two flight attendants saw Loft fade before their eyes they hastily cancelled the flight.

Usually the pair appear simply to check that all is well but on one particular flight they intervened to prevent a potentially fatal accident. Flight attendant Faye Merryweather swore she saw Repo looking inside an infrared oven in the galley and called the flight engineer and the co-pilot for assistance. The engineer immediately recognized Repo's face, then they heard him say, 'Watch out for fire on this airplane.' The warning proved timely. During the flight the aeroplane developed serious engine trouble and was forced to land short of its destination. The oven was subsequently replaced to appease the cabin crew who were becoming increasingly unsettled by such incidents.

This and other episodes are a matter of record in the files of the Flight Safety Foundation and the Federal Aviation Agency. The former investigated several incidents and concluded: 'The reports were given by experienced and trustworthy pilots and crew. We consider them significant. The appearance of the dead flight engineer [Repo] . . . was confirmed by the flight engineer.'

The airline responded to the intensifying interest in their planes by refusing to co-operate with anyone other than the airline authorities. It appears they have learnt the true meaning of 'false economy'. The story inspired a bestselling book, *The Ghost of Flight 401*, by John G. Fuller and a 1978 TV movie of the same name starring Ernest Borgnine and the then unknown Kim Basinger.

Haunted Hollywood

'What the average man calls Death, I believe to be merely the beginning of Life itself. We simply live beyond the shell. We emerge from out of its narrow confines like a chrysalis. Why call it Death? Or, if we give it the name Death, why surround it with dark fears and sick imaginings? I am not afraid of the Unknown.'

Rudolph Valentino

*Another haunted studio is
Universal which was the setting for
the original silent version of*
Phantom of the Opera *(1925)
starring horror screen legend
Lon Chaney Sr whose spirit has
been seen scampering along
the catwalks and gantries with
his cape billowing behind.*

Living legends die hard, particularly those whose larger-than-life personalities dominated the silver screen in Hollywood's heyday. Hollywood Memorial Cemetery (recently renamed Hollywood Forever) is the oldest graveyard in Tinseltown and is reputed to be uncommonly active as far as spectral sightings are concerned. The cemetery backs on to Paramount Studios which is said to be haunted by the ghosts of its most enduring stars, Douglas Fairbanks and Rudolph Valentino, who do not seem content with merely revisiting the scene of their past glories. Curiously, the ghosts do not appear during the day while filming is taking place, but instead wait until the sound stages are quiet and the crew are preparing for the next day's shoot. The most remarkable incident occurred one evening when a technician fell 20 ft from a lighting gantry and was apparently saved from certain death by a spectral Samaritan who broke his fall. He seemed to hover in the air just inches from the ground for an instant, before dropping to the floor, unharmed, in full view of his startled colleagues.

On another occasion two property men suspected their colleagues of playing a practical joke after chairs that they had stacked in a corner of a storeroom mysteriously returned to the centre. They decided to stay overnight in the hope of catching whoever was responsible and that night, to their horror, they heard scraping sounds and saw the furniture moving around the room by itself. The following night they plucked up sufficient courage to attempt another vigil, but the phenomenon did not

Lon Chaney, dressed as Red Death, in the 1925 film
Phantom of the Opera

recur. Evidently the spirits were satisfied that their presence had been acknowledged.

At Culver City Studios, carpenters speak in whispers of a grey figure dressed in a jacket and tie and sporting a fedora hat who walks right through them and disappears through a door in the facing wall. From the description he appears to be the restless spirit of former studio boss Thomas Ince who is credited with establishing the studio system and creating the role of the producer. He died in suspicious circumstances aboard a yacht owned by William Randolph Hearst in 1924. It is rumoured that the rabidly jealous newspaper tycoon was trying to shoot Charlie Chaplin at the time but killed Ince by mistake.

For a generation of silent movie fans Rudolph Valentino personified the 'Latin lover' and after his death at the age of 31 he became the most active ghost in Hollywood. His spirit glides elegantly through the rooms of his former mansion, the Falcon's Lair, gazing longingly from a second-floor window and visiting the horses in the stables. Staff at Paramount studios have sworn they have seen 'the Sheik' admiring the stock in the costume department and walking soundlessly through Studio Five where he lived every man's fantasy, seducing beautiful female film stars and being handsomely paid for doing so. Curiously, his fans appear equally persistent. The ghost of a lady admirer in a veil is often seen bringing phantom flowers to the star's tomb at the Hollywood Forever cemetery.

Another haunted studio is Universal which was the setting for the original silent version of *Phantom of the Opera* (1925) starring horror screen legend Lon Chaney Sr whose spirit has been seen scampering along the catwalks and gantries with his cape billowing behind. Chaney, who died in 1930, was known as 'the man of a thousand faces' because of his uncanny ability to transform himself – by aid of make up and acting – into all manner of the most hideously deformed characters.

TV's original *Superman*, actor George Reeves, is said to have shot himself at his Beverly Hills home in 1959, three days before his wedding, because he could not cope with being typecast. His friends and family maintain that he was murdered. Visitors to the house have reported sensing his apparition dressed in his Superman costume.

Newspapers proclaiming the death of
Marilyn Monroe, 6 August 1962

Another mysterious murder/suicide was that of Thelma Todd who appeared with silent comedy stars Laurel and Hardy, and Buster Keaton. She managed to make the transition to sound pictures but died in 1935 in the garage of her beachside café on the Pacific Coast Highway, near Malibu. The police suspected a suicide, but there were bloodstains which were never satisfactorily explained. The present owners of the property claim to have seen her ghost on the premises and to have smelt exhaust fumes in the empty garage.

The Vogue Theatre, Hollywood Boulevard, is said to be haunted by a projectionist who collapsed and died in the projection booth, a maintenance engineer, and a school teacher and her pupils who were burned to death when their school, Prospect Elementary, which had previously occupied the site, was destroyed in a blaze. The theatre had been a regular venue for studio broadcasts but there have been so many instances of (paranormal) interference with electrical equipment that TV companies are reluctant to hire the theatre any more.

Other haunted Hollywood locations include the Roosevelt Hotel in which several stars made their second home. Guests have frequently complained of hearing a clarinet playing in the early hours only to be told that it is the resident ghost of screen star Montgomery Clift who had stayed at the hotel during the filming of *From Here To Eternity* and had to learn the instrument to secure the role that earned him his third Academy Award nomination. Guests at the time had complained of the unsociable hours he chose to practise and they are continuing to complain long after his death.

More unsettling is the case of the haunted mirror which used to take pride of place in a room Marilyn Monroe had stayed in. Long after Marilyn's death a cleaner suffered the shock of seeing Monroe's face appear in the mirror, forcing the management to remove it and hang it in the hallway. But the ghost reappeared in the mirror whenever a guest paused to check their appearance and it has since acquired a reputation as 'the ghost glass'.

Some ghosts had too good a time during their life to waste the afterlife wailing and moaning. Writer, director and bon vivant Orson Welles continues to enjoy brandy and cigars at his favourite table in Sweet Lady Jane's

On-screen Ghostbuster Dan Ackroyd (middle) has had experiences of ghosts in real life (see page 157)

Bette Davis is said to haunt the rooms of Los Angeles'
Colonial Building, where she lived for many years

Restaurant in Hollywood. Fellow diners, the living ones that is, regularly comment on the smell of cigar smoke but the maître d'hôtel refuses to give a refund.

Actor Hugh Grant is said to have heard the ghost of Bette Davis sobbing and moaning as it sweeps through the luxury apartments in Los Angeles' Colonial Building where she used to live, while another larger-than-life actress, comedian Lucille Ball, is said to haunt her home at 100 North Roxbury Drive; windows have been broken in the Ball house, furniture has moved of its own accord and shouting has been traced to an empty attic. But if the new owners were thinking of calling in the Ghostbusters they might want to think again. *Ghostbuster* star Dan Ackroyd may have been fearless when facing spooky special effects on the big screen but in real life he admits to being unnerved when he realized he was sharing his bed with the ghost of Mama Cass Elliot, one time member of 60s singing group The Mamas and the Papas. 'A ghost certainly haunts my house. It once even crawled into bed with me. I rolled over and just nuzzled up to whatever it was and went back to sleep. The ghost also turns on the Stairmaster and moves jewellery across the dresser. I'm sure it's Mama Cass because you get the feeling it's a big ghost.'

One would imagine that behind the walls of their luxury homes Hollywood's celebrities would enjoy peace and privacy, but the home of actress Elke Sommer and husband Joe Hyams was a living hell to rival anything seen on screen in the *Amityville Horror*. On several occasions the couple and their dinner guests witnessed the spectre of a middle-aged man in a white suit passing through the rooms. The couple were repeatedly forced to flee from the choking fumes of fires which spontaneously and inexplicably broke out at all hours of day and night. Fire Department investigators made a thorough examination of the luxury property on several occasions with particular attention paid to the attic where the conflagrations had begun, but they could find no physical cause for the blazes such as faulty wiring, and expressed disbelief that the fires could have caught hold in that part of the house as there was no inflammable material to feed the flames. Dissatisfied, the couple called in the American Society for Psychical Research who documented a catalogue of anomalous incidents, but they could not appease the spirits. Sommer and Hyams were finally forced to sell their dream home before it burned down with them inside. It was subsequently sold no less than 15 times with many owners living there for less than a year.

Tate was in her bedroom when she saw the spectre of a 'creepy little man', as she later described him, enter her room and appear to search for something. She recognized him as the former owner of the house, Paul Burn, a theatrical agent who had shot himself in the upstairs bathroom after the break up of his marriage to actress Jean Harlow

But arguably the most disturbing Hollywood haunting was that experienced one evening in the 1960s by the late Sharon Tate, actress wife of film director Roman Polanski. Tate was in her bedroom when she saw the spectre of a 'creepy little man', as she later described him, enter her room and appear to search for something. She recognized him as the former owner of the house, Paul Burn, a theatrical agent who had shot himself in the upstairs bathroom after the break up of his marriage to actress Jean Harlow. When Tate fled from the room she came face to face with a second apparition at the foot of the stairs. It was the spirit of a woman who was tied to a pillar with her throat cut. Tate's screams echoed round the walls for it was her own ghost. Shortly afterwards the house became the scene of a sickening ritual murder when Tate was killed by members of the so-called 'Manson Family', who tied her to the staircase and slashed her throat.

Their Final Bow

Hollywood is not the only place to be haunted by dead celebrities whose egos were too large to go quietly. Flamboyant entertainer Liberace (1919–1987) reputedly haunts Carluccio's restaurant off the Las Vegas strip which he once owned and where he still demands that his presence is acknowledged. Regular customers recall the time when the lights failed and all power to the kitchen was cut off until someone remembered that it was Liberace's birthday. After they had drunk to his memory the power came back on. But unfortunately that is not the extent of his activities. Several female patrons swear they have been on the receiving end of the former owner's mischievous sense of humour – they claim to have been locked in the cubicles in the powder room by an unseen hand.

Elvis Presley, arguably the biggest star of all, is clearly not yet ready to bow out gracefully. Las Vegas stage hands have reported seeing the portly apparition in his trademark white sequined suit taking a final bow at the venue he made his own in the early 1970s, the Hilton hotel. Elvis has also been seen revisiting scenes of his former glory, specifically the former RCA recording studios off Nashville's Music Row where the mere mention of his name is answered by falling ladders, exploding light bulbs and odd noises echoing through the sound system.

Not all the apparitions in Las Vegas are those of the entertainers who lived like kings in the 24-hour pleasure palaces. The town's most notorious resident was Mobster 'Bugsy' Siegel who is credited with turning the desert town into the gambling capital of America. On 20 June 1947, Bugsy was 'whacked' by disgruntled business associates who accused him of overspending their ill-gotten gains and skimming some off the top for himself. He has been sighted mooching about his favourite casino in the Flamingo Hotel in Vegas dressed in a smoking jacket and grinning from ear to ear, as well as in the presidential suite which he had made his home. He has also been spotted running and ducking to avoid

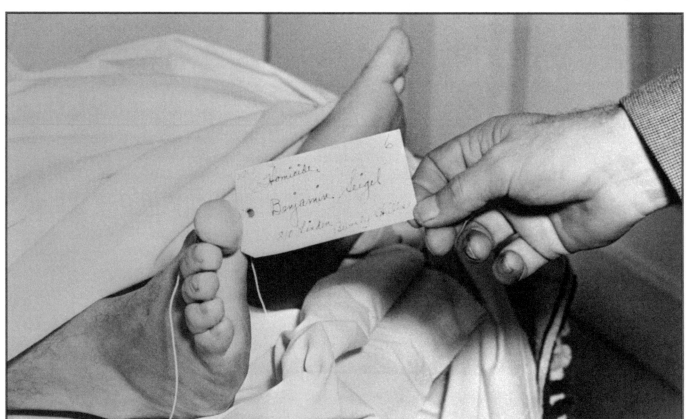

Bugsy Siegel turned up his toes – but didn't stop running in the afterlife

The playful celebrity that was Liberace was said to be just as young at heart after he died

imaginary bullets at his girlfriend's mansion in Beverly Hills, the scene of his murder, although he was shot while seated on the sofa. Perhaps it is his guilty conscience which pursues him into the afterlife.

Spooked Celebrities

Some people can take spirits in their stride while others need to sleep for weeks afterwards with the light on. Oddly enough it's usually the action hero types who discover that their fearless on-screen persona deserts them when faced with the inexplicable.

Jean Claude Van Damme, 'the Muscles from Brussels', admits he was spooked the night he came face to face with a ghost in his bathroom mirror. 'I suddenly felt very cold. I turned round and thought: "I've had a vision or something." It was blue and white and had a very smoky body. Since that moment I've believed in ghosts.'

Movie star Nicolas Cage, who has cultivated an edgy, unpredictable screen persona in such films as *Face Off*, *Windtalkers* and *Lord of War*, admits he was freaked by a phantom intruder at his uncle Francis Ford Coppola's home. 'I was living in the attic, and there were bats there between the walls – you could hear the scratching. One night I was not quite asleep when the door in front of my bed opened and there was this pitch-black silhouette of a woman with big hair. I thought it was my aunt coming to say goodnight. So I said, "Goodnight", and it didn't say anything. Then it moved towards me and my body froze up and I let out this bloodcurdling scream and threw my pillow at it. Then it disappeared. Now, am I saying I saw a ghost? I still don't know. But I saw something that freaked me out.'

The Matrix star Keanu Reeves may have been a messianic hero who saved the world in cyberspace, but he can still wake up in a sweat when haunted by nightmares of a real ghostly encounter during his childhood. 'I was living in New Jersey when I saw and felt this ghost. I

The Matrix star Keanu Reeves may have been a messianic hero who saved the world in cyberspace, but he can still wake up in a sweat when haunted by nightmares of a real ghostly encounter during his childhood

remember just staring at this suit which had no body or legs in it as it came into the room before disappearing. It was a double-breasted suit in white, and I looked at my nanny who was just as shocked as me. I just couldn't get back to sleep afterwards, and I still see the figure in my dreams and nightmares.'

Richard Dreyfuss, star of *Jaws* and *Close Encounters of the Third Kind*, was wide awake when he encountered the spook that cured him of his cocaine habit. 'I had a car crash in the late 1970s, when I was really screwed up, and I started seeing these ghostly visions of a little girl every night. I couldn't shake this image. Every day it became clearer and I didn't know who the hell she was. I had no kids, I was a bachelor. Then I realized that kid was either the child I didn't kill the night I smashed up my car, or it was the daughter that I didn't have yet. I immediately sobered up. I still don't get it, but, hey, it did the trick.'

Life Imitating Art

Even horror movie queens are unnerved when they meet the real thing as *Scream* star Neve Campbell discovered when she bought her Hollywood home without checking its history. 'Someone was murdered in my house six years before I bought it. I had friends round and I left them in the living room to go in the kitchen and they both thought I had just walked back in again. But I hadn't, so what they saw was the woman who was murdered. The previous owner had an exorcist come in, but I don't think it worked.'

Rumour has it that celebrity ex-couple Ethan Hawke and Uma Thurman were forced to abandon their eighteenth-century dream home in Sneden's Landing, New York, only months after they had moved in, because of inexplicable incidents. It appears that they were too scared to describe what they had seen and experienced even after retreating

The young Keanu Reeves experienced a ghostly encounter

Jacob's Ladder star Tim Robbins had a brush with spirits in his new home, and didn't hang around to find out what they wanted

to the safety of their old Manhattan apartment.

Rock star Sting was driven to call in professional ghostbusters when he discovered that his family were sharing their north London home with mischievous spirits. 'Ever since I moved there, people said things happened – they were lying in bed and people started talking to them, or things went missing. I was very sceptical until the night after my daughter Mickey was born. She was disturbed and I went to see her. Her room is full of mobiles and they were going berserk. I thought a window must be open, but they were all shut. I was terrified.' It seems exorcists did the trick as Sting and his kids now sleep soundly without unwanted interruption.

The late John Entwistle, bass player with The Who, enjoyed playing the role of the lord of the manor at his nineteenth-century country estate and was evidently prepared to share it with the previous resident. 'A lot of weird things have happened in the 22 years I've been here.

Among them are sightings of a lady in nineteenth-century clothes walking the grounds, and the camera of an uninvited photographer falling apart. Most recently I was having trouble locating a recording of Keith Moon pounding out a never-used Who song, and so I asked my friendly ghost for a helping hand. A few hours later, when I was about to give up the search, the tapes spontaneously fell off a shelf behind me revealing the Moon recording which had been hidden behind them. I used it.'

One would think that living in a converted church would guarantee peace and quiet but Tim Robbins, star of the supernatural drama *Jacob's Ladder* and writer-director of the (ironically) titled *Dead Man Walking* was evicted from his home, a former chapel, by decidedly unholy spirits. 'It was in Los Angeles, 1984. I had just moved into a new apartment in a converted church. I had two cats. I came home one night – everything was still in boxes – it was dark and the cats were terrified. There were clearly spirits in the room. Then I looked on the wall and there were cockroaches all over it. I moved out the next day.'

John Lennon's widow Yoko Ono discovered a 'lost' Lennon song without supernatural assistance but when the surviving Beatles came to finish it they sensed the presence of the author overseeing the production. Paul McCartney and John Lennon were volatile soul mates and successful songwriting partners during the Beatles' heyday until their acrimonious split in 1970. So it is perhaps not unexpected that the surviving members sensed the late Lennon's presence in the studio when they reformed to record John's *Free As A Bird* using his unfinished demo. McCartney has said, 'There were a lot of strange goings-on in the studio – noises that shouldn't have been there and equipment doing all manner of weird things. There was just an overall feeling that John was around.'

Celebrity Seance

Dave Grohl of rock band The Foo Fighters was sceptical when it came to the subject of the supernatural until his wife, Jennifer, persuaded him to join her in a séance. She had sensed unseen presences at their Seattle home and was determined to discover their cause. Grohl remembers, 'Jennifer asked if there were any spirits in the house. The glass on the Ouija board spelled out: "Y-E-S". I was just looking at Jennifer and she wasn't moving at all. The glass was travelling without her pushing it. Jennifer then asked, "What happened here?" The glass spelled out: "M-U-R-D-E-R-E-D". I asked who was murdered and got the reply: "M-Y-B-A-B-Y".' The couple has since learnt that according to a local legend, a native American baby was murdered there by its mother and buried in a well. The Grohls believe that it is her restless spirit which haunts their house grieving for the child and pleading with the present owners to give it a proper burial.

But it's not just Hollywood celebs and rock stars who admit to being spooked. Princess Stephanie of Monaco has confessed to having written a song with her dead mother, Princess Grace, who had died in a car accident in 1982. 'I found I'd written my own song and recorded it without really being present to the whole thing. Something was telling or guiding me to sit down and just write. I grabbed a pen and pad and the words came flowing out. I can't explain it, but I don't feel as if I wrote them. The words just came into my head as if someone on the other side was writing them down for me.' Her second album contained 'Words Upon The Wind', a song dedicated to her mother. According to her daughter, Princess Grace reappeared when Stephanie succumbed to stage fright during a French TV broadcast. 'Without my mother's help, I could never have done it. I was so petrified that I couldn't speak. Yet as soon as I got in front of the cameras, I could hear my mum telling me to relax and to just remember everything that she had always told me.'

POLTERGEISTS
by Rupert Matthews

CHAPTER 7

The Other World

The word 'poltergeist' is a German term that has been adopted in the English-speaking world. It refers to a particular type of paranormal event. Many other types of inexplicable happening are witnessed by people from time to time, but they are not recognized by formal science.

The word poltergeist is usually translated as 'noisy ghost', but that does not quite capture the full meaning of the term. The ghost is 'noisy' in much the same way as a party thrown by drunken teenagers is noisy. Not only is there a large amount of noise, but there is a rumbustious, anarchic degree of movement and jostling that at any moment might turn to violence.

There is also a feeling of potential mayhem about any place that a poltergeist visits. Nor is the 'ghost' part of the trans-lation completely accurate. There is a bit more to it than that.

In German the word might mean a spirit or a disembodied intelligence as often as it might mean a ghost. While some researchers might maintain that a poltergeist visitation is caused by a ghost, others would strongly disagree. It is but one possible explanation among many.

In this book I shall be using the conventional term 'poltergeist' to describe particular phenomena, but I do not wish to imply that I accept the ghostly interpretation. I think that something else is causing the manifestations.

I shall also be using the word 'visitation' to describe the period of time during which a poltergeist is active. Typically a poltergeist visitation has a beginning, a middle and an end. It lasts for a definite period of time,

Typically a poltergeist visitation has a beginning, a middle and an end

though this can vary considerably, and once it is over it very rarely begins again. I do not mean to imply that the house or the person involved is in fact being visited by some entity that causes the poltergeist activity – that might be the case or it might not. What I do want to say is that just like a visit by an elderly aunt there is, thank goodness, a start and a finish to the career of any given poltergeist you could mention.

Some researchers prefer to use the term 'poltergeist attack', but while some poltergeist events are violent the word 'attack' implies a purpose that might not be there.

'Crisis Apparitions'

A quite different type of ghost goes by the name of 'crisis apparition' among investigators. One such apparition was seen on 7 December 1918 at the Royal Air Force base at Scampton, Lincolnshire. A pilot named David McConnell was ordered to fly an aircraft to the RAF base at Tadcaster because it was wanted there the next day. He left at 11.30am, telling his room mate Lieutenant Larkin that he would return by train and be back in time for supper. At 3.25pm that afternoon Larkin sat reading a book in the room he shared with McConnell. He heard

Speak of the devil: in 1926 three people quite clearly saw the figure of an acquaintance of theirs punting a boat across a lake even though they knew him to be ill at home. They later found out that the man had died at the exact moment that they saw his phantom. See page 170

footsteps coming up the corridor, the door opened and McConnell stood in the doorway wearing flying kit. His flying helmet was dangling from his left hand.

'Hello, my boy,' said McConnell. This was his usual greeting to Larkin.

'Hello,' replied Larkin. 'You're back early.'

'Yes,' agreed McConnell. 'I had a good trip. Well, cheerio.'

He then shut the door and Larkin heard his footsteps retreating down the corridor. Larkin assumed that his room-mate was going to have tea. Or perhaps he was going to file his flight report.

At 3.45pm another lieutenant, Garner Smith, went to Larkin's room and asked him when McConnell would be back, because they had tickets to a show that evening. Larkin replied that McConnell had already returned, but Smith was convinced he had not. The two men went off to check and discovered that McConnell had not yet reported back, nor had the guard on the front gate seen him arrive. Larkin was adamant that he had seen McConnell, so a search began. The search ended when a telegram arrived from Tadcaster: McConnell's aircraft had crash-landed. McConnell had been badly injured and he had died at 3.25pm – the exact time at which Larkin had seen him arrive back in their room.

Hundreds of similar cases are on file. Most of them are difficult to verify because a phantom is often seen by a person who is alone at the time. There is usually only the word of that single person to rely on. However, the McConnell case is different because of the search made by Smith and Larkin. Dozens of men saw Smith and Larkin walking around the Scampton base looking for McConnell. Many of them could verify that the search was made long before anyone heard the news of McConnell's death. Although no one, apart from Larkin, saw the apparition, a number of people could testify that he had reported seeing it well before news of the tragedy had arrived.

Can a mind be read?: JG Pratt and Hubert Pearce in the famous ESP tests conducted at Duke University in 1933-4 by JB Rhine, the 'father of modern parapsychology'. The subjects achieved considerable success in communicating the contents of cards

Another such incident took place in 1926. Miss Godley of County Mayo had gone to visit an elderly man named Robert Bowes, who worked on her estate. He had been forced to take a few days off work due to illness. She took with her the estate steward and a servant named Miss Goldsmith. When Miss Godley saw Bowes she realized that he was seriously ill, so she decided that she would send a boy to fetch the doctor as soon as she got home. As the trio returned home in a pony cart, they were amazed to see Bowes punting a boat across the lake that lay near his home. The boat was about a hundred yards distant, but there could be no mistaking Bowes with his flowing white beard, bowler hat and dark coat. As they all watched, the boat carried Bowes into a reed bed on the far side of the lake and then it vanished from view.

When she got home, Miss Godley followed her earlier plan of sending a boy to the doctor's house. A couple of hours later, the doctor arrived at Miss Godley's house to announce the sad news that Bowes had suffered a sudden seizure and had died about ten minutes after Miss Godley's visit – which was exactly the time at which the phantom Bowes had been seen. This instance is rare in that three different people saw the crisis apparition, instead of the usual one.

Investigators have come up with several ways of explaining how a crisis apparition might come about. One theory is that the person seeing the apparition has the ability to sense things that are beyond the range of the usual five senses – sight, hearing, smell, touch and taste. This ability is usually called extrasensory perception, or ESP.

Those who hold this view believe that the unconscious mind of the percipient of an apparition knows through ESP that the person in question has died or has suffered some accident. This knowledge is then converted into a visible hallucination by the conscious part of the witness's mind.

According to another hypothesis, when people realize that they are about to die, or suffer a terrible accident, they can somehow send a message to someone to whom they feel closely attached. This ability to send a message directly from one brain to another is called telepathy. The mechanism by which this is achieved is unclear, but it is generally thought to be similar to ESP in some way. A third explanation is that when people are on the point of death they can create an apparition of themselves and project it to a distant place, where it is then seen by whichever witness or witnesses happen to be present. Whether such an apparition is a solid manifestation or an intangible shadow is a moot point. Quite how a person could achieve this by mind power alone is unclear.

No matter which explanation is favoured, the matter is most definitely a paranormal one. Conventional science does not recognize the reality of ESP or telepathy – still less does it endorse stone tapes or apparitions projected from a human mind. It would be possible to relate hundreds of accounts of ghosts and apparitions, but none of them have been subjected to close scientific study and there has been no scientific acceptance of the reality of any of the events.

Studying Poltergeists

A poltergeist is neither a classic ghost nor a crisis apparition. As we shall see in the chapters that follow it is something very different again. However, it does share some features with both of those paranormal events. What classic ghosts, crisis apparitions and poltergeists have in common is the spontaneous and unpredictable nature of their occurrence. One of the key reasons why scientists do not study such phenomena is that it is impossible to take one into a laboratory and look at it. None of these phenomena can be made to perform to

No reputable scientist has gone in search of the Yeti or the Bigfoot and few have regarded UFOs as a serious topic for investigation

order, so unlike chemical reactions or living creatures, they cannot be subjected to tests.

And then there is the danger that a scientist might be subjected to ridicule by his fellows, or be starved of research funds by the authorities, if he should announce that he is investigating ghosts. Similar considerations have held back research into all manner of subjects and topics. No reputable scientist has gone in search of the Yeti or the Bigfoot and few have regarded UFOs as a serious topic for investigation. Yet all of these things, and many others, have been seen and attested to by thousands of people.

With poltergeists the researcher does at least have some physical objects to examine. There are hundreds of testimonies to sort through and dozens of living witnesses to be questioned. That should make it possible to launch a detailed and thorough investigation into the mystery – one that might produce some useful answers. When studying unexplained phenomena such as poltergeists it is important to remember that most people are taken completely by surprise when they are confronted by a seemingly impossible set of circumstances. They display a tendency to remember only a few details of the event, and these are not necessarily the ones that an investigator would find the most useful. The inevitable result is that records tend to be incomplete and partial.

What is needed from a researcher is the ability to identify the features that are common to most or all of the episodes. It is sometimes better to create a 'typical' supernatural event from a vast mass of different accounts than to go into enormous detail in one case. Although bizarre or sensational individual incidents make for good newspaper copy or thrilling horror stories, it is often in the aggregate of cases that the answer may be found. It is with these points in mind that we can now begin to study poltergeist visitations and the poltergeist phenomenon.

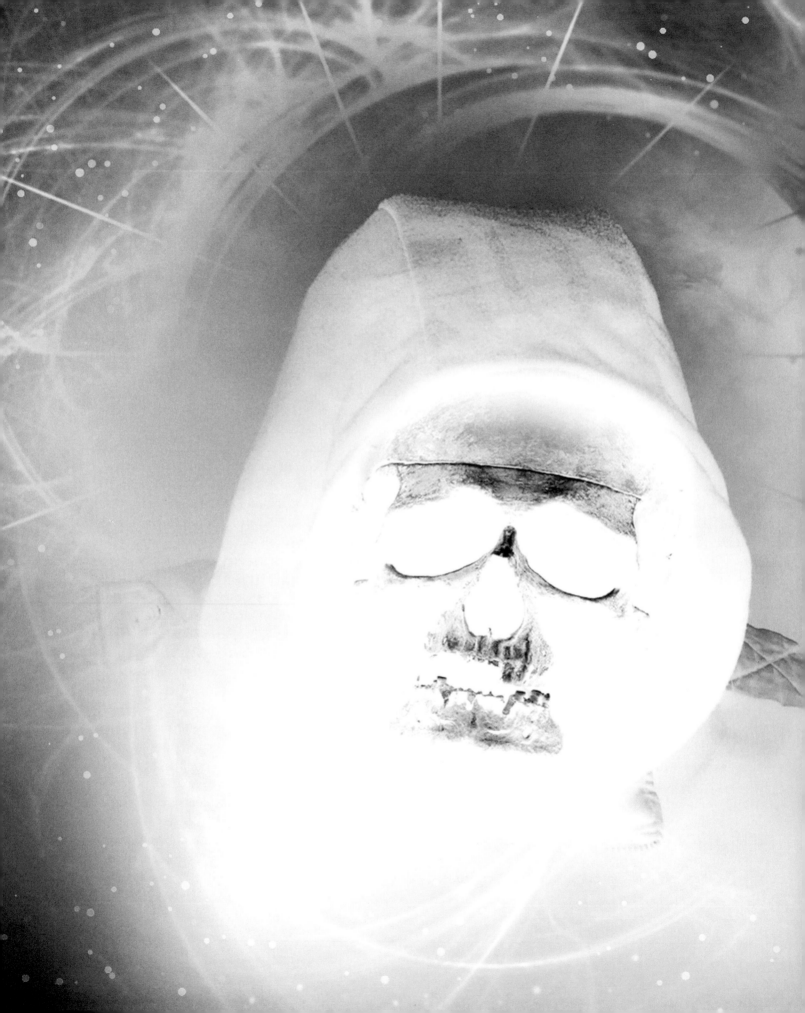

CHAPTER 8

Demons and Witches

t would seem that poltergeists have been around since time immemorial. Many ancient books contain descriptions of incidents that the modern researcher would interpret as visitations by poltergeists.

Unfortunately, most of these accounts took the form of small side stories to the main historic events that were being documented. As a result, they miss out many of the details that the modern researcher would find useful. Nevertheless they serve to show that poltergeists have existed for many centuries and that visitations were much the same a thousand years ago as they are today.

Demons

Such incidents took place within a different culture to our own, of course. Nobody is free from the prejudices of their time, nor can anyone have knowledge of discoveries and inventions that have not yet been made. It is not surprising, therefore, that some of the earliest incidents were seen as attacks by demons. Take for instance the 'demon' that attacked a farmer living just outside Bingen am Rhein in the year 858 in what is now Germany. The demon began by throwing stones at the farmhouse. A few weeks later it began pounding the walls of the house as if with gigantic invisible hammers, making the walls shake and shudder. After that, the spirit began following the farmer about. Although it was never seen, it might suddenly launch a stream of stones at the farmer wherever he happened to be at the time. The demon then learned how to talk. Somehow it managed to create a voice that boomed out of thin air. It accused the farmer of all manner of sins, including the seduction of a local teenage girl.

The hapless farmer's neighbours soon refused to have him in their houses. The local priest was called in. He decided that the demon was too powerful for him and sent a message to the bishop of Mainz asking for help and it was this letter that caused the visitation to be recorded in the episcopal annals of Mainz, which have survived the centuries. The bishop sent a team of priests to exorcize the demon. They went to Bingen equipped with sacred relics, Bibles, holy water and detailed instructions from the bishop on how to go about their work. When the priests arrived at the house, they sprinkled holy water all around them and then began their ceremony. All seemed to be going well until the assembled locals began singing a hymn. This provoked a sudden volley of stones, in the middle of which the demon informed everybody that the lead priest from Mainz was an adulterer who lusted after women. The commotion was so great that the priests retreated with their ceremony unfinished. They returned to Mainz to ask for guidance. The annals do not, unfortunately, record what happened next.

Holy Visitations

Visitations could also be interpreted as the spirits of the dead. In about 1522 (accounts vary) the convent of St Pierre de Lyon suffered a minor scandal when a young nun named Alix de Telieux absconded, taking some jewels with her. A couple of years later news arrived at the convent that the renegade Alix had died. It was said

'In the name of God, go': some poltergeists are thought by witnesses to be demons or devils, prompting the use of holy water and exorcism rituals in an attempt to get rid of the invisible intruder

In 1528 a poltergeist visitation at a convent in France was interpreted by witnesses as being caused by the ghost of a nun

Anthoinette de Grollée was dozing in her room when she felt somebody lift her veil, kiss her lightly and make the sign of the cross on her forehead

The noise was only heard when Anthoinette was present, but she was quite clearly not causing it by any physical means. Eventually young Anthoinette was called in for interrogation by the Mother Superior. The young nun explained about the knocking noises in her room and the feeling of being kissed. She then added that she had been having dreams about the late Alix in recent weeks. The two girls had been close friends before Alix absconded.

The Mother Superior sent a message to the local bishop, who sent a priest named Adrian de Montalembert to the nunnery to investigate. After Montalembert had questioned Anthoinette, it was not long before he heard the mysterious knocking noises for himself. Montalembert decided that the noises were being caused by the unquiet spirit of Alix. He decided to open up communications with the dead nun by calling out questions to her – she could then respond with coded knocks. Once Montalembert began asking questions, the spirit became so communicative as to be almost chatty. It confirmed that it was the spirit of Alix and that it was on some form of temporary release from purgatory so that it could seek salvation. The spirit passed on the lurid details of Alix's sinful life after fleeing the abbey and then it begged for absolution. Finally it asked if Alix's body could be exhumed and reburied in the convent. Only then, said the spirit, would she have demonstrated the forgiveness of those that she had wronged.

After some debate between Montalembert and the Mother Superior, it was agreed that the convent should go to the trouble and expense of exhuming the body and performing the ceremony as requested. The bones were located, dug up and transported to the convent, where they were buried with all the ritual due to a deceased nun of unstained character. For a few days peace reigned and then there began an insistent drumming as if the spirit

that she had succumbed to the sins of the world – but that detail might simply have been added by the ecclesiastical authorities. Then in 1528 one of the young nuns who had remained at the convent had a strange experience. Anthoinette de Grollée was dozing in her room when she felt somebody lift her veil, kiss her lightly and make the sign of the cross on her forehead. She woke up with a start but after finding nobody in the room she decided that she had imagined it.

A few days later Anthoinette heard the sound of somebody rapping on the floor of her room with their knuckles. There was nobody there and there was not enough space under the floorboards for anyone to be hiding. As the days passed the knocking sound got louder and more frequent. Then it began to follow Anthoinette when she left her room. Other nuns began to hear it too.

Desperate plight: the spirit confirmed it was Alix and that it
was on release from purgatory so that it could seek salvation

were demanding communication. Montalembert was
called back.

After asking the spirit how it was getting on, he was
informed that Alix was now released from purgatory
and was free to ascend to heaven. At this point it was
noticed that Anthoinette was floating several feet above
the ground.

There then came a massive thumping noise that seemed
to shake the entire convent to its foundations. This was
followed by another such blow, then a third and a fourth.
As the hammering blows continued a blazing ball of light
erupted in the convent church. It shone out with such
incredible brightness that nobody could look at it. After
33 ground-shaking thuds the noise stopped, the light
went out and Anthoinette fell to the ground. Silence and
peace then reigned at the convent of St Pierre de Lyon.
The spirit never returned.

When a visitation took place at the Dominican
monastery in Berne, Switzerland it was also seen as
a manifestation of a spirit of the dead. However, the
outcome was very different in this case. In 1506 a monk
named Jetzer went to see his prior with a strange and
disturbing story. He said that the bedclothes were being
torn off his bed by invisible hands nearly every night.
Not only that but he was bothered by noises. It sounded
as if some sort of creature was scrabbling around inside
the walls. The prior's initial reaction is not recorded,
but within a matter of days he could not ignore the
problem. The scrabbling noises had become knocking
sounds – no longer confined to Jetzer's cell, they now
invaded the entire monastery. No room was free of the
noises that came at any time of day or night. Despite
the most careful investigation, no explanation could be
found.

The poltergeist that plagued a monastery in Berne led some of the
monks to dishonest dealings that landed them in court

The prior decided to place holy relics into Jetzer's cell in the hope that they would cure the problem. They made it worse. The noises got louder and then doors began to be flung open and slammed shut with great violence. Stones were lobbed about and objects floated up from tables and drifted across rooms. A disembodied voice then began to mutter unintelligibly, but after a few days it managed to make itself understood. The voice said that it was the spirit of Heinrich Kalpurg who had been the prior in the 1340s. The current prior consulted the monastic records and discovered that there had been a prior of that name at that date. Moreover, he had been expelled for unspecified acts of inefficiency and incompetence. The spirit then announced that he had been a grievous sinner – which was interpreted as being a confession that he had been guilty of embezzling monastic funds, or maybe worse. According to the voice, Kalpurg had fled to Paris where he had been murdered in sordid circumstances.

> *The prior placed holy relics into Jetzer's cell in the hope that they would cure the problem. They made it worse*

The prior then ordered continuous masses to be said in the monastery church. God was beseeched to bring peace to the soul of Kalpurg, in order that the monastery might return to normal. The disturbances began to tail off and the monks hoped that their ordeal would soon be over. But events then took a bizarre turn. The prior decided that Jetzer's new-found ability to communicate with the dead would enable him to settle some theological matters. In particular, he wanted to know if the Virgin Mary had been conceived free of original sin. The matter might seem somewhat obscure, but in the early 16th century it was a matter of spirited debate between the Franciscans – who thought that she had – and the Dominicans – who insisted that she had not.

Next time the disembodied voice spoke out in Jetzer's cell the monk asked the prior's question. The voice sounded

Immaculate Conception: the theological dispute over the birth of the Virgin Mary was troubling the Church authorities in the early 16th century, and came to dominate the later stages of the Berne poltergeist visitation

nonplussed. It said it did not know but it would go and ask St Barbara – a saint that Kalpurg seemed to know quite well in the afterlife. A week later St Barbara appeared in Jetzer's cell, clad in shining white robes. Jetzer asked the question again. St Barbara assured him that she would find out.

After another week had passed St Barbara returned, this time accompanied by two angels. She announced that the Dominicans were right in thinking that the Virgin Mary had not been conceived free of original sin.

Jetzer gave the delighted prior the answer to his question. The fame of the monastery and its visitation spread far and wide. But the local bishop was unconvinced. He sent Jetzer a series of complicated questions that he should ask the saint when she next appeared. His aim was to make sure that she was not an evil spirit in disguise. The saint duly reappeared, along with the two angels. As Jetzer began to ask his questions he started to think that something was wrong. He made a grab for the 'saint', who fought back with remarkably unsaintly vigour. In the rough and tumble that followed, Jetzer unmasked one of the 'angels' as the prior, while the 'saint' and the other angel turned out to be senior monks. The prior assured Jetzer that they had only arranged the stunt to test his credibility – and then he declared that Jetzer had passed the test.

Jetzer seemed to accept the prior's story. Indeed, he appeared to be eagerly awaiting his next saintly visit. This time St Bernard of Clairvaux and St Catherine of Siena had come to see him. After a lengthy interview, 'St Bernard' said he would float out of the window and return to heaven. Jetzer took the saint at his word by grabbing him and bundling him out of the window, only for him to tumble the 15 feet down to the cobbled courtyard. 'St Bernard' was the prior. Jetzer then turned on 'St Catherine', who was trying to scramble out of the door. Realizing that he could not shut the door in time, Jetzer stabbed 'St Catherine' in the leg and so proved 'her' to be the procurator of the monastery in disguise.

The bishop now moved in with the full might of ecclesiastical authority. Jetzer was found guilty of conversing with ghosts and he was expelled from the monastery. He took up the profession of tailoring which he had been learning before becoming a monk. The prior, the procurator and the two other monks who had

'Saint Barbara' was called upon to speak on the subject of original sin during the Berne poltergeist visitation

False pretences: what at first seemed to be an apparition of St Bernard turned out to be a monk in disguise

The poltergeist that plagued the Stiff household in 1658 tore bedclothes off in the night and moved a shoe about the bedroom

been unmasked by Jetzer were less fortunate. Convicted of heresy and sacrilege they were executed. The original cause of all the fuss – the invisible spirit of Prior Kalpurg, with its rappings and its disembodied voice – had been forgotten.

Witchcraft

Elsewhere it was witches that got the blame for visitations. In February 1658 trouble erupted at a house in Loddington, Northamptonshire. The house was occupied by the elderly and fairly well-to-do Mrs Cowley, her widowed daughter Mrs Stiff and Mrs Stiff's two teenage daughters.

The first sign of trouble was when the two girls began to find that furniture and other objects in their bedroom had been moved while they were out. Naturally they put this down to some servant playing tricks, so they ignored it. Then one night the bedclothes of the two girls were torn off by unseen hands. This woke them up and caused them some fright.

A couple of days later the family were in the parlour when they heard a noise coming from the hall. When they went to see what had caused the commotion they found furniture from the girls' bedroom stacked up by the front door. While they had been out of the parlour a box had been opened and the flax it had contained had been thrown about the room. The servants were called and everything was put straight, but their efforts were in vain. More and more objects began to be moved about the house by the invisible prankster. During a two-week period the flax was removed from the box nearly every day, even when the box was locked shut; a loaf of bread danced around the kitchen of its own accord; one of Mrs Stiff's shoes took to floating about in the upper rooms as if carried by an invisible maid; and an ink pot flew out of the open window of the parlour. When the servant who saw this happen bent down to pick it up he was hit on the head by the stopper. On top of all that, large numbers of stones flew through the windows in both directions. Several of them hit members of the family and their servants, but nobody was ever hurt. Even when a carving knife was flung at a male servant he came to no harm. The knife reversed itself at the last minute so that the servant was hit by the haft, not the blade.

Some wizards and witches engaged in ritual bathing to prepare themselves for tasks, casting spells and mixing up remedies

During a two-week period a loaf of bread danced around the kitchen, one of Mrs Stiff's shoes took to floating about and an ink pot flew out of the open window

Other tricks were more destructive. A tub of bran was tipped into a box of salt, so that both were ruined; a large bowl of milk was overturned and all the milk was lost; a barrel of beer was ruined when mud and sand were poured into it; and a tub of peas was overturned and strewn around the storage shed.

So far, however, the trouble had affected only the family and its servants. But things changed on a fateful day in April, when the baker's delivery boy – actually a young man aged about 19 – came to call. He went into the kitchen as usual, put his basket down on the table and stopped for a chat with the cook. However, his cheerful chat came to an abrupt halt when a handful of crumbs from the basket rose slowly into the air, hovered for a

Witches were often blamed for poltergeist visitations

Lord of the dance: Old Jenkins made the innkeeper dance quite a jig when he overcharged him for a meal on market day

moment and then drifted across the room. They scattered themselves all over an unfortunate servant. The baker's boy fled and news of the event spread rapidly. Finally the local magistrate, Mr G Clark, was called in and it was he who took down the details of what had been happening.

The people of 17th-century England were firm believers in witchcraft – with good reason. Most rural areas had a local 'wise woman', or a 'cunning man', who was willing to undertake all sorts of tasks for the locals. These sorcerers made medicines from wild herbs to cure sick cattle, potions to help women in childbirth and ointments to aid healing. Some of these mixtures were highly effective because there are a number of genuinely medicinal wild herbs and plants in the English countryside. Even if the medicine itself was ineffective, the wise woman could offer remarkably good advice, such as resting for a couple of days. A busy farmer's wife

might not usually be able to put her feet up for a few days, but with the authority of the wise woman behind her few would argue.

Rather more spectacularly, some cunning men or wise women had mastered arts that sound rather like hypnosis. One cunning man, Pigtail Bridger of Crowborough in Sussex, had the ability to paralyze people with a look. Men who incurred his displeasure would find themselves rooted to the spot and unable to move until he told them they could. Another, Old Jenkins of Hereford, took his revenge in another way. When an innkeeper overcharged him for a meal on market day, Old Jenkins ordered the man to dance. The hapless innkeeper involuntarily danced a jig across the floor of his bar for over an hour until Jenkins tired of the sport and broke the spell, allowing the exhausted man to collapse to the floor.

These wise women and cunning men were powerful figures in pre-modern society. They were treated with enormous respect and sometimes with great fear. After all, it was as easy for a cunning man to feed cattle with poison and make them ill as it was for him to cure them of disease. Giving gifts to the local witch or wizard was a wise precaution. Some of these sorcerers traded on this fear by blackmailing local farmers into handing over a portion of their produce.

Witches and wizards are relevant to the study of poltergeists because a number of them were believed to possess what was called a 'familiar'. Some of these creatures looked like imps, demons or fairies and others had the appearance of hares or cats – the origin of the witch's black cat of popular imagination. It was said that they had the power to make themselves invisible. They would then sneak off around the neighbourhood to eavesdrop on what was going on, afterwards reporting back to their master or mistress. It was also thought that familiars did the bidding of the witch or the wizard that controlled them. The deeds ascribed to familiars sound very much like those of poltergeists. They moved furniture about, threw stones, made banging noises and generally disturbed the peace of the person who had incurred the wrath of the familiar's master.

It was as an attack by a familiar that the visitation at Mrs Cowley's house at Loddington was recorded. Once Mr Clark the magistrate was involved, the machinery of the law rolled into action. First of all, the local wise woman was arrested on the charge of sending a familiar to wreak havoc at Mrs Cowley's house. She protested her innocence but she was thrown into prison to await trial. The wise woman said that she had never had a familiar because she had never learned how to control one. She was not believed, of course, and a strict watch was kept on her. However, the upheavals at Mrs Cowley's home continued unabated. On the very day that the witch was imprisoned a cheese exploded into fragments as if a charge of gunpowder had been placed underneath it and set off. The witch was released. As was so often the case with these early accounts, the end of the story is not recorded. We have the report written by Mr Clark up to the release of the witch, but any documents that he wrote subsequently have not survived.

The death of a girl sparked the Bow poltergeist in 1660

In 1660 another series of paranormal events was blamed on a witch, but once again we do not know how the investigation ended. The case was investigated by Reverend Gibbs, prebendary of Westminster, whose account of the visitation regrettably tails off before the events came to an end. Gibbs was alerted to this instance of 'witchcraft' by an unnamed gentleman from Essex.

The man said that it had all started when he was doing business with a weaver named Paul Fox, who lived in Bow near Plaistow. A few months before the strange happenings began, he had called on Fox to be given the sad news that the weaver's youngest daughter had died a few days earlier. As she lay on her death bed, the girl had complained that a cold hand had touched her repeatedly on the leg. The Essex gentleman muttered his commiserations, concluded his business and moved on.

Some weeks later the Essex gentleman called again on Fox, but this time he was told that the household was being attacked by witchcraft. The gentleman was sceptical and he said so. At that point an upstairs window opened and a lump of wood was thrown out, missing the man by inches. The man denounced the stunt as 'knavery', whereupon the window opened again and a brick was lobbed out, which the man had to move smartly to avoid. Still convinced that some prankster was throwing the objects, the gentleman pushed past Mr Fox and made straight for the stairs. Fox warned him that the upper part of the house was no place to go. He told the gentleman that he and his family had abandoned the entire top floor a week earlier in order to escape the constant noises and the frequent rain of missiles. The gentleman harrumphed and went on up.

As she lay on her death bed, the girl had complained that a cold hand had touched her repeatedly on the leg

He found himself confronted by a scene of utter mayhem. Numerous items of furniture and clothing were scattered about in confusion and bricks and stones were piled up all over the place. The man stepped over the mess so that he could reach the room overlooking the front door. He thought that the person who had been throwing objects at him must be hiding there. As he pushed the door open, a staff that lay on the floor began to move of its own accord. He stepped forward and

Alarming floor show: during the peak activity of the Bow poltergeist, the upstairs storey of the affected house had to be abandoned by the family due to the violent poltergeist activity that took place there

stamped his foot down on the object to bring it to a halt. Something must have been making it move, he thought. He picked it up to look for a wire or a thin piece of string. There was no sign of any trickery. That was when a wooden pole lifted itself up from the floor and whacked him over the shoulders.

As he paused on the landing the door to the room was wrenched open by unseen hands and a mass of clothing, candlesticks and other objects came flying out at him

The man promptly fled from the room, pulling the door shut behind him. As he paused on the landing the door to the room was wrenched open by unseen hands and a mass of clothing, candlesticks and other objects came flying out at him. He ran downstairs to be greeted by the worried Fox family. They all retreated to the kitchen to discuss the terrifying events. Just as they sat down, a clay pipe rose into the air from the sideboard. Then it flew across the room and shattered into a dozen pieces as it hit the wall opposite – the 'witch's familiar' had come downstairs. The Essex gentleman called in Reverend Gibbs, who fortunately knew how to unmask the culprit. He ordained that the object that had moved around the most – a wooden staff – should be slowly roasted over an open fire. This would cause the wizard or the witch who controlled

It was hoped the burning of a wooden staff would bring an end to the Bow poltergeist by revealing the witch responsible

An old woman was seized, but later released

the familiar to come calling, he said. The fire was lit and the staff was placed over it. The Fox family sat down to wait. At first nothing happened and then there was a knock at the door. Paul Fox threw the door open and pounced on the person outside. It turned out to be an elderly woman who lived up the road. She had come to see what the column of smoke was for.

Convinced that they had the witch, Fox and Gibbs tied her up and sent for the magistrate. When the local magistrate arrived he was unimpressed. The old woman was of good character, attended church regularly and was about as far from being a tool of Satan as could be imagined – so he let her go. Gibbs then lost interest in the case so we do not know what happened next.

The Demon Drummer of Tedworth

Witchcraft was also suspected in what is perhaps the most famous of these early cases: the Demon Drummer of Tedworth. The scene of the visitation was the home of John Mompesson, a wealthy magistrate who lived at Tedworth in Wiltshire. The case caused a sensation and it was thoroughly investigated by clergymen and others. Mr Mompesson himself wrote an account of the visitation after it had ended, which finished with the words:

Beggars were a nuisance in the 17th century

I have been very often of late asked the question whether I have not confessed to his Majesty or any other, a cheat discovered about that affair. To which I gave, and shall to my Dying day give the same answer, That I must bely my self and purjure my self also to acknowledge a cheat in a thing where I am sure there was nor could be any, as I, the Minister of the Peace, and two other Honest Gentlemen deposed at the Assizes, upon my Impleading the praying God to keep me from the same, or the like affliction.

And although I am sure this most damnable lye does pass for current amongst one sort of people in the World, invented only, I think, to suppress the Belief of the Being either of God or Devil. Yet I question not but the Thing obtains credit enough amongst those who I principally design should retain a more charitable Opinion of me, than to be any way a deviser of it, only to be talkt of in the World to my own disadvantage and reproach.

The language is old-fashioned, but Mompesson's indignation is clear. He appears to be adamant that he did not invent the strange happenings or fall for a trick.

No doubt he thought that by publishing a true account of the visitation he could quash the more lurid inventions that were circulating. I have based the remainder of this section on Mompesson's comprehensive description of the visitation and the events leading up to it.

In the middle of March 1661 Mompesson was visiting Ludgershall in Wiltshire when the bailiff told him that there was a troublesome beggar in the town. However, two magistrates, Sir William Cawly and Colonel Ayliff, had apparently signed a document that gave the mendicant permission to beg in the streets. The beggar claimed to be a former military drummer in Ayliff's regiment. His habit of beating a drum to attract attention before playing a series of military beats and tattoos to entertain the crowds certainly seemed to support his story. The bailiff, however, found the man a nuisance and wanted him gone.

When Mompesson had the beggar, William Drury, brought before him he asked to see the document that gave him permission to beg. The magistrate quickly concluded that the signatures of Cawly and Ayliff were faked, so he ordered Drury to be thrown into prison and his drum confiscated. He told the bailiff to write to Ayliff asking if Drury really was a retired army drummer of good character, as he claimed. If he was, Mompesson said, he should be released, together with his drum; if not, he

Drury claimed to have been an army drummer

Watchmen were posted outside, but saw nothing even when the starlight was bright

should be charged with vagrancy and illegal begging. Thinking that he had settled the matter, Mompesson got on with his own business in Ludgershall and then went home.

A few days later Drury talked his way out of prison and then disappeared, leaving his drum behind. Not sure what to do with the drum, the bailiff sent it to Mompesson's house, where it was placed in a store room and forgotten about. Five weeks later Mompesson went up to London for a few days on business. When he got back he found his family and servants in a state of some excitement. He was told that a gang of thieves had attempted to burgle the house while he had been away. Everyone was convinced that they had heard the sound of men trying to batter the doors down in order to gain access to the house.

Left in the storeroom: Drury's drum soon became the centre for the poltergeist's unnerving noises

However, when a male servant had peered out of a window with a gun the noises had ceased. Although the servant had seen no bandits, nobody could think of any other explanation.

Three nights after Mompesson's return the noises resumed. Once again, it sounded as if a number of men were trying to batter the front door in. Mompesson roused his male servants, armed himself with a brace of loaded pistols and opened the door. The noises stopped abruptly. Mompesson walked out into the night, his pistols at the ready, but there was nobody in sight. The front door was then shut and locked, whereupon the same sounds started coming from another door. Once again, Mompesson opened the door and lunged out with loaded pistols. Again the noises stopped and once more there was nobody in sight. Mystified, Mompesson stayed up for a while and then went to bed.

Noises could be heard again on the following night, but this time they were different. The sound of a gang of ruffians trying to break in had given way to the patter of footsteps going across the roof of the house. Mompesson went out into the garden and peered up at the roof. The starlight was bright enough to see by, but he could see nobody moving on top of the house. The sound of nocturnal footsteps on the roof continued for three more nights. Then there was silence for the following three nights. On the fourth night a new sound came. It still seemed to originate from the roof, but it now sounded as if somebody was pounding or thumping with a wooden hammer. The noises lasted for about two hours and then they stopped. This went on for five nights and then it ceased. By this time, Mompesson had noticed that the noises started up just after the family had gone to bed – whether they retired early or late. He suspected that someone, or something, was watching them.

After three peaceful nights the trouble began again. This time the thumping noises began on the roof and then moved to the walls of the house. The sounds moved from side to side and up and down as if whatever was doing the pounding was hovering in front of the walls. After several nights of aimless wandering, the pounding noises began to centre around one particular room – the storeroom where Drury's drum had been put. Then the drum began to play itself. By this time it was August and Mrs

The disturbing sounds ceased temporarily when Mrs Mompesson gave birth to her baby

Mompesson was getting close to giving birth. As was then usual among the gentry, Mrs Mompesson retired to her bedroom when the due date for the baby approached. At that point the nocturnal noises abruptly ceased. When she had given birth, Mrs Mompesson stayed in her room for three weeks in order to rest, recover and bond with her baby. Then she came downstairs to show the child off to visitors and relatives. That very night the noises began again, but now they were even more terrifying than before.

The noises began as before, with loud thudding sounds coming from the walls and the roof. But very soon they moved inside the house. It sounded as if some invisible being was thumping its fists against the doors, furniture and walls. Mompesson realized that several of the hammering episodes sounded like military drum beats and calls. This confirmed him in the idea that Drury was somehow to blame. It was very soon obvious that the invisible intruder had lost interest in the drum and had instead developed a fascination with the Mompesson children. None of the accounts state how many children there were, but at least one of them was on the verge of adulthood while the others were younger. Three of the younger children shared a bedroom and it was here that the trouble began to focus. The children's beds would be struck as if with hammers and then the sound of claws scratching the floor would be heard. One night the children's beds were lifted more than two feet up into the air. They were then allowed to fall back to the floor with a terrific crash. Mompesson tried moving the children to a new room but it did no good – the invisible intruder merely followed them.

On 5 November the visitation entered a new phase. It began in the children's room in the middle of the morning. A servant was tidying up the mess from the night before when he saw a wooden board twitch and move. 'Give it to me,' said the man. The board promptly floated up into the air as if carried by unseen hands and then it drifted slowly towards the servant. It stopped when it was about a yard from him. The servant called out for Mompesson, who came into the room. 'Nay,' said the servant. 'Let me have it in my hand.' The wooden board then drifted closer and came to rest in his outstretched palm. He put the board down, but it instantly sprang into the air again and placed itself between his fingers. This happened no fewer than 20 times, at which point Mompesson told the servant to leave the room. As the servant left there was a sudden and overpowering stench of burning sulphur.

The children's bedroom was the scene of some of the most dramatic events in the Tedworth visitation: when the stench of burning sulphur became overwhelming, Mompesson sent for the local vicar

The smell of hell? Mr Cragg, the local vicar, suggested that a prayer meeting might solve the problem

Sulphur being considered to be the smell of hell, Mompesson sent for the local vicar, Mr Cragg. The vicar suggested that a prayer meeting might solve the problem. He then rounded up a group of intrepid neighbours, who were willing to take on in prayer what was by now being called the 'Demon Drummer'. When Mr Cragg arrived the drumming and pounding noises first sounded out from several rooms, but then retreated to the children's bedroom. Mr Cragg led Mompesson and the group of neighbours up to the bedroom. As soon as Cragg knelt down and began to pray, the noises stopped. Encouraged, the neighbours joined in the prayers. When the praying finished, Cragg stood up and turned to say something to Mompesson.

As he did so a chair in the corner of the room began walking forwards on its own. Then a wooden chest started bouncing up and down. The children's shoes leapt out of the cupboard where they were stored, rose about six feet above the floor and then began flying back and forth across the room. The chair continued its advance towards the minister, but it seems to have been only a distraction – a wooden board came up and hit him from behind while he was staring at the walking chair. To his great surprise, the wooden board did not hurt him at all. All he felt was a gentle nudge. As the mayhem continued Cragg and the others fled, leaving Mompesson to face the invisible intruder alone.

Having decided that some sort of decisive action was needed, Mompesson split the children up and sent each of them to stay with a different relative. He hoped that the Demon Drummer would not be able to torment them all at the same time. The plan worked because most of the children were left alone – only Mompesson's 10-year-old daughter was troubled. Early in December, the magistrate brought the children home and changed the family's sleeping arrangements. Mrs Mompesson and the baby slept in one room, the children who did not seem to be affected slept in a second and Mompesson shared a room with the 10-year-old girl. These changes seem to have produced an alteration in the behaviour of the intruder. The loud banging and thumping noises decreased in volume and tempo, but now objects began to move about when nobody was watching. A Bible was frequently moved to the fireside from its place on a shelf, while clothes belonging to Mr Mompesson's mother were taken out of their wardrobe and dumped on the floor.

One day a friend of old Mrs Mompesson's came to visit. The woman said that she had heard of a fairy that had been in the habit of visiting a house in a village a few miles away. It had moved things about in a similar way, but it had also left money behind as if to make up for the nuisance it had caused. Old Mrs Mompesson said that she would be pleased if their drummer would leave money behind. And for the next few days the drumming was replaced by the sound of coins being counted out or jingled in a pouch. To Mrs Mompesson's disappointment, though, no money was ever found.

A household servant named John then went to Mr Mompesson and told him that he had noticed an odd

All hell let loose? A peak in the Tedworth visitation came when a chair, chest of drawers and shoes all flew about the children's bedroom at exactly the same time

thing. Whenever he was holding a knife or a sword, the intruder would cease its activities. Next time the drumming began Mompesson tested the theory. He got John to pick up a sword, whereupon the noises ceased abruptly. This rather curious ploy worked for the rest of the visitation. If the household wanted peace, all that was needed was for John to enter the troubled room carrying a sword.

However, he fell asleep one night while he was holding a sword in his hand. As soon as it slipped from his fingers the pounding noises immediately began. When he bent down to pick the sword up it sprang away from him as if

In its later stages the Tedworth poltergeist developed an aversion to swords and would not manifest itself when they were held

it had been kicked away. This happened twice before he managed to grab it, after which the noises again ceased.

In January 1662 something new happened. The sound of a man singing began to be heard. The eerie voice could usually be heard high up in a chimney. At about the same time a glowing ball of blue light began to be seen at night, gliding gently and silently from room to room. It seemed to be looking for something – or someone. On 10 January Sir Thomas Chamberlain of Oxford arrived with a group of gentlemen. He had come to investigate matters. The new arrivals experienced all of the usual tricks of the Demon Drummer and then a new stunt began – the sound of rustling silk and dainty footsteps was heard, as if a lady in a silk dress were walking through the house on high heels.

One night, one of Sir Thomas's companions made a decision to challenge the intruder. As the sounds of drumming moved through the house the man called out in a firm voice.

'Drummer,' he cried, 'if Satan hath set thee to work give three knocks and no more.'

There then came three incredibly loud knocks, after which there was no more activity for several hours.

A few days later the family Bible was found lying on the floor. It was open at Mark, Chapter 3, which referred to Jesus being able to cast out demons.

By the middle of 1662 the intensity and frequency of the disturbances was fading, but they continued to erupt from time to time. Sometimes a voice would shout out, 'A

Out of this world: some theories formulated to explain supernatural activity suggest that the Earth's magnetic field and its interaction with solar rays may affect the frequency and duration of paranormal events

The Mompesson's family Bible was often moved about by unseen hands during the Tedworth visitation, but Drury was later acquitted of having dealings with an evil spirit ['quendam malum spiritum negotiare'] by the petty Jury

A conversation in prison led to Drury being tried for witchcraft, accused of having caused the poltergeist activity in Tedworth

witch, a witch'. At other times the drumming would return for a few nights or phantom footsteps would be heard around the house. One night John the servant found himself confronted by what looked like a black shadow in the size and shape of a man with two glowing red eyes.

Then in April 1663 came startling news from Gloucester. William Drury had been arrested for theft, but before he had been brought to trial a most amazing thing had happened. When Drury discovered that a man from Wiltshire was visiting the prison he called the visitor over to his cell.

'What news is there from Wiltshire?' asked Drury.

'Why none of concern to thee,' replied the visitor.

Drury chuckled. 'Oh, no,' he scoffed. 'Do not you hear of the drumming at a gentleman's house in Tedworth?'

'That I do, well enough,' replied the visitor quickly.

'Aye,' said Drury boastfully. 'I have plagued him and he shall never be at quiet till he hath made me satisfaction for taking away my drum.'

The man from Wiltshire hurried to tell the magistrates about the exchange. As a result Drury was sent off to the courts in Salisbury to stand trial for witchcraft. Mompesson himself appeared as a witness to testify to the mayhem that had been disturbing his house. In his account Mompesson recorded:

Royal intervention: King Charles II sent two courtiers to Tedworth to investigate the poltergeist activity, but by this time the visitation was drawing to a close and the men witnessed nothing

Stonemason Andrew Mackie and his family were plagued by a particularly active poltergeist in 1695

I indicted him as a felon for the supposed witchcraft about my house. The Assizes came on, where I indicted him on the Statute Primo Jacobi cap.12. Where you may find that to feed, imploy, or reward any evil spirit is Felony. And the Indictment against him was that he did quendam malum spiritum negotiare. The grand Jury found the Bill upon the evidence, but the petty Jury acquitted him.

Despite this, Drury was convicted of being a vagabond and sentenced to be transported to the West Indies to work as a slave on the sugar plantations. As at Ludgershall, however, he somehow got out of prison and again vanished from view.

By this time the Demon Drummer of Tedworth had become so famous that Charles II himself had taken an interest. He sent Lord Falmouth and Lord Chesterfield down to investigate. Nothing untoward happened during the few days that the gentlemen were present, but then all of the accounts agree that things were calming down in any case. It was probably this abortive visit that led to the rumours that the disturbances had never actually taken place. Some even said that they had been the result of some sort of trickery on the part of Mompesson or a member of his household. After the two courtiers had left there were a few further events, but they were minor compared to what had gone before. By the autumn of 1663, whatever had been causing the problems had gone. The Demon Drummer of Tedworth was no more.

The Ringcroft Events

Other poltergeist attacks did, however, continue but witchcraft was not always seen as the culprit. The strange events that took place over a four-month period in 1695 at Ringcroft in Galloway, Scotland came in for as much attention as did the Demon Drummer of Tedworth. This time, however, those on the receiving end of the visitation chose to blame a 'spirit' for the trouble. The case was thoroughly investigated by the local minister, Andrew Ewart, who at various times called in four other ministers to help him, assisted by two local lairds and several gentlemen.

The centre of the visitation was the humble home of Andrew Mackie, a stonemason who lived in the village of

The Mackies' cattle were found roaming loose after each animal had been securely tied up in the byre the night before

On 10 March the four children were about to enter the house when nobody else was at home, but they stopped dead in their tracks when they saw what looked like a human figure. It was sitting hunched up in front of the fireplace, wrapped up in a blanket. The youngest boy, aged ten, recognized the blanket as being his own. 'We have nothing to fear if we bless ourselves first,' he told his siblings. When they still hung back, the boy said a brief prayer and then stepped boldly forward. He grabbed the blanket and gave it a tug. The cloth came away easily, leaving nothing behind but empty air and a stool.

On the following day the minister came to say prayers in the house. He was assailed by a shower of stones. The barrage soon stopped and his prayers were completed. There was no further trouble for a week, but on 18 March the stone throwing began again. The minister was unable to return to the house himself, so he asked Charles Maclellan, laird of Colline, to go in his place. Colline recorded the following statement:

I went to the house, where the spirit molested me mightily, threw stones and divers other things at me, and beat me several times on the shoulders and sides with a great staff so that those who were present heard the noise of the blows. That same night it pulled me off the side of a Bed, knocked upon the Chests and Boards as People do at a Door. And as I was at Prayer leaning on the side of a bed, I felt something thrusting my arm up and casting my eyes thitherward perceived a little white Hand and Arm from the Elbow down, but it vanished presently.

In early April the visitation took a turn for the worse. Bundles of burning straw began to appear around the farm, apparently out of nowhere. At first the fires were confined to the stone-flagged yard, and so did no harm, but then lumps of burning peat began to be thrown instead of stones. One lodged in the thatched roof of a sheep house, which then burned down. Then a lump of stone fell on to a bed shared by two of the children. It was so hot that it scorched a hole in the bedclothes before it could be kicked off. Two hours later it was still too hot to hold.

On 8 April Mackie was digging in his garden when he found some bones. He alerted the local

Ringcroft. As was so often the case, the victims had not realized that something odd was happening until several unexplained events had taken place. Mackie later stated that the trouble had begun one night in February 1695. All of his cattle had escaped from their shed because the ropes holding them in their stalls had been cut or torn. At the time he had blamed intruders. A few days later something else had happened. On that occasion he had found one cow tied so tightly to a roof beam that its hooves were barely touching the ground and it was almost choking.

It was on the night of 7 March that the family realized that something supernatural was afoot. A number of stones were thrown around the house by invisible hands. The doors and the windows were locked and every room was searched, but still the unseen assailant threw stones about. The Mackie family soon discovered that no matter how large the stones were, or how fast they flew through the air, they did no damage when they hit a person or an object. Anyone who was struck by one of the stones felt that somebody had gently pushed it against them and then let it fall.

Sent sprawling: when five church ministers gathered to perform an exorcism at the Mackie farm, the poltergeist responded by lifting one of the churchmen bodily into the air before throwing him flat on his face

Back to the beginning: the Mackie poltergeist ended its visitation where it had started, in the cow byre

magistrate, who at once concluded that the bones must belong to a murder victim. His theory was that the ghost of the deceased person must be causing all of the trouble. Colline was again called in, but despite the most rigorous inquiries no hint of a missing person with any connection to the house could be found.

Then on 9 April Ewart, the local minister, summoned four fellow ministers to the house for an exorcism. The ritual had only just started when the ministers were hit by a deluge of stones. Ewart ignored the attack and continued. But then something lifted him up into the air and pushed him forward, so that he fell flat on his face. Undeterred he managed to finish his service. Unfortunately, it had no noticeable effect.

For several days objects were moved around, stones were thrown and burning peat was hurled in all directions. Then on 26 April the 'spirit' began to talk. 'Ye all be witches,' it announced. 'And I shall take thee down to Hell.' After uttering several other threats the voice turned suddenly more gentle. 'Thou shalt be troubled till Tuesday,' it declared.

On the following Tuesday Colline was again present, having been told about the prediction that the spirit voice had made. When noises began coming from the barn, Colline led Mackie to the doorway and both men peered in. According to Colline:

We observed a black thing in the corner of the same. It increased gradually as if it would have filled the whole House; we could not discern any distinct Form it had, but only that it resembled a black Cloud. It was very frightening to them all and threw barley and mud in their faces.

And then suddenly the thing was gone, never to return.

The Cock Lane Ghost

The cases that we have so far examined remain mysterious and unexplained, even though they were seen as the work of ghosts, witches or demons in their time. However, a mysterious haunting that caught the public imagination in 1762 appears to have been satisfactorily explained in the same year. The train of events that led to the Cock Lane Ghost, as the visitation came to be known, began in 1756 when William Kent married Elizabeth Lynes in Norfolk. The couple then moved to London, but a year later Elizabeth died in childbirth. Her sister Fanny moved to London to care for the baby and to act as housekeeper for Kent. The baby died of some

The famous Cock Lane Ghost poltergeist began its activities when Fanny Lynes invited a neighbour's daughter to stay

The Cock Lane Ghost declared that it was the ghost of Fanny Lynes, claiming she had been poisoned by her lover

came back, but this time they were louder and more insistent. By the time Kent returned from London Fanny was in a state of great fear. She had somehow become convinced that the noises were caused by a demon that had come to kill her.

Kent could see no alternative but to move, so he took rooms in Bartlett Court, Clerkenwell. Before leaving, he asked Parsons for the return of his money. Parsons refused to pay him back and then he taunted Kent with the fact that he was living with Fanny out of wedlock. He threatened to write to Fanny's family in Norfolk and reveal what was going on. Kent consulted his lawyers and launched a legal action to get his money back.

Fanny declared that she had been murdered by Kent, who had daily dosed her drink with arsenic. She had not succumbed to smallpox after all

unspecified illness a few months later – not an uncommon occurrence at the time – but by this time Fanny and Kent had fallen in love.

The law did not permit them to marry at that time but nothing could stop them setting up house together. They occupied the upper floors of a property in Cock Lane which were rented from the man who lived on the ground floor, a Mr Richard Parsons. Being short of cash, Parsons borrowed £20 from Kent. He agreed to pay the sum back at a rate of a pound each month. By the autumn of 1761 Fanny was pregnant, so when Kent had to go away from London for a couple of weeks on business she did not want to be left alone. Her solution was to invite her landlord's 11-year-old daughter Elizabeth to stay with her while Kent was away.

One night, a strange noise was heard in the Kent apartment. At first it sounded as if a large rat was scurrying about behind the wooden panelling, but then it began to sound more like human knuckles banging on wood. It was rather odd. On the next night the sounds

Meanwhile, the move to Clerkenwell proved to be disastrous. Within days Fanny had contracted smallpox and a few days later she was dead. Back in Cock Lane, the strange noises continued. The sounds migrated downstairs from the former Kent room to Elizabeth's bedroom. They were most noticeable at night, when she was in bed, but they would start at all sorts of hours. However, it was soon noticed that they could only be heard when Elizabeth was in the house.

Parsons began charging people to enter his house so that they could listen to the inexplicable noises. Among those who came were Dr Johnson, the Duke of York, Horace Walpole and the Reverend Douglas, who was later to become Bishop of Salisbury. A woman named Mary Frazer was hired to be a sort of chaperone to young Elizabeth. Parsons was perhaps concerned by the fact that a number of strange men went in and out of her bedroom at night. After a few weeks the attraction of the odd noises began to wane and the visitors tailed off. Perhaps in an effort to save her job, Frazer then hit

A trial for slander arose out of the case of the Cock Lane Ghost and fascinated all of London

upon the idea of allowing people to question the 'ghost'. She suggested that the ghost should give one knock to mean 'yes' and two knocks to mean 'no'. If it chose not to answer or did not know the answer, it should make a scratching noise.

The new system proved to be an enormous hit and soon crowds of paying visitors were flocking to Cock Lane. Over the course of the autumn of 1761 the ghost gradually shared a harrowing story with the stream of visitors. It revealed that it was the spirit of the recently departed Fanny – even though the noises had begun when Fanny was very much alive. Quickly dubbed 'Scratching Fanny' by the London crowd, the entity then began to discuss the details of Fanny's relationship with Kent. Most of these were salacious, but one claim stood out boldly. Scratching Fanny declared that she had been murdered by Kent, who had daily dosed her drink with arsenic. She had not succumbed to smallpox after all. When the visitors asked what should be done about the claims, the ghost replied that Kent should hang.

Inevitably news of the accusations reached Kent. He demanded that Parsons and Elizabeth retract the claims.

They countered that the claims came from Fanny's ghost, not from themselves. Kent was invited to Cock Lane, so that he could question the spirit himself. After some debate about who should be in attendance at the event and how it should be conducted, Kent went to Elizabeth's bedroom in Cock Lane. At first the ghost refused to make any noises. It had been growing noticeably quieter in recent weeks, but after a while the familiar knockings began.

Kent examined the bedroom for signs of trickery and then the Reverend John Moore began to question the spirit. After some preliminary queries, Moore got to the main business.

'Are you Fanny Lynes?' he asked. There came one knock for 'yes'.

'Were you murdered by William Kent?' There was another single knock for 'yes'.

'Did anyone else assist Kent?' Two knocks indicated 'no'.

William Kent leapt to his feet. 'Thou art a lying spirit,' he shouted and then he stormed out. He then went to see his lawyers, where he launched a prosecution against Parsons, Elizabeth, Frazer and Moore, on the grounds of conspiracy to slander.

The case progressed and by June 1762 it came to court. The matter revolved around whether a disembodied spirit was making the accusations or whether Parsons was producing the noises. If the 'ghost' episode was shown to be a hoax it would prove that the accusations against Kent were false. Perhaps it was all an attempt to dissuade Kent from pursuing his case for the repayment of the £20.

The court made three journeys to Elizabeth's bedroom. On each occasion the court officials undertook a strict search to make sure that no trickery was possible. On the first two visits no noises were heard. The magistrate leading the investigation told Parsons that unless something happened on the third visit he would be found guilty.

When the court made their final trip the spirit repeated its story about the murder. But this time there was something different about the sounds. Elizabeth's bed was searched and a piece of wood was found. The girl had been rapping with the wood.

Three men were sent to the stocks as a result of the trial

Next day the court found for Kent. Parsons, Frazer and Moore were condemned to stand in the pillory. The news of Elizabeth's attempted trickery spread rapidly and made all the newspapers of the day. So far as 18th-century London was concerned, the concept of ghosts had been thoroughly debunked. Other visitations still took place, but none of them were investigated properly nor were the events recorded carefully. Educated men no longer took them seriously. As a result, some of the accounts that survive are sketchy and superficial while others are solely concerned with disproving the notion of ghosts.

The Bell Witch

However, people in the United States remained rather more open to the idea of the supernatural. As a result, the visitation that affected the Bell family of Robertson County, Tennessee has been recorded in much greater detail than would have been the case in England. The Bell family consisted of John Bell, his wife Lucy and their nine children. They lived in an isolated wooden

Far from the madding crowd: the Bell Farm was isolated, standing more than a mile from the next inhabited dwelling place. When other farmers were called in to help they formed a committee of investigation

Singled out for special treatment: Betsy Bell seemed to be a centre for the Bell Witch in the early stages of its visitation, but the entity later moved outside the house and began to then focus on the father of the family

farmhouse some distance from anything that might be termed a town. Four of the children – John, the eldest, 12-year-old Elizabeth (known as Betsy), 10-year-old Richard and 9-year-old Joel – were affected more than the others.

The visitation seems to have begun in the early months of 1817, though the initial manifestations were so minor and sporadic that it is impossible to be certain. One night the family was disturbed by what sounded like rats or other small animals scuffling about the house. On another occasion, the noises sounded more like a dog scrabbling at the front door. These animal sounds gradually escalated in intensity. By the autumn of 1817 the whole family was aware that something odd was going on. But nothing could be seen. They found that if they got up in the night to investigate the sounds, they could find nothing. If a lamp was lit the noises ceased immediately. No matter what steps were taken, no rats were ever found. It was a real puzzle but at that stage it was still not much of a problem.

That changed in the spring of 1818, when loud thumps and bangs echoed through the farmhouse. Soon afterwards a rather disturbing sound began to be heard. It was difficult to place at first, but the Bells soon decided that it sounded very much like a person smacking his lips in anticipation of a feast. Next came a sound that was

Children living near the Bell farm found that if they threw a stick into a bush, the Bell Witch would usually throw the stick back at them. It became a favourite game for a while until the poltergeist resorted to more sinister activities

The Bell Witch adopted a number of alternative voices, which sang bawdy drinking songs late into the night

more akin to somebody being throttled. It was most upsetting, but worse was to come.

The first physical manifestation took place one night – the bedclothes were hauled off the beds in which the children slept. This happened on several consecutive nights. It woke the children and caused an understandable degree of fright and alarm. After a couple of weeks of restless nights, events escalated when Richard was woken up by something pulling hard on his hair. His screams roused the household, which ensured another broken night's sleep. Then it was Joel's turn. Finally the poltergeist turned on Betsy – her hair was pulled night after night.

It soon became clear that having found Betsy, the invisible intruder had found its target. Not only was her hair pulled repeatedly, but stones were thrown at her – even when she was indoors and nobody else was in the room. Then an invisible hand slapped her face. Her brother, who was talking to her at the time, heard the slap and saw Betsy's cheek redden where the blow had fallen.

This was too much for John Bell. He sent for a near neighbour named James Johnson, who knew his Bible rather better than most people did. It seems that Johnson

After a couple of weeks of restless nights, events escalated when Richard was woken up by something pulling hard on his hair

began by thinking that the children were playing some rather cruel tricks on their father. However, he could not make up his mind if Betsy was in on the prank or was a victim.

When Johnson called at the Bell household all was quiet for a while, but then there came the familiar sound of smacking lips. Johnson swung round angrily. 'Stop it. In the name of the Lord,' he shouted. The sound stopped and nothing else happened during his visit.

The persecution of Betsy continued after Johnson had left. Johnson advised John Bell to arrange for a rota of neighbours to be in the house, where they could keep an eye on things – on the children, in other words. The stone throwing, the face slapping and the knocks and bangs continued unabated, but at least there were witnesses from outside the family. When one visitor expressed the view that the events were all some kind of children's trick he was promptly slapped on the face by an invisible hand. The disturbances then moved outside the house. They began on the track that led to the local church and the school. About a hundred yards from the house the track passed a dense thicket of trees and bushes. As the children walked past this thicket on their way to and from school they would find themselves struck by a flying stick. In common with the stones that had been thrown at Betsy, however, they either missed the children or only touched them lightly if they hit their target. Young Joel took to throwing the sticks back, but they were returned with increased force. It seemed that something in the bushes was catching them. Using his pocket knife (children had such things then), Richard marked a stick and threw it at the thicket – the marked stick came swishing back in an instant. There had to be somebody there. However, when the thicket was searched there was no sign of life.

Back indoors the team of neighbours had become so accustomed to the invisible intruder that they started to play games with it. When they began by tapping on the kitchen table the intruder immediately responded with an identical number of raps. Young Richard later wrote that this behaviour had only made things worse. It had made the spirit seek attention, rather in the manner of a naughty child. Soon, the familiar lip-smacking and choking noises began to be accompanied by grunts, groans, whistles and whispers. At first the whispers could not be understood – they were too faint and indistinct – but within a few days it was possible to discern words and phrases. One of the ghost's first utterings was 'I am a spirit who was once happy. But I have been disturbed and am now unhappy'. The majority of the voice's comments were altogether less pleasant and less informative. Many of them were unprintable, expressing views that few would air in public. John Bell refused to write down most of what the voice said on the grounds that it was blasphemous or of an explicitly sexual nature. The voice expressed its hatred of John Bell, whom it called 'Old Jack Bell', saying that it had come to torment him.

The threat was not idle, for the entity soon turned away from Betsy and focused its attention on John. In addition to the slapping and the stone-throwing, John mysteriously contracted a locked jaw and a swollen tongue. He could sometimes neither eat nor talk for days on end. John Bell was not the only member of the household to come in for harsh treatment. The family had a young slave called Anky, who helped Mrs Bell out with household tasks such as the washing and the cleaning.

The voice would sometimes follow Anky about the house, making comments that today would be classed as racist. The spirit also resorted to more conventional insults. On one occasion the unfortunate girl found herself deluged with a liquid that looked like spit.

When it was asked for more details of who or what it was, the voice at first replied that it was a Native American who had been buried on the site of the house.

When they began by tapping on the kitchen table the intruder immediately responded with an identical number of raps

The visitation was a protest against the building of a white folks' farm on top of its bones, it said. It then discarded that explanation and declared that it was 'Old Kate Batts's Witch'. Kate Batts was a local black woman who earned a modest living as a sort of doctor-cum-social worker to the black community. She acted as a midwife at births, laid out the dead ready for funerals, prepared herbal remedies for the sick and lent a sympathetic ear to those with troubles. Kate Batts was called in for questioning, but she steadfastly denied having anything to do with the upheavals at the Bell household. Fortunately for her, she was believed. She also denied using witchcraft of any type at all, but the voice's insistence that it was 'Old Kate Batts's Witch' stuck in people's minds. Thereafter, the phenomenon came to be called the Bell Witch.

Within a few weeks the voice of the Bell Witch had been joined by others. A gruff male voice declared that its name was Blackdog, a young boy's voice said it was Jerusalem and a woman's voice claimed to be Mathematics. The four voices took to singing bawdy tavern songs and telling rude jokes, while the smell of whisky filled the house. It was as if some loud drunken party was being enjoyed by the Bell Witch and its friends. The voices began to discuss local people with a frankness that was deeply embarrassing. Medical problems were talked about, as well as the sexual behaviour of married couples. Then the voices began to make accusations of drunkenness, violence and theft, none of which could be either proved or disproved.

Needless to say, they caused understandable upset and merriment in the community. The voices then took to repeating long passages from the local minister's Sunday sermon, mocking and joking all the way.

One day, the voice of the Bell Witch announced that it knew the location of a secret hoard of hidden gold. It then whispered the details to Betsy. The boys of the family took shovels and spent hours digging at the specified spot, but they found nothing. When they got back the Bell Witch broke out into loud laughter and

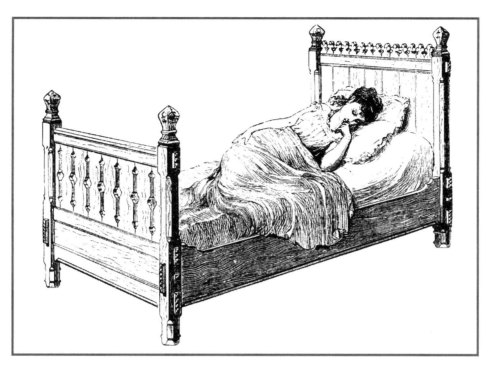

When Mrs Bell fell ill, the Bell Witch caused a bunch of grapes to materialize
out of thin air for her to eat

Betsy Bell's fledgling romance with Joshua Gardner angered the Bell Witch,
leading to a new chapter in the poltergeist visitation

teased the boys about the escapade for days. It had obviously enjoyed the joke.

The Bell Witch enjoyed other unpleasant jokes, too, such as placing pins in beds or on chairs, where people might be expected to prick themselves. The witch also developed a kind of fascination with shoes. They were moved about when nobody was looking and they were wrenched off people's feet when they sat down.

John Bell was the target of the majority of the incidents and he also came in for the most unpleasant treatment. One attack was worse than the rest. He had just stepped out of the front door to begin work on the farm for the day when the Bell Witch grabbed his feet and would not let him walk. Suddenly he felt the invisible hands let go, but he was then punched so hard in the face that he staggered back and had to sit down on a log to recover. The Bell Witch then threw John off the log and shrieked with laughter as it jerked his arms and legs about. He had no means of controlling his convulsive movements. When the invisible entity finally let him go, it stayed in the vicinity singing obscene and offensive songs. Richard had just joined his father so he helped him back indoors, where he took to his bed for a couple of days.

Aggressive as the Bell Witch was towards the father of the family, it could be surprisingly pleasant to the rest of the household. When Mrs Bell was taken ill, the voice hung about weeping and lamenting, 'Poor Lucy. Oh, poor Lucy'. Then it made a couple of pounds of hazelnuts appear at the side of the sick bed. When Betsy saw the nuts she commented, 'Oh, but we have no nutcrackers'. Instantly two pounds of shelled hazel nuts arrived. The sick woman did not fancy the nuts – they are not generally known as a suitable invalid food – so the Bell Witch came back with a large bunch of grapes, which fell from nowhere on to Mrs Bell's bed. The voice said, 'These will be good for her health,' as the grapes landed.

On Betsy's birthday the Bell Witch proved to be very generous. A large basket of fruit, including oranges,

The Bell Witch grabbed his feet and would not let him walk. He was then punched so hard in the face that he staggered back

bananas and grapes materialized out of nowhere. 'Those came from the West Indies,' the Witch announced. 'I brought them myself.' It sounded almost proud. In 1819 Betsy fell in love with a local farm boy named Joshua Gardner. By this time, the disturbances had been going on for about two years. The romance blossomed and an engagement was thought to be imminent. Suddenly the Bell Witch seemed to become aware of the relationship. Not only that, it took a violent dislike to it. The voice of the Bell Witch began following Betsy around the house. It said things like, 'Please, Betsy Bell, don't have Joshua Gardner,' or 'Don't marry Joshua Gardner' – and then it tried insulting the hapless young man. When such pleading did not work, the voice tried a new tactic. When Betsy was out with Gardner, the Bell Witch would keep up a running commentary for the benefit of the rest of the Bell family. It repeated the conversation the two were having, it announced when they were kissing and it described where Joshua put his hands and how Betsy reacted. When Betsy came home, the voice taunted her for her supposedly wanton ways. In the end the pressure got too much and the couple broke up.

Next day one of Joshua's friends arrived at the Bell farm in a blazing temper. Frank Miles pushed his way into the house and shouted out, 'Take any shape you desire, just so that I can get my hands on you.' There followed a few seconds of silence, before an invisible fist punched the young man extremely hard in the face and then in the stomach, causing him to double up in pain and gasp for breath. He left when he had recovered from the beating. The activities of the Bell Witch were heading toward the climax that would ensure its contemporary fame and make it one of the most startling cases in the history of poltergeist studies. On 18 December 1820 John Bell announced that he was not feeling well and that he was going to bed early. Next day he did not wake up and he was found to be in a stupor. The voice of the Bell Witch gloated: 'It's useless for you to try to relieve old Jack. I've got him this time. He will never get up from that bed again.'

After John junior had sent for the doctor he noticed a small bottle that neither he nor anyone else recognized. The Bell Witch spoke out again.

'I put it there. And I gave Old Jack a dose last night while he was asleep, which fixed him.'

The father of the tormented family died the next day without regaining consciousness. On the day of the funeral the witch moved around the house singing songs, one of which was the then popular bar room ditty, 'Row me up some brandy, Oh'.

The apparent murder of John Bell spread the fame of the Bell Witch far and wide. This single act has ensured that the case remains so famous today. No other poltergeist has ever been known to cause the death of a person – or even inflict serious injury. But then the Bell Witch had punched and hit several different people before John Bell died, so it seems to have been abnormal. After the funeral, the Bell Witch went relatively quiet. All of its usual antics were performed, but everybody agreed that they were neither as spectacular nor as frequent as they had been before.

On one occasion, John junior asked the Bell Witch if it could help him to speak to the spirit of his dead father. The Bell Witch refused. 'He is no longer of this world,' it said. After explaining that any evidence of a person surviving death was fraudulent it then instructed John junior to look out of the window. He did so and saw a set of footprints being made in the snow, as if an invisible man were approaching the house. The Bell Witch claimed that the prints were identical to those made by Old Jack Bell in his winter boots. Young John did not bother checking. He had lost interest.

A few weeks later the Bell family was at supper when a loud crashing and rumbling noise came from the

In the firing line: the Bell Witch visitation ended in spectacular fashion when an object like a cannonball fell down the chimney, rolled into the kitchen and then exploded in a cloud of choking smoke

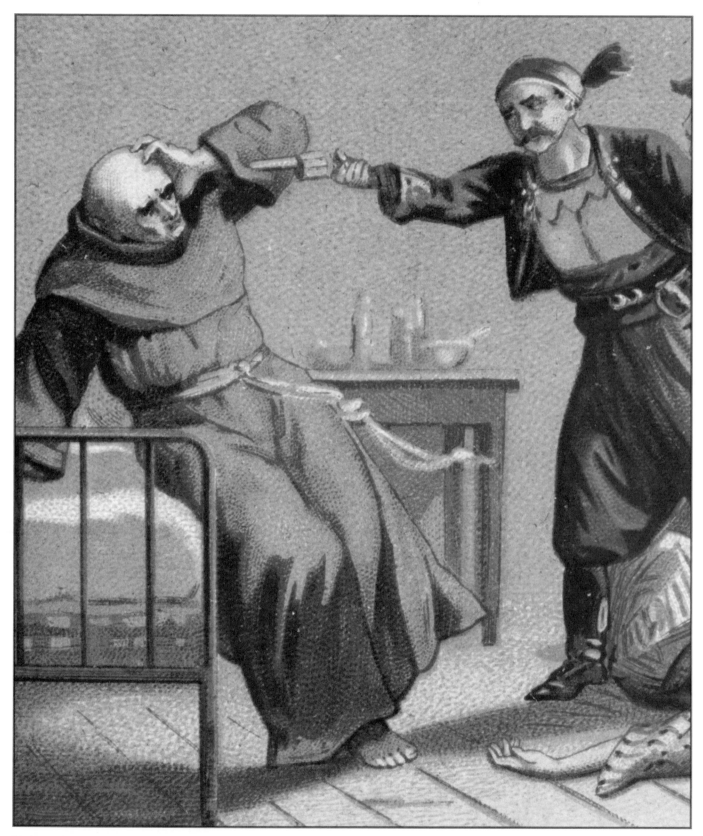

Murder and mayhem: poltergeists tend to have colourful pasts and histories involving much human wrongdoing

chimney. What looked like a large cannonball thumped into the fireplace. It then rolled into the room and exploded in a cloud of choking smoke. The voice of the Bell Witch boomed out, 'I am going and will be gone for seven years.' The smoke cleared and the Bell Witch had gone.

Seven years later it was back. By this time only Mrs Lucy Bell and her two youngest children were living in the farmhouse – the other children had married and moved away. The manifestations began as before, with the sounds of invisible animals scratching about. On a couple of nights bedclothes were torn off again. Mrs Bell and her children decided to ignore anything that happened. They did not even discuss the Bell Witch in the house. After a few days the manifestations ceased. John junior claimed that when the disturbances ceased for the second time he heard the voice of the Bell Witch say that it was leaving for 107 years. By that reckoning it should have been back in 1935, but there is no record of it reappearing.

He heard the Bell Witch say it was leaving for 107 years. By that reckoning it should have been back in 1935

Analyzing the Early Evidence

Looking back on these early cases it is clear that they contain many of the features that are now associated with poltergeist visitations. The first fact that any researcher must face is that at least two of these cases involved obvious and proven trickery by the humans involved. At Berne some of the monks pretended to be ghosts and spirits in order to provide Jetzer with messages that they wanted to be taken as the pronouncements of the saints. In the Cock Lane visitation, young Elizabeth Parsons was caught rapping her knuckles on a piece of wood in order to produce knocking noises. At this distance in time it is impossible to know whether the earlier manifestations in these two cases were also fraudulent or whether the visitations had begun as genuinely paranormal events that were then manipulated by the humans.

Nor do we know if the other cases were genuine or not, even though no fakery was detected. We have to read the records as they stand and judge them accordingly.

Fraud apart, all of the visitations shared one characteristic – they took place in people's homes. Poltergeists do not infest streets or open fields. The presence of humans on a daily and prolonged basis seems to be necessary. They also seem to require the presence of one particular human being if they are to appear. In the Cock Lane visitation it was young Elizabeth Parsons, in the convent of St Pierre de Lyon it was Anthoinette de Grollée, while at the Dominican monastery in Berne it was the monk Jetzer. Modern researchers term this central person the 'focus'. The throwing of stones was also common to each visitation. So prevalent is the throwing of stones that some researchers maintain that a visitation is not really that of a poltergeist unless some stones are thrown about. Although these early accounts do not comment on the types of stone that are thrown, evidence from more recent cases suggests that the poltergeist uses stones that have been picked up at the site of their visitation.

A further feature is shared in almost all of the cases. Although the stones and the other objects that are thrown about are often moved with great speed and violence, when they strike a person they do so gently and they rarely leave a bruise. However, when they hit a wall or a floor – as did the clay pipe in the home of the weaver Paul Fox – they will break or shatter. It is almost as if the poltergeist is determined to get attention, but does not actually want to hurt anybody. The Bell Witch was unusual in actually inflicting injury. Knocks, bangs and raps also occur in most of these early cases. They may vary in volume and number, but nearly every poltergeist will make such noises at some point during the visitation.

It can also be noticed that nearly all of the visitations began quietly and then built up in intensity as time passed. Because of that, the people who were experiencing a visitation did not realize what was happening until things had reached a reasonably advanced stage. The pattern of disturbances only became clear with hindsight. In the Bell Witch case these early events had been mistaken for rats moving about. This conclusion had also been reached at the start of the Cock Lane visitation. The Tedworth visitation was unusual in that the very first events were loud, frightening and unmistakably odd.

In some cases the events appeared to build up to a spectacular climax and then cease abruptly; in others, there was a gradual escalation of events, followed by an equally slow decline. Perhaps these impressions are down to faulty recording – in several instances the documents that we have do not tell the whole story. As with modern events, most of the visitations in these early accounts involve no apparition of any kind. Things move and noises are heard, but nothing is seen. When an apparition does appear it tends to be shadowy and fleeting. A vague black cloud was seen in the Ringcroft case and an indistinct black figure appeared in the Tedworth visitation. Both of them lasted for only a few seconds.

Some of the people in these early visitations attempted to communicate with the poltergeist. In some cases this was achieved by persuading the poltergeist to reply to a series of questions by using a knock code. Other poltergeists developed a voice so that they could speak directly to humans. The disembodied voice seems to be rather more common in the early cases, but that might be because only the more spectacular visitations got written down. One interesting feature of the communications is that they tend toward the sensational and the obscene. When the poltergeist talks about itself, it is usually in terms of murder, crime and exotic sexual escapades. Jetzer's poltergeist claimed to be a former prior of the monastery who had been dismissed in disgrace and then murdered; the Cock Lane ghost also claimed to have been murdered; and the spirit claiming to be that of the disgraced nun Alix de Telieux poured out an enormously colourful account of her sinful life after leaving the convent. No poltergeist has ever claimed to have been a respectable person who has led an utterly blameless and routine life.

However, where the story of the poltergeist could be tested, it proved to be false. The Cock Lane ghost claimed to be the ghost of a person who had been alive when the disturbances began, while the Bell Witch made various claims about itself which were evidently paradoxical.

Another feature of the claims made by early poltergeists about themselves is that they all fitted in very closely with the views of the people on the receiving end of a visitation. For instance, the nuns of St Pierre de Lyon believed that the human soul survived bodily death and that those who had committed sins would go to purgatory before being admitted to heaven – so the poltergeist claimed to be exactly such a soul. The Tedworth visitation occurred at a time when belief in witches as assistants of the devil was at a high point, so the poltergeist ran through the house screaming, 'A witch. A witch'. And when Mr Mompesson thought that the drumming beggar William Drury might be to blame, the poltergeist began playing Drury's confiscated drum.

At the time of the Tedworth visitation it caused a sensation when Drury confessed that he had used witchcraft to cause the mayhem at Mompesson's house. In the event, however, Drury was acquitted of witchcraft at his trial. The records of the trial have not survived, so we do not know what evidence was brought nor why he was acquitted, which is a great shame. It seems obvious, though, that even at that time the evidence was not considered strong enough. There has been some debate among modern researchers as to whether Drury caused the events at Mompesson's house. If so, did he use paranormal means or more mundane tactics? Perhaps it was just that Drury had heard of the Demon Drummer and thought he would try a bit of blackmail. After all, he had a grudge against Mompesson. When all was said and done, Drury was just a beggar who sought alms by claiming to be a retired army drummer. He was not considered to be a wizard, nor did he pretend to be one.

The Bell Witch ceased its visitation in 1828. Just 16 years later a new visitation would capture headlines around the world. It would seem to solve the poltergeist enigma.

The nuns at the convent of St Pierre de Lyon investigated the strange haunting of their home with great thoroughness

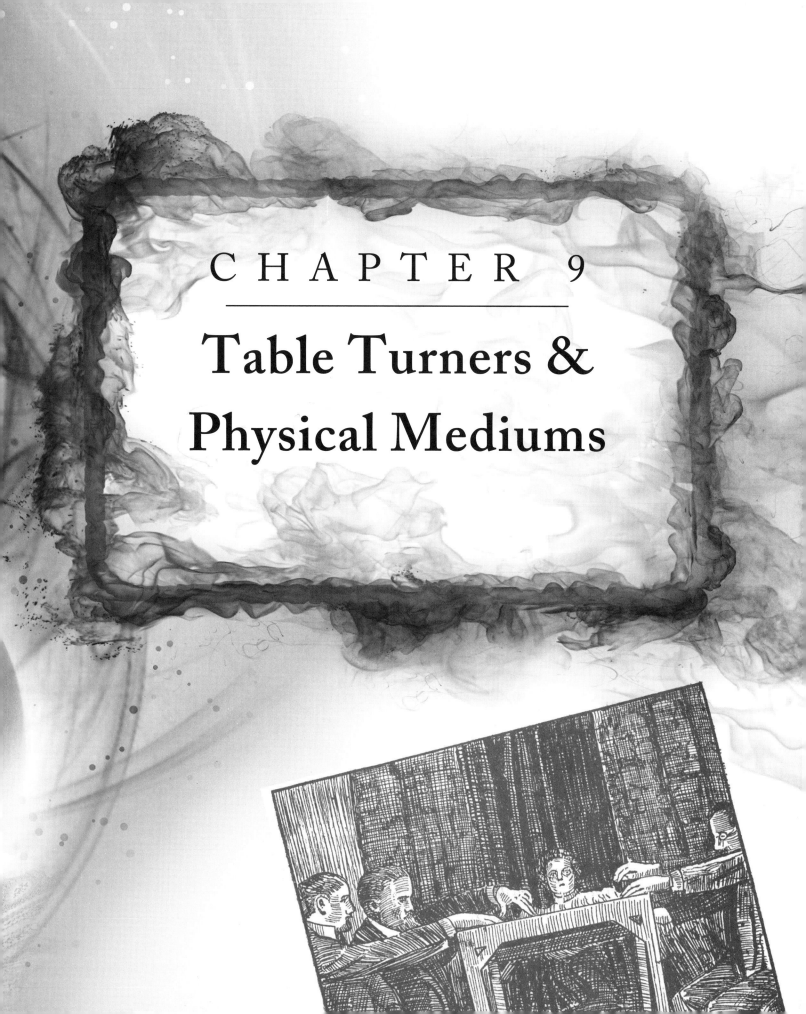

CHAPTER 9

Table Turners & Physical Mediums

f the Bell Witch achieved national fame across the United States, most other early visitations achieved only local notice.

But 1848 saw the beginning of a visitation that would create an international stir. It would dominate discussion of the entire poltergeist phenomenon for more than half a century. The case remains hugely controversial among researchers. It is best to start with a description of what actually happened before looking at how the visitation and the events that flowed from it were interpreted.

The Fox Sisters

In 1847 the Fox family moved into a small wooden house in Hydesville, New York State. They planned on living there until their new home in Rochester was available. At the time the family consisted of John Fox, his wife Margaret, 10-year-old Katie and 14-year-old Maggie. An elder brother named David and an elder sister named Leah were living in Rochester. In March 1848 the Fox family began to hear odd noises, which sounded rather like hollow knocks. These were followed by the sounds of furniture being dragged across the wooden floors. Whenever the noises were investigated, there was no explanation to be found. There were no intruders in the house and no furniture had been moved.

The sounds rapidly increased in volume and frequency and for some reason the two girls decided that they were caused by a ghost. They insisted on sleeping in a bed that had been placed in their parents' room. Katie and Maggie started calling the invisible intruder 'Mr Splitfoot', because all of the demons in the books at their school were depicted with cloven hooves. On the night of 31 March the noises had begun just after the family had gone to bed, which was the usual pattern. On this occasion, though, Katie decided to face the unseen visitor. Sitting up in bed she called out, 'Mr Splitfoot, do as I do.' She then clapped her hands. The knocking noises started, but they ended as soon as Katie stopped clapping. Then it was Maggie's turn to call out, 'Now do just as I do. Count 1, 2, 3, 4.' Maggie clapped her hands four times and she was answered by four knocks.

Mrs Fox decided to take a hand at this point. She asked the invisible knocker to count out the ages of her

When the Fox visitation began the noises were blamed on a demon, nicknamed 'Mr Splitfoot'

Three of a kind: the Fox Sisters, photographed at the height of their fame, were at the centre of a famous visitation that was to lead to the establishment of spiritualism

The Fox poltergeist claimed to be the unquiet spirit of a pedlar who had been murdered in the house

children. The knocks began again as the phantom presence began to tap out the age of each child. A gap was left between each one. Then after a short pause the ghost added three more thumps. Very few people outside the family knew that Mrs Fox had given birth to a child that had died some years earlier, at the age of three. This convinced Mrs Fox that they were dealing with something that possessed intelligence and knowledge. 'Is this a human being that answers my questions?' she called out. There was silence. 'Is it a spirit?' she asked. And then she added, 'If it is, make two raps.' Instantly there were two loud knocks. Over the following few days the Fox girls and their mother worked out a system by which the spirit could answer their questions. One rap meant 'yes', two raps meant 'no' and other numbers stood for various commonly used words. They later devised a code that enabled the spirit to use letters to spell out some of the more obscure words and names.

The Fox's neighbours were invited in to witness their conversations with the spirit. Some of them recorded the results. It gradually emerged that the spirit was claiming to be the unquiet soul of Charles B. Rosa, or Rosma, a murdered man. The spirit used both names. Rosa claimed

that he had been a pedlar in life – and a successful one at that. He said that when he had come to Hydesville about five years earlier the man who had then lived in the Fox house had offered him accommodation. His host had

The wooden house at Hydesville where the Fox family lived was photographed and visited by hordes of visitors fascinated by the tales of communication with the spirits of the dead

then slashed his throat in the middle of the night. The foul deed had been done in the bedroom that was later to be occupied by the two girls, said the spirit. That was why the knockings had begun there. The murderer had then stolen his money and his goods before burying his body in the cellar.

Almost as soon as this story had been revealed, a series of new manifestations began. They took the form of a

A maid was found who recalled a man staying in the haunted house for a single night. He was never seen again

horrific gurgling noise, which was taken to be the sound of the unfortunate Rosa having his throat cut, followed by the sound of a body being dragged over the floor of the bedroom – the scene of the crime. The Foxes and their neighbours went down to the cellar and began digging. They found a few pieces of old bone, but it was never very clear if these were human or not. Then Mrs Fox began asking the locals about pedlars.

She came across a young woman who had worked as a maid in the house five years earlier, when it had been owned by a man named Bell. The woman recalled that one evening Bell had brought a man called Ryan home, who was going to stay the night. She thought he could have been a pedlar. There was no sign of him next morning, so she assumed he had left early.

That seemed to fit in with Rosa's story, apart from the fact that the woman had called him Ryan. Without more ado, Mrs Fox began telling everyone that the spirit's story was true. Bell only lived a few miles away so he was understandably not impressed by the unfolding events. He went to his old home and demanded that the Foxes stop spreading stories about him. They responded that it was the spirit of Rosa who had accused him, not they. Bell then went to the police, who searched their records for any mention of a missing person who had gone by the name of Rosa, Rosma or Ryan. Their best efforts drew a blank. They met with no greater success when they combed the New York State records for missing pedlars.

Although Bell declared himself vindicated, the police still took no action against the Fox family. Thinking there was no smoke without fire, the people of the town began to treat the unfortunate Bell with suspicion and hostility, so he moved away.

Also soon to move were the Fox sisters. As the house in Hydesville became inundated with visitors, sensation-seekers and others, their parents sent them to live with their brother David and their sister Leah in Rochester. The mysterious noises seemed to follow them, because they stopped at Hydesville but broke out in Rochester. When a friend of Leah's came to visit she heard the noises and said she thought it was all a clever trick. An ornament then leapt off a shelf and flew at her head, though it narrowly missed her.

In 1850, Leah suggested that instead of allowing an endless procession of strangers to tramp through her house, they should hire a theatre for a night and invite along everyone who was interested in hearing the mysterious noises. The evening proved to be a great success and it also turned a profit. The girls also discovered that they could communicate with any number of dead spirits, not just the unfortunate Rosa. Leah then suggested that her two younger sisters should put on regular displays.

Before long the Fox girls were touring towns and cities with their show. The knockings and the rappings were now claiming to be the spirits of the dead friends and relatives of people in the audience. The shows became enormously popular and the profits made by the Fox family rose rapidly.

Smoke and mirrors or the real thing? The Fox sisters began charging people to come to watch the antics of their visiting spirits and were soon earning a very good living

Man of influence: the publisher Horace Greeley believed that the Fox sisters were producing genuine phenomena and introduced them to leading figures of the day

If things got dramatic the table would levitate or 'dance' with odd jerking movements. A few table turners claimed to be able to talk to the spirits

Table Turning

It was not long before other people began to claim that they could produce similar phenomena to the Fox girls. First of all, the Fox sisters' imitators came up with something that would later go by the name of 'table turning', though table turning was only a part of what happened. According to its followers, table turning could be reproduced successfully in most homes on most occasions. The Fox sisters did not restrict themselves to stage appearances; their audiences could sometimes be relatively small. The method they used on these occasions was copied by the table turning fraternity. A group of at least four, but no more than 12, adults sat round a table with their hands placed flat on the table top, palm side down. The people were then expected to chat amiably amongst themselves – they could even crack jokes – while they called upon the spirits to move the table.

In successful table turning sessions the table would move about the room. It might even produce knocks or raps, as if it were being hit by a hard object. Most sessions went no further than random movements of the table, together with a few strange knocks. If things got more dramatic the table would levitate or 'dance' with odd jerking movements as it hopped about. A few table turners claimed to be able to talk to the spirits by using a code of rapping or jumping movements. One thing was generally recognized among table turners – for a session to be successful it was necessary for all of those present to believe that the table would move. If even one of the participants expressed scepticism, the manifestations would be weak or absent altogether.

During 1852 and 1853 table turning became a popular parlour game across North America and Europe. But scientists stepped in to denounce the explanation

Horace Greeley, the publisher, then became involved. He introduced the Fox sisters to high society and ensured that they got a generally favourable coverage in the press. The Quaker community of New York State also took an interest in the girls and many of them became convinced that they really were able to communicate with the dead. By 1855, the girls' activity had become known as 'spiritualism'. All of this sparked off a hot debate, not only among religious leaders but in the whole of society.

If the phenomena were genuine, as many thought, were they caused by spirits, demons or other supernatural beings?

Michael Faraday in his laboratory: Faraday was a chemist and physicist, expert in the fields of electromagnetism and electrochemistry, but he was a sceptic when it came to table turning

that spirits were involved. Instead, they ascribed the phenomenon to electricity, the rotation of the earth or magnetism. It was the ageing physicist Michael Faraday who came up with a way of scientifically testing the phenomenon. As expected by the table turners, though, the presence of the sceptical Faraday put a damper on things. A few minor table shuffles did take place at one sitting, but Faraday's equipment had detected an involuntary spasm in the arms of one of the sitters, just as the table had moved. That was enough for Faraday, who immediately announced that table turning was due to the involuntary movements of the sitters. The scientific world took up Faraday's conclusions and trumpeted them widely. Everyone ignored the fact that Faraday's findings did not explain the levitations, the jumps or the knocks. So far as the press and the scientists were concerned, table turning had been explained away. Despite this setback, it continued to produce some impressive phenomena for those prepared to continue with it.

Some of these people discovered that they had a special gift for producing dramatic results. Not only did the table move but so did other objects in the room – but these results remained unpredictable and unreliable. In time, however, the table turning practitioners who went down this route devised a procedure that stood a far better chance of producing interesting phenomena – they called it a seance. But that development was not going to come to fruition for another two decades or so. Meanwhile, other events began to catch the popular imagination.

Physical Mediums

In 1854 an exciting new development took place. The Davenport brothers of Buffalo, New York claimed to be able to produce manifestations that were far more impressive than anything that mere table turning, or even the Fox sisters, could produce. The Davenports went on the stage with their demonstration of bizarre effects. When their show began, the brothers were tied to their chairs. This was a way of showing everyone that they were not able to physically influence any of the phenomena that would be witnessed. Objects would then move about, musical instruments would play and other apparently impossible events would take place.

No business like show business: the dashing Davenport Brothers put on a stage show that was later revealed to be a fraud

Meanwhile another New York State resident claimed the ability to communicate with the spirits. This was 15-year-old Cora Scott, who became better known under her married name of Cora Hatch. Cora's abilities started just after the death of her father, when she was 13 years old. She began to fall into trances, during which she

Cora Scott claimed to be able to pass on messages from the dead. Her feats were remarkable – no evidence of trickery was ever found

Master magician: it was the great illusionist Jean Robert-Houdin who unmasked the Davenport Brothers, demonstrating on stage how they had achieved the seemingly impossible and thereby becoming their nemesis

A publicity illustration for the Davenport Brothers and their cabinet: the scale of the apparent activity
has been exaggerated – in reality the men were out of sight during most of the show

would speak in foreign languages or write messages that
had apparently come from the spirits of the dead. Later
on she seemed to acquire the ability to make contact with
deceased experts in the sciences and the arts. She was
then able to pass on their knowledge to the world. In

view of her lack of knowledge of these subjects, the level
of expertise she displayed was truly remarkable

For some years Cora displayed her abilities to small
groups of people who were interested in the emerging
cult of spiritualism. However, after her marriage to

A table levitates during a seance – such physical activity was common during early seances

they came to grief in London. An English stage conjuror who had read about Houdin asked a sailor to show him how to tie a knot that could not be wriggled out of. He then went to the Davenport show in the hope of being called up on stage to test the knots. After several visits he was eventually selected. He used the opportunity to tie the brothers up with his special knot and then he sat back to watch. The Davenports were unable to perform, their secret was unmasked and a near riot followed as the audience demanded their money back. The Davenports later enjoyed a reasonable career as conjurors and illusionists, but they never earned as much as when they had claimed that the spirits were assisting them.

Meanwhile the seance had come into vogue. People could now produce dramatic manifestations such as knocks, levitations and the movement of objects. In most cases seances produced no more than these physical manifestations. However, some seance leaders claimed the ability to contact spirits – they would later become known as 'mediums'. These mediums might go into trances, during which they claimed to speak with the voices of spirits. At other times, they could interpret knocking sounds as messages or they might write messages on scraps of paper.

By the 1880s a number of people claimed to be gifted mediums, who were able to contact any named spirit almost on demand. They were now charging for their services, often obtaining large sums of money from those who wished to talk to their deceased loved ones. At the same time public interest in table turning and seances was waning. They were no longer popular as parlour games.

As we have seen, the Fox sisters had started the whole spiritualism movement.

But in 1888 they made a truly startling announcement: they insisted they had faked the whole thing.

The background to this move by the sisters, now middle-aged women, was complex.

For a start, they were no longer earning much money. The success of their stage show, managed by their elder sister Leah, had long since faded. Added to that, Kate had taken to drink and had become so violently unpredictable that her ex-husband's relatives were starting legal action to have her children taken away from her. Maggie,

Benjamin Hatch she followed the Fox sisters and the Davenport brothers on to the stage.

Her public success was enormous. It was no doubt helped by her youth and good looks. As well as appearing on stage, Cora also wrote books while she was in her trances: these sold well. After several years, Cora's gifts began to fade. She was no longer able to enter trances as easily as before, nor were her feats as impressive.

Meanwhile, the Davenports met with disaster when they went on a tour of Europe in 1864. Their show in Paris was watched by the most famous European illusionist and conjurer of the time, Jean Eugène Robert-Houdin. He suspected trickery and he said so. Within a month, Houdin had worked out a method of reproducing the supposedly impossible feats of the Davenports. He put on a stage show in which he replicated the Davenport show and then he explained how it had been done. The performer must first of all have an assistant behind the scenes. Then he must have the ability to slip out of the knots while he was inside the cabinet or sitting behind the tablecloth.

The Davenports denied that any trickery was involved, but they moved to Britain to continue their tour. Sadly,

An illustration showing the early stages of the Fox sisters' activities. One of the girls speaks to the spirit in the Hydesville home, while the rest of the family look on

meanwhile, had suffered a crisis of faith after converting to Catholicism.

First of all she had abandoned her beliefs and then she had re-embraced them. Finally, after a quarrel with Leah, the sisters went to a newspaper. They offered to come clean about their fraudulent activities in return for a cash sum of $1,500. The newspaper paid up and on 21 October 1888 the confession was made to a packed audience at the New York Academy of Music.

It was Maggie who did all the talking; Kate just sat silently listening. According to Maggie the initial incidents back in Hydesville had begun as a school prank.

When we went to bed at night we used to tie an apple to a string and move the string up and down, causing the apple to bump on the floor, or we would drop the apple on the floor, making a strange noise every time it would rebound. Mother listened to this for a time. She would not

understand it and did not suspect us as being capable of a trick because we were so young.

She then went on to explain that the mysterious rappings that had taken place in private meetings and on stage had been faked using a method devised after the girls had moved to Rochester.

My sister Katie was the first to observe that by swishing her fingers she could produce certain noises with her knuckles and joints, and that the same effect could be made with the toes. Finding that we could make raps without moving our feet – first with one foot and then with both – we practised until we could do this easily when the room was dark. Like most perplexing things when made clear, it is astonishing how easily it is done. The rappings are simply the result of perfect control of the muscles of the leg below the knee, which govern the tendons of the foot and allow action of the toe and ankle bones that is not commonly known. Such perfect control is only possible when the child is taken at an early age and carefully and continually taught to practise the muscles which grow stiffer in later years. This, then, is the simple explanation of the whole method of the knocks and raps.

> ### Reaction to the public revelation was fiercely divided. Some claimed that the earlier noises had been much louder and from different parts of the room

She then proceeded to produce a series of sample raps. First she produced them as she would have done in a meeting, with her feet under a table. Then she removed the table cloth and showed the audience how she slipped her shoes off so that her toes would have the necessary space in which to move and produce the noises. Maggie continued to explain:

> *A great many people when they hear the rapping imagine at once that the spirits are touching them. It is a very common delusion. Some very wealthy people came to see me some years ago when I lived in 42nd Street and I did some rapping for them. I made the spirit rap on the chair and one of the ladies cried out, 'I feel the spirit tapping me on the shoulder.' Of course that was pure imagination.*

Maggie went on to launch a devastating attack on spiritualism and all those who practiced table turning or conducted seances. She said the entire movement was a fraud and all of those involved were guilty of trickery and deceit.

Reaction to the public revelation was fiercely divided. Among those present were some who had been present at the original events in Hydesville and others who had seen the Fox sisters in the early days at Rochester. They insisted that the noises that Maggie had produced on stage were nothing like those they had experienced at the time of the disturbances. They said that the earlier noises had been much louder and had come from different parts of the room, not just from the table. They also claimed that the original noises had been of a different quality or type altogether.

On the other hand, the scientists and the sceptics in the audience hailed the confession as an explanation of the entire affair. They used Maggie's statement to denounce the spiritualist movement and explain away all of the phenomena that emerged at table turning sessions or seances. So far as science was concerned, the matter was settled.

Kate Fox's reaction was interesting. In letters written after the public confession she denounced her sister for her attacks on spiritualism and spiritualists. She died soon after of an alcohol-related disease. About a year later Maggie recanted her confession. She announced that the original phenomena in Hydesville and Rochester had all been genuine. The later fakery had, she said, been the fault of Leah, who had wanted to maintain the flow of money coming in from the stage show even after the

The huge death toll of the First World War led to a renewed demand for communication with the spirits of the dead

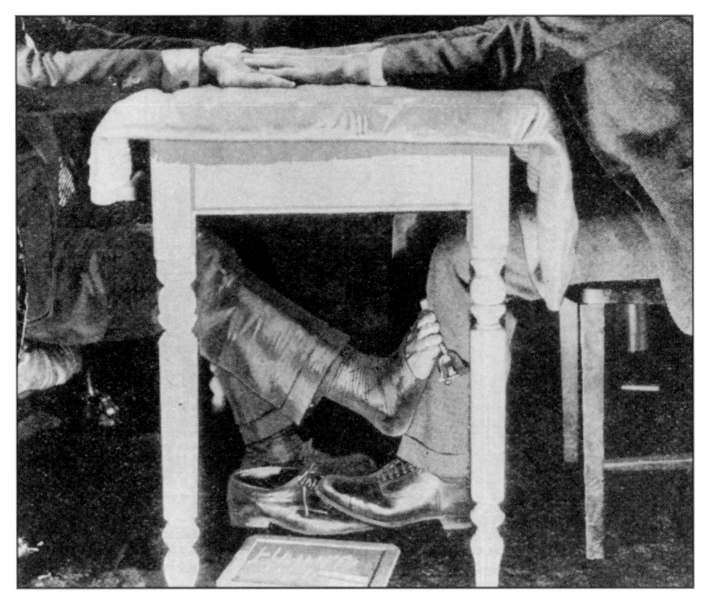

A fake medium could ring a bell and fake a handgrip under the table while his own hands were securely held. Such simple trickery could be surprisingly effective in dimly lit rooms

manifestations had faded. Maggie then spoke in support of mediums. She said that their work was as valid and genuine as her early manifestations had been.

The spiritualist movement, as it had become, continued in a low-key fashion over the next two decades. Scientists tended to ignore it and most of the public treated it as an interesting curiosity that had neither been proved nor disproved. So things might have continued had it not been for the outbreak of the First World War.

During the four years of carnage on the Western Front, millions of men were killed. Fathers, sons and husbands were slaughtered in huge numbers. Before 1914, soldiering had been viewed as a reliable career for anyone who chose it, but most men were not called upon to face the horrors of war. Suddenly ordinary men were marched off to face the enemy. So many were lost in battle that there was a massive public reaction.

At first, the First World War had a beneficial effect on spiritualism. Large numbers of the bereaved sought solace

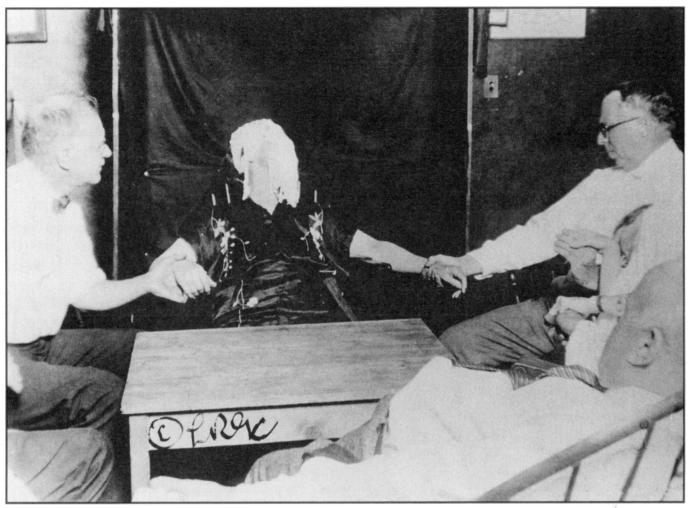

This seance shows what purports to be ectoplasm issuing from a medium's face. In most cases the 'ectoplasm' turned out to be muslin or some other cloth

from their grief in the belief that their dead relatives had passed over to a better place. Many rediscovered their faith in Christianity, but others turned to mediums in the hope of making direct contact with their lost ones. Those mediums and spiritualists who had continued with their work after the Fox confessions found themselves inundated with demands for assistance. Soon, large numbers of new mediums appeared on the scene, all offering to help people communicate with the dead soldiers. Bereaved relatives flocked to the mediums, some of whom charged high prices for entry to their seances. The more accomplished mediums produced truly dramatic effects. Ghosts walked the rooms, voices spoke and disembodied hands appeared to move objects about.

Denouncing the Fakes

It looked as if spiritualism was on the rise, but some viewed the developments with scepticism. The high earnings of some of the more dramatic mediums aroused suspicions. Harry Houdini was among those who were disinclined to believe in the reality of what was going on. Houdini had taken his stage name from Jean Eugène Robert-Houdin – who had been instrumental in unmasking the Davenport Brothers.

While Houdini is best known for his dramatic feats of escapology, he was also a gifted illusionist and stage conjurer. He attended a few seances after his mother died and became quickly convinced that trickery was involved. As a result, he spent some time devising ways in which

Psychic investigator Harry Price plus 'friend' as photographed by William Hope founder of the Crewe Circle, a group devoted to 'spirit photography', in 1932 – unknown to his host, Price had marked the photographic plates and thus proved the picture was a fake

certain that he knew how the 'medium' was performing the trick – then he would stand up and declare his real name. He would first announce how the trick was done and then he would go on to reveal the fraudulent devices and mechanisms that were being used. Finally, the policeman would arrest the medium while the reporter took notes. Houdini would later exploit his success by going on stage to replicate the stunts that he had unmasked. Amazingly some of the discredited 'mediums' appeared with him.

Houdini's campaign against Mina Crandon, or 'Margery', turned out to be both spectacular and contentious. It began in 1924, when she claimed a prize of $2,500 from the magazine *Scientific American*. The magazine had offered the reward to anyone who could convince their committee that they were able to produce 'physical manifestations of a psychic nature under scientific control'. The manifestations produced by Margery were impressive and no evidence of trickery was found. Convinced at last, the committee was on the point of declaring for Margery and awarding her the prize. But Houdini had just published a book based on his anti-medium campaign. Armed with his expert knowledge, he decided to take a hand.

The events that followed were controversial. Houdini decided to submit Margery's claim to a series of tests. They involved asking Margery to reproduce the effects she had achieved in her seances, but using equipment supplied by Houdini. There were several minor incidents, but nothing on the scale that she usually achieved. Margery accused Houdini of making it impossible for her to succeed by sabotaging her equipment. Houdini denied the charge. He claimed that Margery had tampered with the mechanism herself in order to provide an excuse for failure. A second round of tests was arranged, but in the meantime a sceptic attending one of Margery's routine seances had witnessed one of her tricks. By gripping a long dark rod in her mouth she had been able to manipulate objects on a table. *Scientific American* decided that Margery had failed the test.

All of this had been played out in the full glare of publicity. Houdini's campaign, and the activities of other sceptics, resulted in numerous 'mediums' being exposed. Several of these tricksters were prosecuted for having

he could replicate the manifestations that he had seen. Then he practised the tricks until he was certain that he was correct.

His next task was to consult various lawyers in order to establish whether these mediums could be taken to task. He was informed that they would be guilty of fraud if they took money after falsely claiming to be able to contact the dead. Houdini began a systematic campaign of unmasking the heartless mediums who charged the bereaved exorbitant fees for attending their seances. After booking himself into sessions under an assumed name, he attended with a newspaper reporter and a police officer. The campaigner waited until he was

Scourge of the phoney spiritualists: Harry Houdini poses for a fake spirit photograph in order to demonstrate how the forgeries were produced. Photos such as this were highly popular until the trickery involved was revealed to the public

The church of dead souls: spiritualism continues to exist as a movement. Some branches operate as an organized church, while others prefer a less formal structure to their activities

obtained money under false pretences. This effectively destroyed the credibility of the physical mediums – that is, those who produced knocks and raps or moved objects around during seances. Interestingly, one of those who played a minor role in the denouncing of fake mediums was an amateur historian named Harry Price. Price would later go on to lead a colourful and rather controversial life as an investigator of the paranormal. He would be called in to deal with several poltergeist cases and his work would become instrumental in defining and categorizing different types of haunting.

Table turning had already been dismissed as a fad – now the holding of seances disappeared as a pastime as well. Thereafter seances and the like retreated to the world of fiction. They either became the stuff of horror stories or they were treated with comical contempt. Physical mediumship was then abandoned by the spiritualist movement. The practice and the beliefs that surrounded the movement had developed in a different ways, one of which was the founding of spiritualist churches. However, when physical phenomena were no longer a part of the discipline the relevance of the movement to the study of poltergeists vanished.

Where Does This Leave Poltergeists?

Looking back at these events from the early 21st century, some things are clear that were not so obvious at the time. Contemporary accounts of the original experience of the Fox sisters at Hydesville read very much like those of other early visitations. The disturbances began fairly quietly with some odd noises in the girls' bedroom. Then the noises became louder and more insistent: the girls decided that they were caused by a ghost. When whatever it was began to communicate through coded rappings it announced that it was a ghost. So it was fitting in with the expectations of the viewer. Not only that but the ghost was not the phantom of some boringly

normal inhabitant of Hydesville, but that of an exotic pedlar. And he had been murdered as well. Finally, when the Fox girls moved to Rochester, the noises went with them. It all sounds very familiar. Read in isolation, the experiences of the Fox sisters might be viewed as a typical poltergeist visitation.

It is what happened next that is unusual. Unlike most recipients of the attentions of a poltergeist, the Fox sisters did not find it troublesome – in fact, they welcomed its activities. They then went on to invite people round to witness the manifestations. When the 'ghost' had an audience it accused a local man of murder, which led to quite a degree of fuss and resentment. This is reminiscent of the behaviour of the Cock Lane Ghost. However, when the Fox sisters went on stage and started to earn money from the phenomena that surrounded them it was something that had never happened before. Those who saw the stage act were divided. Some thought it was genuine, others imagined that the girls were involved in trickery. Again, it might be useful to compare the Fox sisters' case with that of the Cock Lane Ghost. In the latter instance, the phenomena were on the wane when the start of a court case put pressure on the ghost to perform. That was when Elizabeth Parsons was caught cheating. Similarly, it was when the Fox girls were earning considerable sums of money that they were suspected of trickery.

Maggie Fox's later confession is an interesting matter. Once again, she was offered money, but this time it was to denounce the supernatural elements of her story. Her account of how she and her sister created rapping and knocking noises is quite obviously true in the context of the later years of the girls' stage careers. Those who had not known the girls at Hydesville soon believed, therefore, that the entire phenomenon had been a fraud. But those who had experienced the earlier manifestations were not convinced. They maintained that the earlier noises had been louder and different. At a later date, when the financial pressure was off, Maggie took back her confession. She said the original events had been genuine.

In the case of the Fox Sisters, the most reasonable interpretation of events would be that a real poltergeist – whatever that might be – had initially been involved.

On the payroll? The appearance of what purported to be the spirits of the dead in white robes at 19th-century seances are now generally held to have been fraudulent

Maggie's later confession does not really ring true. It is hard to imagine how the bouncing of an apple on a wooden floor could be mistaken for loud bangs.

In any case, many of the noises occurred when both girls were in the room. It would have been clear that they were not bouncing apples about. And how was it that the girls were too young to have been suspected of trickery? As we have seen, Maggie was 14 years old at the time and her sister was 10. If they had been three or four years old the comment might have made sense, but teenagers are notoriously prone to fibbing and pranks.

It is noticeable that Maggie remained vague about the later phenomena in her recantation. By the time of her confession many of her friends were mediums, or were otherwise involved with spiritualism. Understandably, she became alienated from them because of her denunciation of their activities. Perhaps she wanted to regain their friendship.

That raises the issue of the mediums and spiritualists who followed the Fox Sisters' lead. Some were undoubtedly fraudulent, such as the Davenport Brothers. However, others might have actually believed that they were creating phenomena when the cause of their psychic powers was more down to earth. For example, young Cora Hatch might have been genuinely declaiming knowledge quite beyond anything she possessed in her normal state. There is no reason to ascribe this to spirits, though. She might just have been recalling things she had heard many years earlier, which her conscious mind had forgotten. Hypnotists recognize that those in a trance can recall the details of a past event much more clearly and easily than they do when they are awake.

The phenomena experienced at table turning sessions and some seances are rather more interesting. Happenings like the sound of knuckle raps and the levitation of tables and small ornaments have often been associated with poltergeists. The actions of many poltergeists are, of course, much more dramatic than this. However, the events that were reported at 19th-century seances are very reminiscent of the low-key activities of poltergeists. Unlike the later physical mediums, the table turners were not making money out of their activities, nor were they convincingly shown to be faking.

It was when the 'mediums' moved beyond traditional poltergeist behaviour that they were found to be frauds. The ability to speak to the spirit of a known dead person is not something that is generally associated with poltergeist cases. Poltergeists will usually claim to be the spirit of a person nobody has ever heard of. If they say they are the soul of a real person, it is often a person who died so long ago that nobody is around who can remember them clearly. Or again, as in the Cock Lane Ghost affair, the claim to be a real person is a false claim. Nor does a poltergeist visitation normally involve the sighting of ghosts. Apparitions tend to be vague, temporary, almost shapeless and usually black. Human figures clad in white, diaphanous robes appeared at seances held by mediums, but they are not associated with poltergeists.

With only the accounts left by 19th- century table turners and attendees at seances to work with, it is impossible to be certain. However, it does seem that some of the low-key phenomena were genuine, at least in the sense that the people involved did not cause them. Similarly, the more dramatic instances of physical mediumship can probably be discounted as clever conjuring tricks by people intent on making money out of the bereaved. It appears that the entire spiritualist saga had been something of a blind alley for those investigating hauntings and poltergeists. As we shall see in a later chapter, however, the events that followed the Fox Sisters' experiences might actually hold the key to unlocking the poltergeist mystery.

Meanwhile, the events at Hydesville, and in seance rooms around the world, did have one important and lasting effect. They convinced the scientific establishment that the entire poltergeist phenomenon was a nonsense that was not worth investigating. In earlier years poltergeist visitations had often attracted educated gentlemen or clergymen who were interested in observing and recording what happened. For some time after the Fox Sisters' experiences this ceased to be the case. Many of the visitations that took place over the following years were effectively ignored and not recorded properly. As far as the majority of scientists are concerned, things have not moved on at all. Poltergeists and the manifestations they produce are not real, according to conventional science. It was not until the later 20th century that a few scientists began to break ranks by being prepared to treat the subject seriously.

The general public, on the other hand, came to a rather different conclusion. They came to believe that any strange events of the poltergeist type were the work of ghosts or spirits. It is to some of those cases that we must now turn.

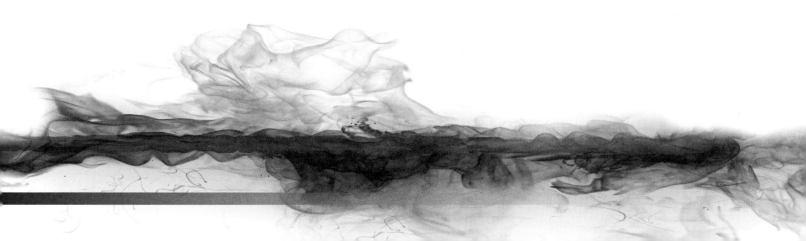

CHAPTER 10

Classic Victorian Hauntings

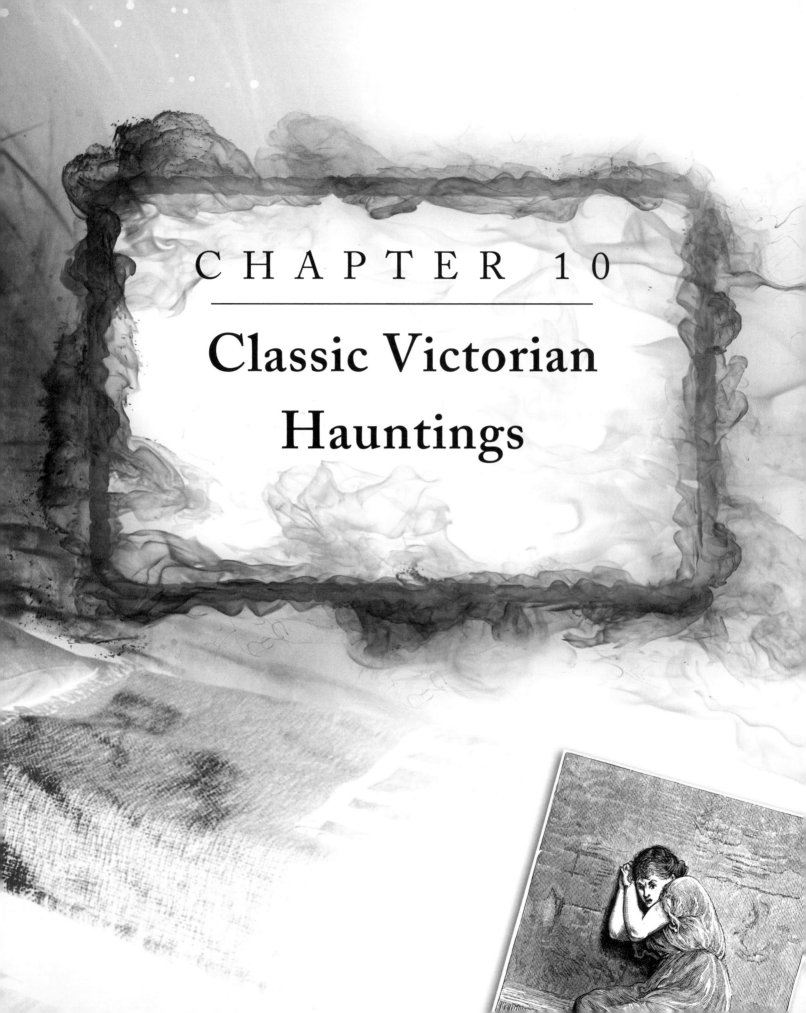

Neither the furore over the Fox Sisters and their experiences nor the growth of spiritualism seemed to have much effect on the frequency of poltergeist visitation or the forms that it took.

As with some of the earlier cases, the records that we have are somewhat scanty and incomplete. They often centre on the apparently supernatural occurrences that took place while ignoring the background to the phenomenon.

This is perfectly understandable, but the modern researcher can find it frustrating.

The Great Amherst Mystery

But not all of the cases that were reported after the time of the Fox Sisters are so fragmentary. Take, for instance, the events that took place in Amherst, Nova Scotia between 1878 and 1879. They would become known as the Great Amherst Mystery. While the visitation was going on the writer Walter Hubbell spent some time in the affected house. He went there with the avowed aim of writing up the 'haunting' in book form, so that it could be published. Some have thought that Hubbell's aim of making money gave him a motive to exaggerate the tale, but whenever the book can be cross-referenced to other contemporary sources its contents seem to be genuine.

The affected house was a relatively small one. It was occupied by Daniel and Olive Teed and their two sons George and Willie. Also in the house were Olive's two younger sisters Jennie and Esther Cox, plus her brother William. Daniel's brother John also lived in the fairly crowded house. When he came to investigate the 'haunting', Hubbell thought it was significant that

Jennie, aged 22, was very pretty but that Esther, aged 18, was plump and plain. Despite this, Esther was the one with a long-term boyfriend. He was called Bob MacNeal and he was known locally as a bit of a tough who was suspected of some petty pilfering.

In August 1878 Daniel Teed's cow stopped giving the usual amount of milk. He suspected that somebody had been milking the cow surreptitiously. Esther loved drinking milk so he imagined that either she or her boyfriend were to blame. A few days later Bob MacNeal packed his bags, abandoned his lodgings and left Amherst without leaving any forwarding address. Esther was understandably distraught. The visitation began one week later.

On the evening of 4 September, Esther climbed into her bed in the room that she shared with Jennie. Almost at once she screamed and leapt out again saying that there was a mouse in the bed. Jennie stripped the bed, but could find no sign of any mouse. On the following evening, both girls heard what sounded like a mouse scurrying about under Esther's bed. Jennie peered under the bed and spotted a small cardboard box. The box suddenly moved so Jennie thought that the mouse must be inside it.

She pulled the box out so that it stood in the middle of the floor. The box gave a sudden jerk and fell over. But when the lid fell open the girls could see that there was nothing there. They set the box upright again and once more it flipped over. Daniel Teed came in at this

The humble cottage of a shoemaker: it was in this small wooden house in Amherst, Nova Scotia, that a most dramatic poltergeist visitation took place in 1878 and 1879

point. He told them that they were imagining things and ordered them to bed.

On the following evening, Esther complained that she felt unwell. She went to bed early but a few minutes later she was heard screaming. Jennie ran to see what was wrong. When she got there Esther's face was flushed bright red and her hair was standing on end. Then her body began to swell up. Jennie called for Daniel, who dashed in with John and William. At that moment there was a terrific bang, as if somebody had fired a cannon just outside the house. The men ran outside, found nothing and came back indoors. Esther was fast asleep and her appearance was normal.

Two nights later Esther felt ill again. This time Jennie accompanied her to the bedroom and saw her face turn

red for herself. She called for the men, who came in just as the bedclothes flew off Esther's bed. They drifted through the air to collapse in a pile in the corner. When John went over to look at them, a pillow rose into the air and hovered for a moment before hitting him hard on the head. He immediately fled. On the following day he sent a message asking for his clothes to be sent to a nearby boarding house, where he had taken up residence. He never returned to the house. After John had left the invisible cannon fired again, twice this time. Again Esther collapsed into sleep and once more her appearance returned to normal.

Daniel Teed summoned Dr Carritte as soon as he could. The doctor could find nothing wrong with Esther, but as he finished his inspection the girl's pillow flew across the room. Dr Carritte put it back, but again it left the bed and hurtled through the air. Then a scratching noise began to be heard. It was apparently coming from inside the wall above Esther's bed. As the appalled doctor watched, scratch marks began to appear on the wall as if made by an invisible claw. The marks gradually became more controlled until they took the form of writing. The words could be clearly seen: 'Esther Cox, you are mine to kill.' This was followed by a series of knocks and bangs that continued for two hours.

Over the following three weeks, the knocking noises gradually increased in frequency and volume. They were especially loud on the day after Dr Carritte had given Esther a dose of morphine to help her sleep. Then Esther broke down and told the doctor and her sister that there was more to Bob MacNeal's sudden departure than met the eye. On the day before he left she had been out for a drive in the country with him in a borrowed pony and trap. Once they had reached a remote spot, Bob had tried to persuade her to have sex with him. When she refused he pulled out a gun and seemed intent on raping her. A farm cart had then lumbered into view and Bob had fled.

Jennie started to blame Bob MacNeal for the haunting. Her words were followed by a very loud thump on the wall. Dr Carritte remarked that the 'ghost' seemed to understand everything they said. He was rewarded with three distinct knocks. The doctor then decided to ask the ghost some questions. He suggested that one knock should mean 'no', two knocks should signify 'do not know' and three knocks should stand for 'yes'. There came three knocks as if the ghost were agreeing, but the subsequent question and answer session made no sense at all.

The knocking noises continued for some weeks. They became so loud that they could be heard from outside the house. A crowd often gathered to listen. In December Esther fell ill with diphtheria and the manifestations stopped. She went away to stay with relatives while

The family's neighbours were alarmed by the fires because all of the houses in the town were built of wood, so they demanded that Esther be sent away

she recuperated and during that time there were no disturbances, either in Amherst or at her temporary home. They began again when she returned to Amherst. Soon after she got home, Esther called the rest of the family into her room. She said that a disembodied voice had announced that the house was going to be set on fire. At that instant a lit match appeared out of thin air and dropped on to Esther's bed. Jennie put it out. Another match fell and was put out. Then over a dozen lit matches materialized at various points around the room. They all fell to the floor. And then the knocking noises began again.

Over the next week several small fires broke out. The first fire left one of Esther's dresses smouldering while a second set a barrel of tinder ablaze. The family's neighbours were alarmed by the fires because all of the houses in the town were built of wood, so they demanded that Esther be sent away. A restaurant owner in the town named John White thought this was uncharitable, so he offered Esther a live-in job. Nothing happened during the first two weeks of Esther's new job. Then one day, as she was scrubbing the floor, the brush leapt out of her

The poltergeist grabbed the brush from Esther Cox's hand when she was scrubbing the floor

Supernatural target practice: one day metal objects flew at Esther Cox as if she were a powerful magnet. The effect lasted for several days, but stopped when she began wearing insulated shoes

hand and floated up to the ceiling. It hovered there for several seconds before dropping. On the following day the oven door flung itself open repeatedly. Then Esther seemed to become a powerful magnet. Cutlery and other objects would fly across the room to stick to her. One knife cut her as it made contact and she bled profusely.

White thought that an excess of electricity might be to blame. He had a pair of shoes with insulated soles made and he asked Esther to wear them. The magnetic activity ended but Esther developed severe headaches and bad nosebleeds, so she refused to wear the shoes. However, the magnetism did not return. Instead the wooden furniture in the restaurant began to slide about of its own accord. This began to put customers off, so White reluctantly told Esther she had to go home. In fact, Esther went to stay with an elder sister who was

Esther Cox was put in prison after a barn burned down, but it is possible that the fire was begun by the poltergeist

chairs in the room started to hop and dance about. The visitation seemed to escalate rapidly over the next few days, as if Hubbell was indeed resented. No fewer than 45 small fires broke out, Esther was stabbed by pins on 30 different occasions and small objects floated around the house more than ever before. But Hubbell persisted. He eventually persuaded the spirits to communicate with him by using a code of raps. The more dramatic activity then tailed off.

> *No fewer than 45 small fires broke out, Esther was stabbed by pins on 30 different occasions and small objects floated around the house*

The spirits refused to talk about themselves, so Hubbell was unable to discover anything as to their origin or their motives. He did, however, get them to tell him what they would do next – things like moving a chair or floating an ornament around the room. They also told him what he had written down and they even knew the dates on the coins in his pocket. Hubbell visited the Amherst house several times over the following months. He closely questioned witnesses about the events that had occurred before he arrived and then he interacted with the spirits and watched the manifestations. The manifestations were always at their strongest when Esther was having her periods, he noticed. He linked this to the fact that the visitation had begun just after the attempted rape. However, he was unable to formulate a theory as to quite how these features were all connected. After collecting all the evidence that he needed for his book, Hubbell suggested that the afflicted household might earn some money by putting Esther on the stage. Perhaps she could get her spirits to perform in public, as the Fox Sisters had done. The enterprise proved a failure, because the spirits never turned up. In any case the visitation seemed to be winding down – the incidents were not as frequent and they were becoming less severe.

married to a farmer near New Brunswick. As before, the manifestations ceased while she was away – though Esther said she began to hear voices when she was alone. When she returned to amherst in June 1879 the visitation began again. This was the point at which Hubbell took an interest. He wrote and asked if he could come to stay in the 'haunted house' as a paying guest. Daniel Teed agreed so Hubbell moved in.

The writer had been in the house for less than five minutes when his umbrella rose from the corner where he had left it and floated across the room to fall at his feet. Undeterred, he sat down to talk to Teed, whereupon a nearby chair lurched across the room and banged into his. Esther then came in from her bedroom, where she had been resting. She said that the spirit voices had told her that Hubbell was unwelcome. Hubbell said he had come to stay and he was not leaving. At that, all the

After a few months of peace, Esther left home to take a job on a farm run by a couple named Davidson. Soon after she arrived, the Davidson's neighbours reported a series of petty thefts. The stolen objects were found in the Davidsons' barn. Mr Davidson suspected Esther but he was uncertain if he should report the matter. Then his barn burned down and Esther was thrown into prison, accused of arson and theft. She was released after four months. It was never entirely clear if the fire had been caused by Esther, by accident or by the 'spirits'. Whatever the truth the visitation was very definitely over by the time Esther left prison. She went on to lead a conventional and entirely blameless life.

The Fowler Visitation

Another well-documented, late-19th-century case took place in a house near the village of Appleby in what was then Westmorland, but is now Cumbria. One of those involved kept a diary and wrote down the events as they happened, allowing us to follow the progress of this particular visitation in detail.

The house in question was a former flour mill which, like so many in England, was abandoned in the 1880s when cheap grain was imported from North America and milled at the dockside. In 1887 the semi-derelict old watermill was bought by a businessman from Manchester named Fowler. His plan was to turn it into a comfortable country home for his family, which consisted of his wife and two daughters – Teddie aged 12 and Jessica aged 14. After he had moved his family in, Fowler would have to spend part of his time in Manchester. He intended to occupy a small apartment over his business when he did so. But the old mill had to be converted into a home before the family could move in.

Most of the changes were cosmetic, but one modification was more substantial than the others. It was to have a huge impact on the lives of the mill's occupants. The mill's water wheel had formerly been linked to a large axle that had entered the mill through the side wall overlooking the river. After entering the 'wheel room' the axle had been connected to the mass of cogs and gears that powered the milling machinery. The room was lit by a large window, while a door gave access to some stone steps and a gantry from which the water wheel could be inspected and repaired. A door led from the wheel room into the kitchen.

Fowler hired a gang of workmen to remove the wheel and all of the machinery. He then had the door bricked up, but he left the window as it was. The wall separating the wheel room from the kitchen was torn down and replaced by a flimsy partition that stood much closer to the outside wall.

This created a far larger kitchen that now had the advantage of a window overlooking the river. A storeroom now occupied the greatly reduced wheel room – but the family still called it the wheel room. The building work was finished in early May 1887 and the family moved in. About two weeks later, Teddie complained of feeling ill. When she began to run a slight fever her mother put her to bed and decided that she should rest there for a day or two. That evening the other three members of the family were eating supper in the kitchen when the sound of breaking glass came from the wheel room.

Mr Fowler went into the room to find that a pane of glass in the window had been smashed. At first he thought that a large bird must have flown into the window and broken it, but he soon decided that the pane had been smashed deliberately. He peered out but he could see nobody, so he walked through the kitchen and out into his garden. From this vantage point he could see the stream in both directions and the path that ran along the far side. Again, nobody was in sight. Fowler then returned to the wheel room and began clearing up the broken glass. He quickly found the missile that had smashed the window. It was a large stone, identical to those found in the rocky bed of the stream, and it was still wet. Fowler put the incident down to stray vandals and returned to his family.

Ten days later the family were again at supper in the kitchen when they began to hear the sound of somebody knocking on the far side of the partition. The knocking noises got louder and more insistent and then moved to the door that led from the kitchen into the storage room. Thinking that some prankster was at work, Foster walked over and opened the door. The noises stopped at once. When Foster looked round the room there was nobody there. Three days later Mrs Fowler and Jessica

Trouble at mill: a former flour mill in Appleby was the scene
of a well-documented poltergeist attack in 1887

were working in the kitchen when they heard voices coming from the wheel room. The voices were not loud and neither Mrs Fowler nor Jessica could catch what they were saying. They knew that nobody was in the wheel room, and so they fled the house. While they were standing in the garden wondering what to do a man who worked on a neighbouring farm came walking down the lane. Mrs Fowler told the man that she was worried that somebody was in the house. The farmhand went in and searched diligently but found nobody.

That night the voices in the wheel room started again while the family were at supper. This time they were louder. The family could tell that a man and a woman were speaking, though they could not understand what they were saying. Then there came a sound like a saucer falling to the floor and breaking. Mr Fowler quickly opened the door to the room. The voices stopped. There was no broken saucer, nor anything that could have explained the noise. Worrying as the events were, the time had come when Mr Fowler needed to go to Manchester to look after his business. He would be leaving on the following Monday and he would have to stay in Manchester for several days. Although he did not want to leave his family alone, he dreaded what would happen if he announced that the house was haunted. His solution was to sent for an employee named Dick Carter, whom he knew to be level-headed. Carter and his wife would stay at the mill in his absence.

Before Carter arrived, Fowler screwed two stout metal bars across the door that led from the kitchen to the wheel room, so that it could not be opened from either side. As he did so a stone smashed through the window and landed in the wheel room. Fowler then fixed a wire mesh over the outside of the window. On the Monday, Fowler told Carter what had been going on. He expressed his fear that the house was haunted. Carter promised to keep a close eye on things and Foster then left for Manchester.

That evening the people gathered in the kitchen comprised Mr and Mrs Carter, Mrs Fowler, Teddie and Jessica. The two women were clearing up when the manifestations began. This time they were far more dramatic than before. It all began when a cup fell off the dresser, followed by a pair of saucers and another cup.

Then a jug of beer tipped over and spilled its contents all over the floor. This was followed by the fire irons, which began dancing about in their holder. Finally, pieces of coal started flying out of the coal scuttle. The girls screamed and dived for cover, followed quickly by Mrs Fowler. But Carter stood up and surveyed the mayhem around him. He had promised to keep an eye on things, so he was determined to remember everything that happened. His employer would expect a report. Suddenly, everything fell still. But not for long.

Noises started to come from the sealed-up wheel room. At first it sounded as if the boxes in the wheel room were being thrown about but then came the sound of hammering and banging. Carter ushered everyone out of the house before getting into a small boat and crossing to the far side of the river. He wanted to get a good view of the wheel room window. He watched as packing cases moved back and forth. Then an empty pram floated up to the ceiling before moving off to one side. The pram drifted past the window five times and then the movements and noises ceased. After 20 minutes of silence, Carter rowed back across the stream and entered the house. All was quiet, so he waved the others in. Carter sat up all night in the kitchen while the others went to bed. There were no more incidents, so he was able to doze off.

Next morning, he climbed up a ladder and peered into the wheel room. All of the packing boxes had been piled up against one wall and the pram was perched on top.

Nothing happened for the rest of the week, but when Fowler came home the disturbances broke out again. Once more the packing cases and the pram were moved around the sealed room and loud hammering noises were heard. Then the voices came back. It sounded as if the man and the woman were having an argument, but as before the actual words could not be distinguished. This lasted for an hour and then quiet returned. Over the months that followed the disturbances continued unabated. There might be a few days when nothing happened, but then the noises and the movements would come back. Mr Fowler's diary entries for a few weeks in August/September are typical. The references to everyday life have been omitted, but the entries that describe the visitation read as follows:

Saturday, August 13

Four jugs broken in kitchen. Several knocks on door. Scraping sound on wheel room window.

Monday, August 15

Cat frightened at something in kitchen, and has run away.

Thursday, August 18

Five spoons found on floor of kitchen this morning, on dresser over night. Jess had a plate thrown at her. Noises in the wheel room.

Sunday, August 21

Quiet, except for jug of water upset, and knives found in sink.

Friday, August 26

A noisy night last night. On guard outside wheel room. They kept it up for nearly two hours. Ink bottles thrown to floor.

Monday, September 5

No sleep last night. On guard all night. Hell is in the wheel room. Wife stayed up part of time.

'Hell is in the wheel room': peering into the locked store, Mr Fowler saw that unseen hands had piled up the crates and boxes, finally balancing a pram on top of the pile

The Appleby events were put down to a death that had resulted from a bar-room fight some years before the haunting began

It is hardly surprising that the Fowler family wanted to take a holiday after such a summer. Mr Fowler's married sister lived on the Isle of Man and he arranged for them all to visit her for a couple of weeks in September. Before leaving he made a point of putting all the loose objects away. Then he made a careful note of where everything was before locking every door. Finally, he asked a neighbour to keep an eye on the place. They agreed to make a daily check on the outside doors and windows.

In the event, the Fowlers were away for four weeks. When the time came to return home, Teddie asked if she could stay on with her aunt. So Mr and Mrs Fowler and Jessica returned without her. The house was exactly as they had left it. There were no further manifestations of any kind.

Once the trouble was over, Fowler felt more inclined to talk about the events. He spoke to the local curate, who agreed to do some research. The curate discovered that one of the former workers at the mill had been a

Welshman named Tom Watkins. Watkins had been employed to look after the machinery in the wheel room. He often slept in the room when the mill was busy. When the Welshman had formed a friendship with a local woman, the woman's husband had taken exception to the way in which the 'friendship' was progressing. One night a fight had broken out between Watkins and the husband in the local inn. It had ended with the woman's husband dying from a blow to the head. Watkins was arrested, but he was released after it became clear that the other man had attacked him first. Watkins and the widow then moved off to Wales. Their subsequent fate was unknown. The visitation was promptly put down to a haunting that was connected to these events. The ghosts that had been heard arguing in the wheel room were assumed to be those of Watkins and his lover.

The Dagg Farm Visitation

Two years later a farm in Canada became the target of a visitation. Once again the events were carefully recorded by one of the protagonists. The farm was owned by George Dagg, who lived there with his wife Susan, his four-year-old daughter Mary and his two-year-old son Johnny. Also living at the farm was a teenage boy named Dean, who had been hired as an odd job boy, and an 11-year-old orphan named Dinah McLean, whom the Daggs had taken in.

On 15 September 1889, Dean found a $5 bill on the floor. He gave it to Mr Dagg who recognized it as one of the two notes that he had put into his private bureau on the previous day. When he went to put it back he found that the other note was missing as well. After this note turned up in Dean's room Dagg suspected the boy of theft. But he decided to say nothing – the boy had turned in one note and so might have got cold feet about the attempted crime. That afternoon Mrs Dagg discovered that a piece of human excrement had been smeared across the floor. Because it had happened so soon after the note incident, the event was blamed on Dean. Dagg forced him to clean up the mess and then dragged him off to the nearby town to see the magistrate. Three more streaks of excrement appeared while they were gone, so Dean was clearly not to blame.

The Dagg Farm poltergeist seemed to focus its attentions on an orphan named Dinah who was living with the family

The mysterious phenomena escalated rapidly, both in number and intensity. Apart from the disgusting streaks, which continued to appear for a few days, stones began to be thrown. The missiles not only smashed a number of windows but they also hit young Mary. Then food began to be moved about in the dairy, particularly butter.

Several small fires started around the house, which had to be put out, and then pools of water formed on the floor, which had to be mopped up. Within a few days

When the Dagg Farm poltergeist promised to leave on a specific day, neighbours crowded round to witness the event

She led Woodcock to the shed, but nothing seemed to be amiss.

Then Dinah called out, 'Are you there, mister?'

This prompted the disembodied voice to reply with a stream of swear words.

When the voice fell silent, Woodcock asked, 'Who are you?'

'I am the Devil,' came the gruff voice. 'I'll have you in my clutches. Get out of this or I'll break your neck.' It then poured out a new torrent of obscenities.

Woodcock sent Dinah to fetch George Dagg while he continued to talk to the voice, which merely swore at him rather than making any meaningful replies. When Dagg arrived in the woodshed, he asked a perfectly understandable question: 'Why on earth have you been bothering me and my family?'

'Just for fun,' came the reply.

'There is no fun in throwing a stone at young Mary,' protested Dagg.

'Poor wee Mary,' exclaimed the voice. 'I did not intend to hit her. I intended it for Dinah. But I did not let the stone hurt her.' More obscenities followed. Then the voice apologized for the fires.

Woodcock stayed on the Dagg farm for several days, during which time the poltergeist activity continued unabated. On one occasion the two younger children claimed that they had seen the ghost. They said it looked like a thin man with a cow's head, complete with horns.

Woodcock tried to get the spirit to communicate in writing, thinking that this would be better evidence than his own notes. The spirit happily picked up a pencil and wrote furiously on a piece of paper. When Woodcock bent over to read what had been written, he saw that it was another stream of swear words. He complained, whereupon the voice said, 'I will steal your pencil'.

The pencil then lifted into the air and flew out of the door. On the following

the manifestations began to centre on Dinah. Her lovely long hair, which she wore in a plait, came in for a lot of tugging and pulling. One particular tug was so violent that the plait was almost severed, which forced Dinah to have her hair cut short. Then Dinah claimed that she could hear a voice muttering softly. The others could not hear it at first, but within a day or two they too could hear a gruff male voice. When words could be distinguished they were obscene swear words.

It was at this point that a local man named Woodcock came to the Dagg farm. He asked if he could stay with them while he investigated the haunting. George Dagg agreed to the arrangement. Woodcock wanted to start with the most recent phenomenon so Dinah told him that she had seen something moving in the woodshed.

Mopping up: clearing up after the poltergeist became a regular chore at the Dagg Farm

The final manifestation of the Dagg Farm poltergeist came in the form of a kindly old man with a long beard, dressed in white, who talked to the children of the house and cuddled them before floating off into the sky (see page 252)

Ballechin House in Scotland hit the headlines in the 1890s when a poltergeist took up residence and plagued a number of guests who later wrote to *The Times* newspaper about the events

Saturday the voice said that it had decided to leave the Dagg farm the next day. Word got out and early next morning neighbours and friends started arriving. As each one entered, the voice cracked jokes or made amusing comments about the person. It showed a quite astonishing level of knowledge about the locals and their lives. After a while one person, probably Woodcock, remarked that the voice was no longer swearing.

'I am not the person who used the filthy language,' the voice declared. 'I am an angel from Heaven sent by God to drive away that fellow.'

Woodcock pointed out that the voice sounded exactly the same as before, whereupon the voice swore profusely before returning to its humorous remarks. The voice later claimed to be the ghost of a local person who had died about 20 years earlier at the age of 80. Later in the afternoon, the voice changed from being gruff and male to being soft and feminine. It began to sing hymns and said that it would be leaving soon. The fairly substantial crowd that had been questioning it objected and asked it to stay. At 3am the voice said that it really had to leave, but that it would visit the children once more before it left for good. Then it fell silent.

The next morning Mary, Johnny and Dinah came running excitedly into the house. They said they had seen 'a man with a beautiful face and long white hair and beard dressed all in white' in the farmyard. The figure had bent down to cuddle Mary and Johnny while Dinah watched. He had called Johnny 'a fine little fellow' and then he had lifted him up. The man had then let the children go and had smiled at them. Then he had floated gently up into the air, heading upwards as if to heaven, before vanishing. The visitation was over.

The Haunting of Ballechin House

By the 1890s attitudes toward poltergeist activity had begun to improve. The events surrounding the Fox Sisters at Hydesville had faded from memory. Once again reputable people were open to the idea that there were still unexplained phenomena taking place that needed to be investigated. As yet nobody had coined the word 'poltergeist' but a similarity between some cases of hauntings was beginning to be seen.

The activities surrounding Ballechin House near Dunkeld in Perthshire constitute a typical instance from this transitional period. In the 1890s the house was owned by a Captain JMS Steuart, who rented it out, together with the extensive grouse shoot that went with it. In 1896 the house and the shoot were let for a year to a Spanish nobleman, who moved in with his family in time for the grouse season to begin. The nobleman, who preferred to remain anonymous, invited several British friends to spend time at the house. He also hired local staff to run the house, though he brought his own personal servants from Spain. Finally he hired an English butler named Harold Sanders.

The haunting of Ballechin House began as soon as the Spanish family moved in. After 11 weeks of mayhem the Spanish family fled. The events were witnessed by many of the British guests, some of whom were very well connected socially, and the story spread rapidly. Some of the rumours were extremely lurid – they lost nothing in the telling as they passed from person to person. In the end the butler, Harold Sanders, contact The Times newspaper in an attempt to set the record straight. Sanders was the soul of discretion, so he mentioned no names and identified people only by their initials. Presumably this allowed those in the know to identify who he was talking about, but did not allow anyone to

Butler Harold Sanders wrote a detailed account of his experiences at the hands of the poltergeist at Ballechin House

be picked out by the general reading public. The Spanish nobleman's guests included Colonel A; Major B and his two daughters Miss B and the other Miss B; Mr and Mrs H with their daughter Miss H; Mrs G and finally 'the old Spanish nurse'.

After setting the scene and describing the arrangements in the house, Sanders said that one night there was 'a tremendous thumping on the doors, heavy footsteps along the passages and similar disturbances heard by every inmate of the house, including the servants.' He went on in some detail:

The same thing happened with variations almost nightly for the succeeding two months that I was there, and every visitor that came to the house was disturbed in the same manner. One gentleman (Colonel A) told me he was awakened on several occasions with the feeling that someone was pulling the bedclothes off him. Some heavy footsteps were heard, and others like the rustling of a lady's dress; and sometimes groans were heard, but nearly

I could feel something breathing on me. I tried to reach some matches on a chair by my bedside, but my hand was held back by some invisible power

always accompanied with heavy knocking: sometimes the whole house would be aroused. One night I remember five gentlemen meeting at the top of the stairs in their night suits, some with sticks or pokers, one had a revolver, vowing vengeance on the disturbers of their sleep.

During the two months after I first heard the noises I kept watch altogether about twelve times in various parts of the house, mostly unknown to others (at the time), and have heard the noises in the wing as well as other parts.

When watching I always experienced a peculiar sensation a few minutes before hearing any noise. I can only describe it as like suddenly entering an ice house, and a feeling that someone was present and about to speak to me. On three different nights I was awakened by my bedclothes being pulled off my feet. But the worst night I had at Ballechin was one night about the second week in September, and I shall never forget it as long as I live.

I had been keeping watch with two gentlemen, one a visitor the other one of the house. We heard the noises I have described about half past two. Both gentlemen were very much alarmed; but we searched everywhere, but could not find any trace of the ghost or cause of the noises, although they came this time from an unoccupied room. (I may mention that the noises were never heard in the daytime but always between midnight and four in the

Hair-raising moment: the events at Ballechin House reached a climax when butler Sander's bedclothes floated into the air and his bed was jerked violently about the room, causing him to break out into a cold sweat of fear

morning – generally between two and four o'clock.) After a thorough search the two gentlemen went to bed sadder, but not wiser, men, for we had discovered nothing. I then went to my room, but not to bed, for I was not satisfied, and decided to continue the watch alone. So I seated myself on the service stairs.

I had not long to wait (about twenty minutes only) when the knocking re-commenced from the same direction as before, but much louder than before and followed, after a very short interval, by two distinct groans which certainly made me feel very uncomfortable for it sounded like someone being stabbed and then falling to the floor. That was enough for me. I went and asked the two gentlemen who had just gone to bed if they had heard anything. One said he had heard five knocks and two groans, the same as I had; while the other (whose room was much nearer to where the sounds came from) said he had heard nothing. I then retired to my bed, but not to sleep, for I had not been in bed three minutes before I experienced the sensation as before, but instead of being followed by knocking, my bedclothes were lifted up and let fall again – first at the foot of my bed, but gradually coming towards my head. I held the bedclothes around my neck with my hands, but they were gently lifted in spite of my efforts to hold them. I then reached around me with my hand, but could feel nothing. This was immediately followed by my being fanned as though some bird was flying around my head, and I could distinctly hear and feel something breathing on me. I then tried to reach some matches that were on a chair by my bedside, but my hand was held back as if by some invisible power. Then the thing seemed to retire to the foot of my bed. Then I suddenly found the foot of my bed lifted up and carried around towards the window for about three or four feet, then replaced to its former position. All this did not take, I should think, more than two or three minutes, although at the time it seemed hours to me. Just then the clock struck four, and being tired out with my long night's watching, I fell asleep.

No wonder the unfortunate man would never forget his experiences. Once the butler had gone into print, others involved also contacted *The Times* newspaper. Miss B wrote a letter a few days later in which she reported:

I wakened suddenly in the middle of the night, and noticed how quiet the house was. Then I heard the clock strike two and a few minutes later there came a crashing, vibrating batter against the door of the outer room. My sister was sleeping very soundly, but she started up in a moment at the noise, wide awake. We heard the battering noise again two nights later when we were in the bedroom of our host's daughter waiting for the ghost.

It was as if someone was hitting the door with his fist as hard as he could hit. I left my room at once, but could find nothing to account for the noise

Major B then wrote in, having first taken the trouble to contact Colonel A, whose bedroom had been separated from his own by a wall with an interconnecting door.

He wrote:

On August 24th at about 3.30am, I heard very loud knocking, apparently on the door to Colonel A's room, about nine raps in all. Three raps came quickly one after the other, then three more the same, and three more the same.

It was as if someone was hitting the door with his fist as hard as he could hit. I left my room at once, but could find nothing to account for the noise.

It was daylight at the time. I heard the same noises on the 28th and 30th August at about the same hour viz. between 3 and 4am.

Colonel A. corroborated the story, writing:

What I heard was what you heard, a terrific banging at one's bedroom door, generally about from 2 to 3am, about two nights out of three.

Major and the Colonel were on opposite sides of a partition door, yet both heard the same bangs and both

Mrs G and her daughter were awoken by supernatural noises at 1am in Ballechin House

Ballechin was investigated after the haunting, and events were blamed on the ghost of a nun named Ishbel

thought they were coming from the other side. Mrs G also wrote to the newspaper.

I, my daughter, and my husband were put in rooms adjoining, at the end of the new wing. At 2am a succession of thundering knocks came from the end of our passage, re-echoing through the house, where it was heard by many others. About half an hour afterwards my husband heard a piercing shriek; then all was still. The next night and succeeding ones we heard loud single knocks at different doors along our passage. The last night but one before we left, I was roused from sleep by hearing the clock strike one, and immediately it had ceased six violent blows shook our own door on its hinges, and came with frightful rapidity, followed by deep groans.

The most dramatic aspects of the visitation seem to have ended as soon as the Spanish family moved out. However, the correspondence in The Times intrigued a Miss Goodrich Freer, who proceeded to rent the house with the intention of investigating what she firmly believed to be a haunting by a ghost. Very soon after arriving, Miss Freer and her friends unpacked a ouija board and tried to contact the 'spirits' in a seance. They were rewarded by apparently being contacted by a spirit

that called itself Ishbel, which instructed them to 'go at dusk to the glen up by the burn'. Miss Freer duly went to the specified place and waited. She recorded what happened next in a journal:

Against the snow I saw a slight, black figure, a woman, moving slowly up the glen. She stopped and turned and looked at me. She was dressed as a nun. Her face looked pale. I saw her hand in the folds of her habit. Then she moved on, as it seemed, on a slope too steep for walking. When she came under the trees she disappeared.

A typical Ouija Board of the type that is used to try to establish
communication with the entity causing a poltergeist visitation

Mr Bartholomew Chaundry died when he fell over the banisters of Bethony Manor in Oxfordshire
when drunk. A later poltergeist visitation in the house was blamed on his restless spirit

Miss Freer appears to assume that the nun was Ishbel. However, did 'Ishbel' vanish in supernatural fashion or simply slip out of sight in the dark shadows that are to be found under fir trees at dusk? In the days that followed, Miss Freer and her guests reported hearing footsteps, bangs, knockings, crashes and groans in the house at night. Then Miss Freer, but nobody else, saw the ghostly nun three more times in the grounds of the house. On one occasion the ghost appeared to be weeping. Miss Freer undertook some research into the history of Ballechin House and found that about half a century earlier it had been home to a bad-tempered old man who had habitually threatened to 'come back and haunt' any local folk who annoyed him.

The Haunting at Bethony

Another lady who took it upon herself to investigate a 'haunting' was a Miss Sharpe, who lived at Bethony, a manor house near Tackley in Oxfordshire. In 1875 a former owner, Mr Bartholomew Chaundry, died after he fell over the banisters from the first floor. He landed in the hall and broke his neck. There were no suspicious circumstances, because Chaundry was a notorious drunk who was well known for falling over when he had been drinking heavily. Nevertheless, Miss Sharpe thought that the death might have had something to do with later events.

Miss Sharpe lived alone, though various friends and relatives came to visit from time to time. She also took in the village poor when they were ill – at least three of them died in the house, though she does not seem to have thought this significant. The house also contained a number of servants, but in her account of the 'haunting' Miss Sharpe does not say how many, nor does she name them. The first sign of something odd happening came on 24 April 1905 when the sound of a door being slammed shut was heard. Other doors were heard being slammed, even when no door was found to be shut. After a few days of this, an odd sound rather like that of heavy metal chains being dragged over the roof was heard at night. Then came the faint sounds of muttering voices. The actual words could not be made out, but the voices definitely seemed to be male.

One day there came the sound of an enormous explosion. The entire house shook to the blast. 'I thought

Lights similar to stars and flashing, firework-like explosions featured in the haunting of Bethony Manor. The lights could dim suddenly and then flare up again

it was an earthquake,' recorded Miss Sharpe. No other properties in the area had been affected and no sign of any explosion could be found. The blast seemed to herald the start of the real visitation. From that day onwards Miss Sharpe, her servants and her guests were subjected to phenomena that became more frequent and more insistent. Day after day Miss Sharpe recorded a succession of sounds. The noise of a man in heavy boots clumping up the staircase, then back down again, was particularly common. A sound like a workman battering at stone with a pickaxe was often heard for hours on end. On other days it was as if a football were being kicked against the walls repeatedly. The sounds of tearing paper were occasionally heard, as was the noise of a woman in a heavy silk skirt walking about. On some days an incessant light tapping would sound out in the Blue Room, a sitting room. Indeed, as the months passed it became clear that most of the phenomena took place in or adjacent to the Blue Room.

Objects were moved about – clothing was a favourite of the 'ghosts' – and bedclothes were torn off sleeping guests in the middle of the night. Others had their beds shaken violently from side to side. Strange sights were also seen. Lights, akin to small stars, were sighted floating through the house at night, while bright flashes would illuminate rooms for a second or two, then fade. Conversely candles would sometimes 'misbehave'. Although they could be seen to be as alight as ever, the light from them could dim as dramatically as if a cover of smoked glass had been put over them.

Then the apparitions began to appear. The first one to appear was what looked like the shadow of a burly man. Miss Sharpe took this to be the man in heavy boots who tramped up and down the stairs. The shadow became firmer until it assumed the definite shape of a big man in farming clothes. After materializing several times in a bedroom the burly farmer was seen no more. He was replaced by the more sinister figure of a tall, thin man

Lights, akin to small stars, were sighted floating through the house at night, while bright flashes would illuminate rooms for a second or two, then fade.

wrapped in a black cloak. This spirit exuded a feeling of derision and scorn that was felt by everyone who saw him. Miss Sharpe did not content herself with merely recording the events in her diary – she also carried out tests. Thin threads were strung across rooms where the apparitions walked but they were never found to be broken, even after one of the figures had walked right through them. She sealed up rooms where noises were heard in order to make sure that nobody could get in or out, but the noises continued.

After some nocturnal disturbances upset a young niece who was visiting, Miss Sharpe decided that the disturbances had to stop, so she called in the local vicar.

On 12 July 1907 he conducted a prayer meeting in the house and sprinkled holy water in every room. According to Miss Sharpe the atmosphere in the house changed suddenly and definitively, and the manifestations ceased at once. In January 1908 strange noises began to be heard again. The most frequent sound this time was that of an invisible dog running about, its claws scritch-scratching on the wooden floors. Miss Sharpe sent for the vicar again and the service was repeated on 21 February. The manifestations ceased again, this time for good.

The Case of 50 Berkeley Square

The visitations that I have discussed so far were fairly well documented because somebody on the scene chose to write down what was happening. Most incidents from the middle and later 19th century are not so well recorded. A typical instance was the case of 50 Berkeley Square, in London's prestigious Mayfair area, which was said to be the most haunted house in London. By the 1870s numerous stories were circulating about the house, but most of them refer to some sort of nameless horror on the top floor and a room at the back of the house that was said to be the most haunted of all.

One man met his death, the story goes, when he fell from an upper floor at No. 50 Berkeley Square and impaled himself on the railings below. The body was discovered by a patrolling policeman

Another victim of events in No. 50 Berkeley Square was found on the top floor. Apparently he died from sheer terror

In one version of the story a pair of sailors had spotted that the house was empty, so they broke in. After making free with the food and drink, they went upstairs to sleep. Early the following morning a passing policeman found the body of one of the sailors impaled on the railings outside the house. He had clearly fallen from a broken window high above. The policeman then broke into the house to search it. He found the second sailor on the upstairs floor – he was a gibbering wreck. The sailor muttered something incoherent about the horror that he had seen, but he never recovered his wits and died soon afterwards.

Another tale has it that the house was left empty for many years by the owner, who refused to rent it out to anybody. He employed a housekeeper who was instructed to keep the house in good order, but she was absolutely banned from going up to the top floor. The haunted room was kept securely locked and only the house owner had a key. Once every few months the owner would visit the forbidden room. He would lock the housekeeper in the kitchen and then climb the stairs.

Talk of the town: Victorian London was agog with rumours of ghostly goings-on at No. 50 Berkeley Square, one of the most fashionable addresses in the city

After unlocking the door he would go into the room and sit there for several hours. Then he would carefully lock the door behind him again and let the housekeeper out of the kitchen.

It was rumoured that a man who knew the owner once asked for permission to enter the haunted room. Against his better judgement the owner handed over his keys and the man travelled to London. The housekeeper prepared the man's supper and then retired to bed. In the middle of the night the bell connected to the pull in the haunted room gave a gentle tinkle that awoke the housekeeper. Thinking that the guest might want a snack or a new chamber pot, she slipped on a dressing gown. At that point the bell was almost yanked off the wall by the violence of the tugging on the wire. The housekeeper hurried up the stairs with a light. She found the man stone dead on the floor with a look of absolute terror on his face.

Although such stories were widely known, there is absolutely no documentary evidence for any of them. It is known that for much of the preceding 40 years the house had been occupied by a rather eccentric man who did little to maintain it. No doubt the house did look like a haunted house at times. However, the origin of the stories seems to have been a poltergeist visitation in the 1850s. Nothing was written about it at the time, but later on those involved recollected that furniture had been moved about by unseen hands and various thumps and knockings had been heard. It is not much of a record of a poltergeist visitation, but it is sadly typical of much of the material from the time.

Poltergeists in the News

In the second half of the 19th century, the population of Britain became almost universally literate for the first time. Accordingly, a large number of newspapers and magazines flooded the market. While earlier journals had been written by the gentry for the gentry, these new publications were aimed at the masses. It took a huge amount of material, from the sentimental to the sensational, to satisfy the appetites of this new reading public. Reports of mysterious happenings were particularly popular. Looking back, it can be seen that a good number of these stories describe some sort of

Blankets, mattresses and clothes spontaneously burst into flames at the home of Mr and Mrs Moulton in Bedford in 1856

poltergeist activity. The lack of any form of serious investigation meant that the details were sketchy, but the articles are an indication that the poltergeist phenomenon was continuing throughout these decades.

In August 1856, for instance, the news-papers in Bedford covered an odd story – it came to light at a judicial hearing. Mrs Moulton's husband was away for a few days on business, so on 12 August she decided to take the opportunity to fumigate their house. Together with the housemaid, Anne Fennimore, Mrs Moulton obtained the required sulphur and borrowed the 'burning jars' made of earthenware that would be needed. The jars were filled with sulphur, distributed around the house and ignited. At first all went well and the fumes began to fill the house, but then one of the burning jars suddenly toppled over, scattering flaming sulphur over the floor. The two women put the blaze out without much difficulty, though the floorboards had been singed, and the rest of the process passed off without trouble. However, as the women were preparing for supper that evening Mrs Moulton smelled burning again. She tracked it down to a spare bedroom where a mattress was on fire. She put the fire out with a jug of water and then called for the maid. Neither of them could think how the mattress had caught fire when none of the burning pots had been in the room.

Then they both smelled burning again. This time the smoke trail led to a blanket chest in another bedroom. The lid was opened to reveal a smouldering blanket, which was quickly extinguished. Then smoke came pouring out of a wardrobe. Opening the door, they discovered that a dress was on fire. There were no more incidents that day, but on the following morning some bed linen burst into flames. That was enough for Mrs Moulton – she sent an urgent telegram to her husband, demanding that he cut short his business trip and come home at once. Over the next few days at least a dozen small fires broke out around the house. A neighbour came round to keep Mrs Moulton company, but when she picked up a cushion from the sofa to plump it up, it burst into flames in her hands.

Mr Moulton returned on 16 August. It was raining heavily so his overcoat got very wet as he walked back from the railway station. He hung the sodden garment up as he came in. A few hours later it was still just as wet, but it caught fire and the flames had to be beaten out. Mr Moulton sent for the police. While the policeman was talking to Mr Moulton, the handkerchief in his pocket suddenly burst into flames. Not knowing what to do, the policeman left after suggesting a judicial hearing. By the time the hearing took place in late August the fires had stopped occurring.

Witnesses were called to testify to the reality of the fires, but none of them were able to say what had started them. Mrs Moulton suggested that the spilled sulphur had somehow been to blame, but nobody could imagine quite how. The jury recorded a verdict of accidental damage.

Then in 1878 the *Glasgow News* reported the arrest of a 12-year-old girl named Ann Kidner. A hayrick in her home village had been set on fire and the local policeman had come along to investigate. His suspicions were aroused by Ann's behaviour. Sobbing uncontrollably, she kept on saying that she had not touched the hayrick. The policeman immediately frogmarched her off to the farmhouse of John Shattock who owned the hayrick. Young Ann worked there as a scullery maid.

When Shattock heard the news of the fire, he was upset but strangely unsurprised.

He was also unwilling to blame the girl. As the policeman sat down at the kitchen table to discuss the matter, a loaf of bread rose into the air, drifted across the room and came to rest on a sideboard. The policeman's reaction was to arrest Ann and haul her off to prison. However, the magistrate ordered her release a few days later.

In December 1904 and January 1905 the *Louth News* kept up a running commentary on a series of bizarre events at Binbrook Farm near Great Grimsby. The case

Mr Moulton was drenched after being caught in heavy rain as he walked home, but his wet clothes were soon inexplicably on fire

Chickens at a farm in Lincolnshire were strangled by a poltergeist active in 1904

The 1904 poltergeist delighted in knocking over furniture when nobody was in the room

began as one of suspected vandalism after some chickens had been found dead in the chicken house one morning. As the newspaper reported, the birds had been killed in an outlandish manner:

They have all been killed in the same weird way. The skin around the neck, from the head to the breast, has been pulled off, and the windpipe drawn from its place and snapped.

After this had happened a couple of times, the farmer, Mr White, set a watch on his chicken houses – which between them held over 250 birds. This made no difference because the chicken killings continued even though no person or animal was ever seen approaching the chicken houses. Then it seemed that the farmhouse had been broken into during the day. Furniture was found tumbled about, clothes had been hauled out of drawers and tossed about and ornaments had been moved from their usual places. The mystery deepened when the farmer and his family realized that nothing had been stolen. This happened at least a dozen times.

On 25 January the family gained a witness to the bizarre events when the village schoolteacher called. As he sat talking to Mrs White, the smell of burning wool drifted into the room. They hurried out into the passageway and found a blazing blanket on the tiled floor. The blanket had not been there when the teacher had entered the house a few minutes earlier and there was no fireplace in the passage that could have set it on fire. Nor was there anyone else in the house. The teacher was sure of that. The climax to the visitation came three days later on 28 January. A reporter from the *Louth News* took down farmer White's account of the incident:

Our servant girl, whom we had taken from the workhouse and who had neither kin nor friend in the world that she knows of, was sweeping the kitchen. There was a very small fire in the grate: there was a guard there, so that no one can come within two feet or more of the fire, and she was at the other end of the room, and had not been near the fire. I suddenly came into the kitchen, and there she was, sweeping away, while the back of her dress was afire. She looked around as I shouted, and, seeing the flames, rushed through the door. She tripped and I smothered the fire out with wet sacks. But she was terribly burned and she is at the Louth Hospital now in terrible pain.

The reporter then went to Louth Hospital. He was not allowed to talk to the girl, but the doctor told him:

The girl was burnt extensively on the back and lies in a critical condition. She adheres to the belief that she was in the middle of the room when her clothes ignited.

That was the end of the visitation. The girl recovered and went to work elsewhere. By this time only 24 chickens were left alive.

I have included the following item to illustrate the fact that reports of the poltergeist phenomenon were not confined to the shores of Britain at this time. In December 1891 an outbreak of unexplained fires filled the newspapers in Toronto, Canada. The affected household was that of Robert Dawson and his wife. Also living in the house was 14-year-old Jennie Bramwell. Jennie's parents had died some years previously and she had been living in an orphanage. As was usual in those days,

The visitation of 1904 in Louth came to a dramatic ending when the clothes of the servant girl caught fire as she swept the kitchen

Mystery firestarter: Jennie snapped out of her trance and pointed out to Mrs Dawson the flames that were licking the ceiling. They managed to put them out, but an hour later they discovered another fire had broken out spontaneously

she had been trained in the skills useful to a domestic servant. The Dawsons had taken Jennie in a few months earlier and they were very pleased with her work and her character. In fact, they were considering adopting the girl and had been in touch with the orphanage about how they should go about it.

Jennie then fell ill. She could not get out of bed for several days and she kept slipping into a trance-like sleep that had the local doctor baffled. But on 11 December she made a sudden recovery, so she got up and returned to her usual routine. All went well until the following day, when a change came over her. She was chatting to Mrs Dawson in the sitting room when her eyes suddenly glazed over. When Mrs Dawson realized that the girl was not listening to her she thought that Jennie's mystery ailment had returned. Then Jennie seemed to snap out of it. She looked at Mrs Dawson in bewilderment and then her eyes went towards the ceiling. 'Look at that,' exclaimed the girl. Mrs Dawson looked up and saw that flames coming from seemingly nowhere were licking at the ceiling. They managed to put the flames out by throwing water at them. An hour later, Jennie drew Mrs Dawson's attention to another fire that had broken out spontaneously.

Mr Dawson did not at first believe the stories that he heard on his return. However, he soon changed his mind when the wall-paper beside him burst into flames as he sat talking to Jennie. Then a dress caught fire, followed by a sofa. In all 45 fires broke out in the following seven days. Jennie was in the room on each occasion, but she was nowhere near any of the outbreaks when they occurred. Then Jennie announced that she wanted to go back to the orphanage, so she packed her bags and left. No more fires broke out in the Dawson household and none occurred at the orphanage.

The New Breed of Researchers

The visitations that were recorded in the second half of the 19th century gradually convinced researchers that some types of haunting could not be classed as ghosts. Ghosts could be seen but they were not heard and they could not move things around. Yet there were records of spirits that moved objects and made noises. However, at this time most researchers were more interested in spiritualists and mediums, or in those humans who claimed extraordinary powers such as the ability to levitate or to see into the future. But fascinating as these paranormal abilities might be, they do not represent poltergeist activity.

By the 1890s a few researchers were willing to go into haunted houses in order to view events for themselves. The term 'poltergeist' was not yet in widespread use, but these researchers looked back over recent cases of physical ghosts and began to draw some conclusions. As before, it was clear that poltergeists inhabited the places

But as the new breed of researchers went out into the world to search for physical ghosts, they were armed with rather more knowledge than the well-meaning vicars and curious gentlemen who had gone before them

where people lived – they did not favour open spaces. Poltergeist manifestations had also changed little since the earlier reports – there were still knocking noises, bangs, thumps and moving objects. The only apparently new phenomenon was the lighting of fires. The Amherst poltergeist used matches, then a new invention, but in other visitations fires were started without matches.

It was also increasingly apparent that most of the 19th-century poltergeists selected a focus person. This feature can also be discerned in earlier cases, but the records from the 19th century tend to be more detailed. The people who were present in the house are listed as well as the phenomena that took place. Where this focus could be clearly identified it was usually found to be a young person, usually a girl, who was undergoing some sort of stress. Esther Cox had undergone an attempted rape just before the Amherst visitation began, while Jennie Bramwell had heard that she might be adopted. Other apparent focus persons may or may not have been in a similar position. Ann Kidner, for instance, was working as a servant on a farm some way from home. She might have been very unhappy, or she might have been quite content – the records do not offer any clues. But at least we know that she was not living happily at home with her family.

And as before there is the possibility of trickery. Miss Freer's experiences at Ballechin House seem just a little too convenient. Seeing a ghostly nun in a glen after being instructed by a ouija board message to go there is very odd. Even more so when the 'ghost' appeared at dusk, close to where there were some shadowy trees into which it could 'vanish'. Perhaps her friends were having some fun with her. But as the new breed of researchers went out into the world to search for physical ghosts, they were armed with rather more knowledge than the well-meaning vicars and curious gentlemen who had gone before them. They still did not know what was causing the events, but they were prepared to be open-minded. Their researches would add massively to the available knowledge.

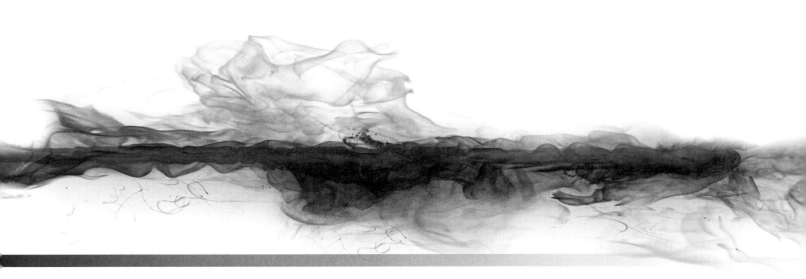

CHAPTER 11

Enter the
Investigators

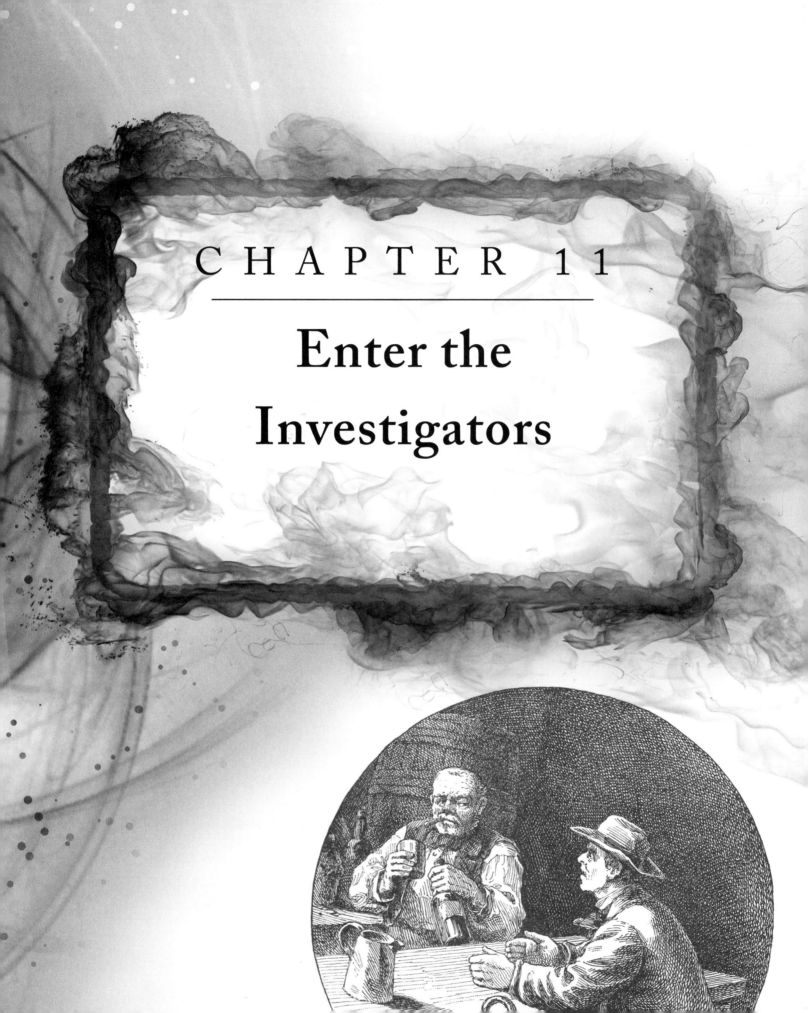

n the later 19th century specific organizations were created for the purpose of investigating anomalous phenomena. In Britain, these included the Ghost Club and the Society for Psychical Research (which quickly spread to the United States, Australia and continental Europe).

These organizations were mostly concerned with the idea that the soul survived physical death, but they also launched investigations into other odd phenomena – including what we would today call poltergeists – and amassed a large amount of data.

The Central Person, or 'Focus'

By about 1900 it was being recognized that physical hauntings, as many called them, were quite different from other hauntings. In particular, it began to be noticed that there was usually a central person, who was called the 'focus'. One of the earliest scientific researchers was the great criminologist Professor Cesare Lombroso of Italy.

He kept copious notes and produced many theories about the possible cause of events.

Throughout the 1890s his studies of anomalous events encroached more and more on his official work. He soon became better known for his paranormal investigations, which were reported in the press, than for anything else. In November of 1900 Lombroso was in Turin when he read about a haunting in the local newspaper. It had taken place in a wine bar and restaurant in the Via Bava, whose proprietor was a Signor Fumero. This seemed to be a classic poltergeist visitation because the reports included accounts of furniture moving about, wine bottles smashing and ornaments dancing by themselves. Lombroso decided to investigate, so he went round to see Signor Fumero.

The investigation got off to a somewhat comical start when Lombroso knocked on the wine bar door one morning. He began by asking Fumero if the newspaper reports were accurate. Fumero replied, 'Oh yes, we did have a ghost. But it has gone away now. The famous Professor Lombroso came here a few days ago. He sorted the business out. There is nothing to see here.' Lombroso was most surprised to hear that he had supposedly already called, so he introduced himself and handed over his card. Fumero glanced hurriedly around the street, then ushered Lombroso inside. It turned out that the police had been called in a few days earlier. They had witnessed the bizarre events for themselves, but had assumed that Fumero was faking the visitation. They told him to stop the charade at once or they would arrest him for criminal damage, fraud and other unspecified crimes. Unnerved by this reaction, Fumero had decided to avoid any additional problems by claiming that Lombroso had visited his premises and solved the haunting. Now that Lombroso really was in his shop, he begged the famous professor to investigate.

Fumero ushered Lombroso down to his wine cellar. As the two men entered, a bottle flew across the room and struck Lombroso on the foot. Then three empty bottles rolled across the floor at great speed, smashing themselves to pieces against a table leg. The glass splinters joined a sizeable pile of other debris. Lombroso took a candle and began to walk around the cellar. He wanted to make sure that nobody was hiding there. His progress was

Seeker after truth: Professor Cesare Lombroso was a criminologist who began to study the paranormal in the 1890s and produced a number of influential theories about the events he investigated

On the shelf: the poltergeist at the wine shop in Turin was most active down in the cellar where the wine bottles were kept safely stowed away on wooden racks

halted when a bottle floated off a rack and drifted slowly through the air, before suddenly smashing itself on the floor. A second bottle repeated the manoeuvre, then a third, a fourth and a fifth. Lombroso decided to retreat upstairs with Fumero to discuss events. As they left another bottle smashed itself.

Once upstairs, Fumero explained that while most of the phenomena occurred in the cellar, strange events had taken place throughout the shop. Chairs had danced about in the front room, plates had floated around the kitchen and ornaments were always being found in the wrong places. Finally Fumero showed Lombroso a machine that had been thrown across the workroom by unseen hands. The main metal plate was badly bent. Lombroso decided that such a feat could not be achieved with a person's bare hands – indeed, a burly

The work of
unseen hands:
while Lombroso
was in the Turin
wine cellar, bottles
of wine floated
off the racks by
themselves, hovered
in mid air and then
smashed themselves
on the floor

blacksmith armed with the tools of his trade would have had trouble replicating the damage.

Fumero told Lombroso that he had noticed one curious feature in the weeks since the disturbances began. Although the 'ghost' was in the habit of hurling bottles, knives and plates at people, the objects always missed by the narrowest of margins. For instance, a bottle of wine had recently been thrown at him with some force. But while it had been so close to his head that his hair had been splattered with wine when it had smashed itself against a wall, he had not been hurt. Nor had anyone else. It was as if the ghost wanted to frighten people but not actually hurt them.

Lombroso set about his investigation with methodical patience. He interviewed everyone involved and made a list of all of the incidents. Having studied all of the data,

Happy return: the Turin wineshop went back to normal after one of the waiters was sacked

She reported that while she had been away she had suffered a recurrence of a strange illness that she had suffered as a teenager – she saw people who were not really there

he came to the conclusion that the focus in this case was Fumero's wife, a nervous and skinny woman who was aged about 50. He suggested that Signora Fumero might like to take a short holiday as an escape from the stress of the haunting. The woman agreed with eagerness and made arrangements to stay with a cousin.

The 'haunting' stopped as soon as Signora Fumero left. When she came back, the manifestations began again. She reported that while she had been away she had suffered a recurrence of a strange illness that she had suffered as a teenager – she saw people who were not really there. Lombroso was convinced that he had found the focus but he wanted to double-check his theory, so he asked Signora Fumero to go away for a second time. However, the woman was reluctant to go in case this triggered her hallucinations. She believed that she was being driven from her home by the 'ghost', so before she left she launched into a long and bitter tirade against whatever it was.

This time the manifestations did not cease once the woman had left, but they changed dramatically. The disturbances now centred around the main bar and the

kitchen areas. Not only that, they seemed to be confined to the pieces of kitchen equipment that had been used most often by the absent Signora Fumero. The objects used by the staff remained unaffected. When Signora Fumero returned the new pattern of disturbances continued. If she laid a table, the plates and the cutlery would immediately fly off towards the floor. If one of the staff laid a table nothing happened to it. Lombroso went back to his notes and studied them again. It was true that the problems appeared to revolve around Signora Fumero, but there was another factor. The disturbances only seemed to take place when a particular member of staff was on duty – a boy of about 14 who was thin, pale and rather introspective. When Lombroso asked Fumero to give the boy a day off the disturbances ceased. The trial was repeated, and again all was quiet. Fumero sacked the boy and the haunting came to a halt.

Lombroso accepted the conventional view that a poltergeist visitation is caused by a ghost, or the spirit of a dead person. He also believed that focuses were mediums who were not conscious of their ability to communicate with the dead. In the case of the Turin wine shop, he suspected that either the young waiter or a spirit that acted through him had a grudge against Signora Fumero. This would have explained why she was the target of the visitation while the actual focus was the young waiter. Lombroso died nine years after this investigation, having done much to popularize his theory that poltergeist activity occurred when an angry or mischievous spirit managed to 'break through' into our world using an unconscious medium, the focus.

Ghost in a Blacksmith's Shop

In Austria, the local branch of the Society for Psychical Research was presented with a poltergeist case in the summer of 1906. Herr Warndorfer was sent to investigate. He found a small blacksmith's workshop run by a Herr Zimmerl, who was assisted by two teenage apprentices. Zimmerl's problems began in July, when tools and pieces of metal were found to have been moved. Things escalated rapidly, to the point that objects moved

Beware of flying objects: Herr Zimmerl's blacksmith's workshop in Austria was the scene of a poltergeist visitation that was investigated by the Austrian Society for Psychical Research in 1906

No smoking: the poltergeist at the Austrian workshop wrenched the pipe from the mouth of Herr Warndorfer while he was sitting smoking it. It hovered in mid air for a few seconds before flying off

about when the men were in the workshop. By the end of July tools and iron bars were being flung about violently, though nobody was hit or injured.

Nevertheless, the manifestations were causing a nuisance. More than one customer narrowly avoided being struck by a flying lump of iron and the apprentices refused to work alone. Herr Zimmerl sent for the police, who at first assumed that one of the apprentices was causing the mischief. However, after they had seen some of the flying objects for themselves they pronounced themselves baffled, so they left. Which was when Herr Warndorfer arrived. He spent several days at the workshop, during which time he too witnessed the flying missiles. Although he was struck three times by tools or pieces of iron he felt only the lightest of touches and was quite un-injured. One day Herr Warndorfer had his pipe wrenched from his mouth by unseen hands. It hovered in front of his face for a second or two before flying off across the room. Warndorfer was intent on spotting any trickery so he kept a careful eye on Zimmerl and his apprentices. He found no evidence of any fraud or fakery, though the mayhem continued unabated.

Harry Price

In Britain, the cause of poltergeist research was taken up and advanced by the controversial Harry Price. Nobody has ever equalled Harry Price's stature as a ghost hunter. His carefully researched books contain a vast wealth of information and his lengthy investigations used the very latest technological gadgets. He was adept at finding natural explanations for alleged hauntings and he did not hesitate to speak out when he suspected trickery or fraud. At the same time, he would happily declare a phenomenon to be genuine if he thought that was the case. He billed himself as the greatest ghost hunter alive and he was accepted as such by the public and the media.

His fellow researchers into psychic phenomena were not so sure. In the later part of his career Price was accused of fraud and trickery on several occasions. But while many suspected him of faking some of the phenomena he was supposedly investigating, nothing was ever conclusively proved. It is certain that he hammed up or exaggerated some of his claims in order to get the newspapers and the

Ghost hunter extraordinaire: the British psychic investigator Harry Price who dealt with numerous poltergeist cases during his long and often controversial career looking into the paranormal

radio interested in his work or to boost sales of his books.

But that is quite a different thing from saying that he faked psychic phenomena. It is possible that some of the more diligent and retiring researchers resented Price's colourful showmanship. Perhaps they alleged trickery when all he was guilty of was announcing results without having conducted the tests that others thought were necessary.

> *Price instantly realized that a poltergeist was at work. After the dramatic opening barrages of coal and coins, the poltergeist had started creating fires*

Price was born in London in 1881. Little is known about his parents. He received a good, but unspectacular education at the Haberdashers' Aske's Hatcham Boys School. During his time at school he read voraciously and his interest ranged over a vast array of subjects. He first displayed a liking for being in the public eye when he was a teenager. For instance, he enjoyed amateur dramatics and he wrote articles for the local press on various historical subjects. He also took an interest in the archaeological excavations in Greenwich Park, London, though how deeply he was actually involved is unclear.

After leaving school he worked as a paper salesman, but he continued to write for the newspapers. He also carried on playing an amateur role in archaeological digs. When he got married he dropped archaeology in order to become an amateur conjurer. He joined the Magic Circle in 1922. Inspired by Harry Houdini's unmasking of false mediums, Price also began using his conjuring skills to expose fraudsters. Like Houdini, his targets were the heartless people who were claiming to be able to communicate with the spirits of deceased loved ones. In order to further these investigations, Price established what he called the National Laboratory of Psychical Research, with himself as chairman.

In 1934 the National Laboratory was to become the University of London Council for Psychical Investigation, with Price as honorary secretary. Price continued his researches, radio broadcasts, writing and stage shows up to his death in 1948.

The Battersea Mystery House

On 19 January 1929 Price paid his first visit to the Battersea Mystery House that is featured in the introduction to this book. He found the Robinson family at breakfast. The house was home to 86-year-old Henry Robinson and his four adult children: Frederick, Lillah, Kate and Mary. Mary had been married to George Perkins, who had died a few months earlier. She had recently moved into the house with her 14-year-old son Peter. Frederick Robinson was the effective head of the household because the elderly Henry was mostly confined to his bed.

When Price called, Frederick began by showing him the broken glass in the conservatory and a couple of smashed ornaments. He then explained that he and his sisters were about to leave for work, while young Peter had to go to school. Price asked if he could come back after work along with a reporter from the London Evening News: Frederick agreed. When Price and the reporter, a Mr Grice, arrived late that afternoon, Frederick told them what had been happening. Price instantly realized that a poltergeist was at work.

Broken crockery was a frequent sight in the Battersea Mystery House investigated by Harry Price

After the dramatic opening barrages of coal and coins, the poltergeist had started creating fires. The Robinsons had a washerwoman who came in to launder the family's clothes and household linen. When she had unlocked the outhouse on 19 December she had been confronted by a heap of burning coals in the middle of the floor. She ran to fetch Frederick, who could not imagine how they had got there. Frederick and the washerwoman were the only two people with a key to the building, and neither of them had set the fire. Three days later an hour of mayhem began at 9am, when a loud banging noise was heard coming from the walls of the house. It was as if somebody was pounding on them with sledgehammers. Then the window in old Mr Robinson's bedroom exploded as if a large stone had been thrown through it. No stone was found, but the shards of glass were scattered all over the floor. The elderly man was understandably in a state of abject terror. Frederick ran out to ask a neighbour, Mr Bradbury, if the old man could stay at their house for a day or two. Bradbury agreed and he came round to help Frederick move the old man. As they were lifting old Mr Robinson from the bed a heavy chest of drawers began swaying from side to side and then crashed face down on to the floor.

As soon as the old man had left the house the hat stand in the hallway began rocking from side to side. Frederick ran to grab it, but it was wrenched from his hands by some invisible force. It was then flung against the stairs so violently that it broke in two. Bradbury came back at this point. He later told Price what had happened:

One of the women [Lillah] said that she was afraid to stop in the house, and that she was also afraid to go into her room to pack up her clothing. We went with her into her room, and she told us that she had been awakened by loud bangings on the door, and the crashing of glass. We stayed there until she had packed her bag and then returned to the back bedroom. Mr Robinson showed us pennies and coal on the conservatory roof.

The four of us – all men – were looking at these when suddenly from another bedroom came a great crash and downstairs we heard a woman scream. We ran to the room and there we saw a chest of drawers lying on the floor. It was all very strange. Mr Robinson then took us to the kitchen and showed us the damage done there.

Over the following two weeks the damage caused by the poltergeist had been less intensive, but the house was steadily becoming a shattered wreck. Panels had been smashed in three interior doors and nearly every window at the back of the house had been destroyed. Two more windows were damaged at the front. A tea tray and several plates and cups had been smashed and several ornaments had been thrown about and broken. Frederick Robinson showed Price and Grice around the house. He explained the damage and how it had occurred. When they walked into the house they stood for a moment in the scullery. As they did so there was a thump from the kitchen. They hurried through and found a wooden-handled gas lighter lying in the middle of the floor. It was normally kept on the gas stove. The reporter raced off to file a report just in time to make the stop press of his newspaper's evening edition.

Next day Price and Grice met to review and discuss the evidence. In the meantime, Grice had been doing some research. He had discovered that the house that backed on to Robinson's home was no normal house. It was, in fact, a private care home that was run by a psychologist who specialized in the care of men suffering from what was then called 'shell shock'. This term covered a range of mental disorders such as post- traumatic stress, nervous breakdown and intermittent insanity. The link between the various disorders was that they had all been brought on by the First World War.

At first it had been thought that shell shock was caused by the physical concussion of constant artillery fire. But

As they were lifting old Mr Robinson from the bed a heavy chest of drawers began swaying from side to side and then crashed face down on to the floor

by 1917 it began to be recognized that the problem was linked to the intensive strain of being in a war situation. It was also seen that more than one condition was involved. The term shell shock was dropped by doctors

well known that men suffering from shell shock were capable of erratic and often bizarre behaviour. Were the happenings at the Battersea Mystery House somehow related? Grice suggested that the missiles that had been

March of the furniture: a terrified Mrs Perkins was chased out of the dining room and along the corridor by a procession of chairs that marched as if they were sotldiers on parade

and the military, but it continued in common usage.

Although the First World War had been over for more than 10 years by the time Price called at the Battersea Mystery House, hundreds of men were still so incapacitated by shell shock that they were unable to work. The poorer families cared for such men at home, but those with more money might place their relatives in private institutions such as the one in Battersea. It was

falling on the Robinson household could have been thrown by the patients at the home. The distance from one house to the next was only 80 yards, which was well within range of a catapult – the rear garden of the clinic was even closer. Price was not convinced by this theory, and neither was Grice, but they agreed to alert the doctor to what was going on. The doctor proceeded to keep an eye on his patients, but nothing untoward ever took place.

In any case, when Price and Grice returned to the Robinson household it was clear that events had moved on considerably. On 20 December the police had arrested Frederick Robinson. He had been taken to a secure hospital where a psychologist was examining him as to his mental state. Apparently the police had suspected him of plaguing his own family and faking the events. A policeman was put on duty outside the house to guard against sightseers. However, the removal of Frederick had not affected the visitation – the loud thumps and bangs continued as before, accompanied by flying objects. On the Saturday evening the manifestations had stepped up to a new level of activity.

It all started when Mrs Perkins went into the dining room to lay the table for dinner. As she did so one of the dining chairs slid back from under the table as if pulled by invisible hands. It turned to face Mrs Perkins and then began to advance towards her. A second chair then repeated the movement, forming up behind the first. A third followed, then a fourth and a fifth. Understandably, Mrs Perkins quickly retreated into the hallway. But she was pursued by the chairs, which advanced in single file like soldiers on parade. The bizarre procession followed Mrs Perkins to the foot of the stairs and then the chairs turned around and marched back into the dining room. When Mrs Perkins summoned up the courage to go back into the room she found all of the chairs piled up on top of the dining table. After some minutes, during which nothing else happened, Mrs Perkins lifted the chairs down and began laying the table. She then went through to the kitchen to fetch some plates. When she returned the chairs were all stacked up on top of the table again. She took them down, but again they arranged themselves on top of the table. At that stage she was totally unnerved, so she went out to get the policeman who was on guard. He came in, looked at the chairs and

However, the removal of Frederick had not affected the visitation – the loud thumps and bangs continued as before. On Saturday, the manifestations stepped up a level

accused Mrs Perkins of putting them there herself. She scolded him and sent him outside again.

Next day it was Kate Robinson's turn to witness a series of bizarre events. It began in mid morning, when her brother's attaché case flew at her across the kitchen. She retreated to the hall, where an umbrella sprang from the hall stand and floated across the room. Later, when she was in the kitchen with Peter, the chairs started vibrating – then the kitchen table fell over. Kate and Peter ran outside and watched through the windows as the kitchen chairs jigged about and then all fell over at the same time.

There was much to tell Price and Grice when they visited the house on the following Monday. As they were talking to Kate and Mrs Perkins in the kitchen there came a loud thump from the scullery. Price and Grice hurriedly burst into the room to find a pair of lady's boots on the floor. Inside one of them was a bronze cherub. It was one of a pair of ornaments that were kept on the mantelpiece in the sitting room. The disturbances continued for the rest of the week, though not at the level that had been witnessed the previous weekend. On the following Friday Kate Robinson and Mrs Perkins decided to abandon the house. Young Peter was sent off to stay with relatives in the country on a long-term basis while the two women moved in with friends in Battersea.

That weekend the crowds gathered in Eland Road to gape at the Mystery House.

There were so many people squashed together that mounted police officers and several constables were in attendance. However, nothing was seen or heard. Price then got permission to spend some time alone in the house. On the following Monday, the Daily Express contacted him to see if he would allow a well-known medium to join his investigation. Price agreed, so when he went to the house on Wednesday of that week he was accompanied by the medium and a *Daily Express* reporter named Salusbury. Price does not seem to have had a high regard for the medium. In his review of the case written a few years later he says that the medium declared that she felt excessively cold when she entered the house. As Price points out, it was the middle of winter and the house had been locked up for several days without a fire being lit.

The party toured the house, going from room to room. The medium sensed nothing apart from the cold, which she thought was supernatural. After visiting all of the upstairs rooms the trio went back downstairs. They all noticed that a piece of yellow soap was now lying in the middle of the hall floor. All of them were certain that it had not been there earlier and none of them could explain how it got there. Mrs Perkins later identified it as a piece of soap from the washroom. Frederick Robinson was released by the police on the following day. He moved straight back into the house and Kate and Mrs Perkins followed a day or two later. When old Mr Robinson died a couple of weeks after their return the family finally abandoned the Mystery House and rented another one nearby. There were no further disturbances in Eland Road and the family had no problems in their new home.

Looking at the Battersea case with hindsight, it can be seen that the visitation followed the pattern that was by then becoming familiar to investigators. It began relatively quietly, with a few small pieces of coal being thrown. The disturbances then escalated, very quickly in this case, until they reached a dramatic crescendo – furniture started marching around the house. They ended abruptly when Peter Perkins was sent to live with relatives in the country. Apart from the appearance of a stray bar of soap nothing else happened after Peter left. This would seem to indicate that Peter was the focus of this particular poltergeist visitation. He certainly had some of the attributes of a focus. He was a teenager and his father had recently died, which had forced him and his mother to move into a rather crowded house with

relatives. The situation cannot have been anything other than stressful. We also have no way of knowing how well or badly Peter got on with his relatives. The activities during this poltergeist visitation fit the general pattern. Objects were thrown about, furniture moved of its own accord and bangs and thumps were heard. Despite the mayhem, nobody was hurt.

When a poltergeist took the form of a talking mongoose it was generally accepted that the limits of credibility had been reached

Gef the Mongoose

By the time of the Battersea Mystery House case many people were willing to accept the fact that unexplained events can sometimes take place. But when a poltergeist took the form of a talking mongoose it was generally accepted that the limits of credibility had been reached. The events took place at Doarlish Cashen on the Isle of Man during the 1930s and Price went along to investigate. However, because of the general mirth that the case had generated it was small wonder that he was rather cool about it in later years. Writing in 1945 he dismissed it as 'the talking mongoose case that I investigated, with negative results, in 1935'. Because he needed to earn a living from his investigations, Price did not relish being associated with a famous source of amusement, and so he probably preferred to keep his distance. However, a reappraisal of Price's notes, and those of other investigators, shows that the Doarlish Cashen visitation was a relatively straightforward poltergeist case, albeit with some very peculiar features.

In September 1931 the isolated farmhouse of Doarlish Cashen was home to the Irving family. There was James Irving, his wife Margaret and their 13-year-old daughter Voirrey. James was a retired salesman who had bought the smallholding to indulge his love of growing fruit and vegetables while creating an income to supplement his modest pension. At 60 he was several years older than his wife. Voirrey was a quiet girl who did well at school but did not make friends easily. She was particularly keen on wildlife, having read a great deal about the subject.

Doarlish Cashen: Voirrey Irving and her father stand outside the isolated farmhouse
on the Isle of Man that was the venue for the case of Gef the Talking Mongoose,
one of the most peculiar and enigmatic poltergeist visitations of the 20th century

Living on the Isle of Man enabled her to study a wide range of wildlife at close hand.

The visitation began with the usual low level activity. In this case it took the form of scurrying noises, accompanied by growling and barking as if some sort of animal was making a home for itself under the floorboards. Now and then there came a loud cracking noise that made the walls shake and the pictures move slightly. The Irvings decided that some sort of animal had taken up residence in their house, though the cracking phenomenon was a mystery. After several weeks of this, James Irving decided to see if the animal would respond to any of his animal impersonations – something for which he had quite a name in the area. He began with mammal noises, because the mystery animal seemed to be a mammal of some kind. The mysterious intruder accurately copied the calls of foxes, hedgehogs and badgers, but then it moved on to mimic local birds as well. In November the 'animal' began repeating rhymes sung by Voirrey, though in a very high-pitched and squeaky voice. There was no animal on earth that could do that.

By February 1932 the strange creature had learned how to talk in a more normal, human-like voice. It could also speak for itself – it did not just repeat what the Irvings said. Most of the talk was of a purely domestic nature.

The voice reminded Mrs Irving to do the ironing or suggested that Mr Irving should go to the shops. However, the intruder did sometimes talk about itself. It announced that its name was Gef and that it was a mongoose who had been born in Delhi on 7 June 1852. It stuck to this story throughout the visitation. The Irvings seem to have taken Gef's claims at face value. They believed that they were dealing with a talking mongoose of astonishing intelligence – they always spoke about the visitation in those terms. It was James Irving who brought the talking mongoose to Harry Price's attention. Price was busy on other projects, but he thought the case sounded interesting so he sent a friend, Captain MacDonald, to investigate.

The visitation began in the form of scurrying noises, accompanied by growling and barking as if some animal was making a home under the floorboards

MacDonald arrived at Doarlish Cashen on 26 February 1932. Although he stayed for more than five hours, and gathered much information from the Irvings, he experienced nothing odd. Eventually he got up to leave, saying that he would return on the following day. At once Gef's voice called out, 'Go away. Who is that man?' Then came a string of indistinct mutterings. When MacDonald returned, nothing much happened at first. Then a stream of water emerged from a wall – the Irvings told MacDonald it was Gef 'performing its natural functions'. A short while later Gef began talking to Margaret while she was upstairs. MacDonald, who was downstairs, called out to Gef, but the talking mongoose replied, 'No, I won't stay long as I don't like you.' MacDonald tried creeping up the stairs, but Gef heard him and called out, 'He's coming.' No more was heard of Gef that day.

A reporter from the *Daily Dispatch* in Manchester then paid a short visit. He heard the voice of Gef, but no other manifestations took place while he was there. When an old family friend named Charles Northwood went to visit the Irvings in March 1932, Gef became a little more

Gef was rarely seen, but when he was encountered he seemed to be a perfectly normal mongoose-like creature

Marking his territory: a stream of water that inexplicably spurted from the walls
was explained by the Irving family as being Gef the mongoose urinating

voluble. The story of Gef the talking mongoose had appeared in the newspapers and Northwood seems to have been concerned about his friends, so he arranged to visit for a few days. Before he arrived, he asked James Irving if he thought Gef would be active during his visit. Northwood was perhaps initially disappointed, because Gef was quiet when he first arrived. He did not speak or scurry about and he did not sing his favourite song, Carolina Moon, even when it was played on the gramophone. But when Voirrey went into the kitchen to prepare lunch she heard Gef whisper, 'Go away, Voirrey, go away'. After lunch Gef's voice became louder and Northwood heard him call out, 'Charles, Charles, Chuck,

Chuck.' Gef then returned to his usual domestic chatter about farm affairs. When Northwood suggested that his son Arthur might like to visit, Gef reacted violently. 'Tell Arthur not to come,' Gef shouted. 'He doesn't believe. I won't speak if he does come. I'll blow his brains out with a thrupenny cartridge'. There followed a long period of silence. Then Gef shouted at Northwood, 'You don't believe. You are a doubter.' This outburst was followed by loud bangs and crashes. Then there was silence again until after Northwood had gone.

In the months that followed, Gef performed only when the Irvings were alone. He had apparently taken up residence in a wooden box in Voirrey's bedroom – it

Gef invited Margaret to put her hand through a hole in Voirrey's bedroom wall. On her first attempt she felt a little paw with three long fingers and a thumb

was here that he was heard most often. Gef also began to indulge in the more physical antics that were associated with poltergeists. He moved chairs around, he bounced a rubber ball in time to music on the gramophone, he opened drawers and rummaged about in them and he struck matches. More unusually, Gef began killing rabbits and leaving them for the Irvings to find. He would announce a kill from his wooden box, which Voirrey began calling 'Gef's Sanctum', and then he would tell the Irvings where he had left it. The dead rabbit was always there and it made a welcome addition to the family larder. Gef also took to eating food that had been left out for him. He ordered what he wanted – it was usually bacon, sausages or chocolate – and said where it should be put. The food would be taken as soon as the Irvings were not looking.

Gef was generally friendly and chatty, though his temper changed at times. When asked who he was, he once said, 'I am a ghost in the form of a weasel,' but on another occasion he said, 'I am the Holy Ghost.' He was perhaps being more truthful when he said, 'You will never get to know what I am.' Sometimes he was amusing – he would say, 'I am the eighth wonder of the world,' for instance, or 'I can split the atom.' But he could also be mildly abusive when he called people names and told them to leave the house. The reporter from the *Daily Dispatch* returned so that he could carry out a detailed investigation. This time he was rather more sceptical. He noticed that Gef spoke only when Voirrey was in the same room. Although he did not actually put his opinion into words, it is clear that he suspected that Voirrey was responsible for the voice.

Gef preferred not to be seen, though all three members

of the family caught glimpses of something that could have been Gef. However, he invited Margaret to put her hand through a hole in Voirrey's bedroom wall on a couple of occasions. On her first attempt she felt a little paw with three long fingers and a thumb. When she had another try she felt Gef's mouth complete with his small, sharp teeth. Voirrey once took a photo of Gef, but the print was indistinct. It just showed a blob, which might have been a mongoose, or a weasel – or anything else for that matter.

In March 1935 Gef left Voirrey a memento. It was a tuft of what he said was his hair. James Irving sent the scraps of fur to Price, who had been monitoring the case. Price then had them analyzed by London Zoo. The results showed that the hair had probably come from a domestic dog with slightly curly hair and a fawn colour. He consulted MacDonald who confirmed that the Irvings had a pet dog named Mona, which had wavy hair of a brown colour. Price decided that it was time he investigated the goings-on at Doarlish Cashen for himself.

He took Richard Lambert, editor of *The Listener* magazine, along with him to the Isle of Man. Gef did not appear during their stay so neither Price nor Lambert came away with any first-hand testimony. The two men did, however, collect witness statements from everyone who had experienced the phenomenon. They also took plaster casts of footprints that had apparently been left by Gef. The casts were sent to London Zoo, who replied that the footprints could not be precisely identified, though they might belong to a weasel or a raccoon. The experts were more definite about the hair samples that had been taken from the Irvings' pet dog Mona. They were absolutely identical to the fur that had supposedly come from Gef.

This fact has often been used as evidence that the Gef visitation was a fraud from start to finish. However, it must be said that many poltergeists are habitual liars. If Gef had claimed that the dog's hair was his own his behaviour would have been typical of a poltergeist.

As well as being investigated by Price, Gef was also studied by Nandor Fodor of the International Institute for Psychical Research. Fodor did not believe that Gef was either a mongoose or a ghost. He had a theory that

Nandor Fodor did not believe that Gef was either a mongoose or a ghost. He could only be a poltergeist

poltergeists were created by the focus person, perhaps unconsciously. So the manifestations were generated by a human mind that was undergoing subconscious turmoil. He became convinced that the Gef visitation fitted in with his theories, but few others shared his views.

The Irvings reported that by the autumn of 1935 Gef was not as active as he had been. Early in 1936, he seems to have vanished altogether. The Irvings later sold up and moved away. In 1946 the farmer who had bought the property, Leslie Graham, shot and killed a weasel-like creature on the property. He contacted the newspapers and said that he had, 'killed Gef the talking mongoose'. The newspapers showed Voirrey a photo of the animal, but she said it was not Gef. She seemed very certain of the fact.

Gef's antics had come in for some serious and detailed investigation during the five years that they had lasted. It

is therefore possible to look at the case and its background in a more detailed way than was possible in earlier visitations. Gef showed all the characteristics of a typical poltergeist, in spite of his claims to be a mongoose. That is, the visitation had begun with infrequently heard low noises, which had become louder and more numerous over a period of some weeks. Finally, the manifestations had become more dramatic. The voice had started as animal grunts and barks and had then become high-pitched. At first it was only able only to repeat what was said to it, but eventually it was apparently able to speak for itself with intelligence.

As in other poltergeist cases, it seems that Gef became what the Irvings expected him to be. Right from the start, the Irving family had interpreted the noises as being those of an animal. Even when the intruder began to speak, they remained convinced that they were dealing with a clever animal.

So when Gef finally talked about himself it was to announce that he was indeed a clever animal. Another feature of the case that seems to link it to other poltergeist visitations is the way in which the manifestations continued for a while and then tailed off. Gef was around for about five years in all, but he never seems to have produced the hugely dramatic stunts that some poltergeists of shorter duration have managed to achieve. This inverse correlation between duration and intensity of activity seems to be a feature of the cases that have been subjected to study. The longer a visitation has lasted the less impressive the manifestations have been.

The Irving family's circumstances were carefully noted by several visitors. There were elements that would characterize other poltergeist visitations. James Irving was a boastful fellow who liked to spin yarns to his neighbours about his exploits as a salesman. He had married late and he dominated his family. The household had been run according to his whim, with little regard for the wishes of Margaret or Voirrey. Margaret tolerated James's bossiness. She was seemingly content as long as she was generally left alone. Young Voirrey also seems to have accepted a subordinate role at home. At the same time, she shone academically at school and indulged her passion for wildlife studies in the fields and woods around her home. However, the remote nature of her

Ploughing a lone furrow: Voirrey lived in a remote part of the Isle of Man and her father discouraged her from bringing friends home which meant she spent a lot of time on her own communing with nature and indulging her passion for wildlife

home and her father's attitude did not allow her to bring school friends home. This was perhaps why she did not have any really close companions of her own age. Voirrey was undoubtedly the focus of this visitation. Many people who have been the focus of a visitation were finding life frustrating or stressful. Perhaps that was true in the case of Voirrey.

Another feature that surrounded the Gef visitation was a vague suspicion of trickery and fraud. It is one that has been seen in several other cases.

The reporter from the *Daily Dispatch* suspected that Voirrey might be making the voice of Gef, but he was never able to catch her out. Price also suspected fraud in the later stages of the case. Another reporter, this time from the Isle of Man Examiner, thought that James Irving was to blame. The journalist noted that when on one occasion Gef had given a rather indistinct squeak, James had said, 'There, you heard him. He said, "They don't believe." You heard him. That was Gef.' Gef had certainly said no such thing so James was guilty of exaggeration. But this was at the time when Gef's visits were getting less frequent and impressive. Perhaps James wanted to ensure that the reporter did not go home disappointed.

The Case of Olive Wilkins

Altogether more conventional was a later case from Price's files, yet in some ways it was quite unique. The events involved a Dr Wilkins of Sunderland and his family and they took place in 1942. It all perhaps began in 1940, though, when Dr Wilkins' daughter Olive fell in love with a flight lieutenant in the RAF. She was only 19 and he was a few years older. The airman proposed, but Dr Wilkins and his wife were reluctant to give permission for the marriage to go ahead. Not only was Olive quite young but there was also a war on and her prospective husband was on active service. There was every possibility that their daughter might become a very young widow. After some debate, none of it bad-tempered, the young couple finally got married in the autumn of 1941. They set up home in a rented flat in Sunderland, where Olive had a job as a secretary. If her new husband was on duty, Olive would often go to her

parent's home for supper. Because the rented flat was small, she had left many belongings – such as books, a tennis racket, old toys and the like – in her old bedroom.

The bedclothes had been carefully turned down. Mrs Wilkins was certain she had not touched the bed and nobody had a key, except herself

On 26 February 1942 Mrs Wilkins borrowed a kilt pin from her daughter's jewellery box, so that she could secure a wrap. Nothing in the bedroom was out of place. After spending the day in town, Mrs Wilkins returned home, took off her wrap and went to her daughter's former bedroom. She was going to replace the pin while she remembered. As she entered the room she stopped dumbfounded. The bedclothes had been carefully and neatly turned down, just as they would have been if the family had still had a maid. Mrs Wilkins was certain that she had not touched the bed and nobody had a key to the house except herself, Dr Wilkins and Olive – both of whom were at work.

Three days later Mrs Wilkins was in the kitchen preparing dinner when she heard the front door open. The familiar sound of her husband's footsteps approaching across the hallway was heard, accompanied by the click-clack of her daughter's heels. The kitchen door opened and in came Dr Wilkins alone.

'Where is Olive?' asked Mrs Wilkins.

'I don't know,' replied Dr Wilkins. 'Gone home I suppose.' She was not with him, nor had he heard her footsteps.

Four days later, Mrs Wilkins went into Olive's room to find that the bed had been disarranged just as if it had been slept in. Two days later one of Olive's books had been removed from the bookcase and then left open on the windowsill. It was just as if somebody had glanced at it before putting it down. A week later Mrs Wilkins again heard the front door open. This time only one set of footsteps could be heard coming across the hallway. There was no mistaking Olive's tread, though. She went up the stairs, along the landing and into her bedroom. Then she came out again and went into the bathroom. The toilet flushed and then there was silence. After a while Mrs Wilkins went up but there was no sign of her daughter. When Dr Wilkins got home he was sent hotfoot round to Olive's flat, where he found the young couple sitting down to supper. Olive said that she had not been round to her parent's house at all. A couple of weeks later, Olive really did come round after work. She brought the happy news that she was pregnant. One month later her husband was posted overseas.

> *If Mrs Wilkins went into the hall the footsteps would stop at once, but if she did not the sounds would move up the stairs to Olive's bedroom*

Olive's pregnancy developed along perfectly normal lines as the weeks passed. But at the home of Dr and Mrs Wilkins the poltergeist-like activity increased in frequency and variety. The bedclothes in Olive's old bedroom came in for particular attention.

They were found rumpled as if they had been slept in, stripped from the bed and folded neatly or turned down ready for a person to get into. Not only that – the drawers in Olive's dressing table had often been found open. The clothes they contained had often been rearranged or placed on the bed. Underwear was a favourite target for this treatment, but skirts and blouses were also moved about. Again and again Mrs Wilkins heard the sounds of her daughter opening the front doorand walking across the hallway. Sometimes it really was her, but most of the time it was not. If Mrs Wilkins went into the hall the footsteps would stop at once, but if she did not the sounds would move up the stairs to Olive's bedroom. By the time Olive entered the final month of her pregnancy something was happening every day. Sometimes it was twice a day.

The marriage of Olive Wilkins to an airman was a happy, but fraught event that may have triggered poltergeist manifestations

Thus far the disturbances had been restricted to the upper part of the house. Then one day Mrs Wilkins came home from shopping to find that something strange had taken place in the dining room. A photograph of her daughter and son-in-law that had been kept on the mantelpiece had been moved to the table. Fearing that this sudden change marked some problem, Mrs Wilkins telephoned her daughter's place of work. She discovered that she had gone into labour and had been taken to hospital. The next day Olive was delivered of a healthy baby girl, who was named Enid. The manifestations ceased at once and they never returned.

This case is interesting for a number of reasons. The disturbances at the Wilkins' home were in some ways typical of a poltergeist. They began slowly and they built up to a climax. Objects were moved about and unexplained sounds were heard. The manifestations also centred on a young person whose life had been recently disturbed.

In other ways the case was quite unique. The disturbances were very obviously linked to Olive's old home and her former bedroom. They were also centred on things that she had used before she was married.

The stress that Olive had been placed under must have been considerable. She had recently married, she was pregnant and her husband had been sent away to a dangerous place. Interestingly the disturbances began when Olive discovered that she was pregnant. At such an emotional time she must have been drawn back to the security and safety of her old home, her toys and her bedroom. It would seem to be the case, therefore, that this entirely understandable longing manifested itself in poltergeist-type incidents. However, it is possible that Mrs Wilkins was the focus and that it was her anxiety for her daughter that was the emotional impulse behind the manifestations.

The cases studied by these early investigators were useful in that they revealed that a number of features regularly occur in poltergeist visitations. But however dramatic these earlier cases were, they are as nothing compared to the cases that have occurred since. In more recent decades the recipients of a visitation have been more willing to report what has been happening, while researchers have conducted investigations with ever greater thoroughness.

CHAPTER 12

Major Investigations

Doctor and Minister se
...euchie girl

ALLO...

Mr Stevenson and the
prayed. The strange h...
completely stopped.

Mr Stevenson discuss...
simple case of a minis...
with a person and
apparently being ans...

By the later 20th century the poltergeist phenomenon was beginning to be better recognized by the general public. That is not to say that it was better understood. Although the term 'poltergeist' was being widely used by lots of people, it was being loosely applied to a range of phenomena.

The result was that most people still tended to view a poltergeist as a form of ghost, not as a distinct type of paranormal event. Added to that, most mainstream scientists continued to be reluctant to spend time and money investigating poltergeist visitations. Those few scientists who were prepared to deal with visitations seriously were not always able to get to the scene of a poltergeist visitation while it was still happening. Their frustration was shared by a large number of amateur investigators. As a result, phenomena were not always investigated as thoroughly as might have been hoped.

The house in Sauchie where Virginia Campbell lived during the poltergeist outbreak

Even so, these people were doing their best and a useful amount of evidence and data was compiled.

The Sauchie Poltergeist

In the case of a poltergeist that occurred in the Scottish village of Sauchie in 1960 it was Dr A Owen, a fellow of Trinity College, Cambridge who launched an investigation. He visited the scene while the visitation was in progress and interviewed most of those concerned.

The focus of this poltergeist was apparently 11-year-old Virginia Campbell. She and her mother Annie had recently moved to Sauchie from Donegal in Ireland, following the divorce of Annie from Virginia's father. Virginia and Annie moved in with relatives, which meant that Virginia had to share a room with her 9-year-old cousin Margaret.

The move seemed to go well, though, and Virginia settled in comfortably at Sauchie School. Then on 22 November, just after Virginia and Margaret had gone to bed, something strange happened. The girls claimed to have heard the sound of a ball bouncing around in their room, but this ceased when Annie went up to investigate. Next day some furniture was found to have been moved.

That night the bouncing ball noises were back, but this time they were louder and more insistent. Over the following days the manifestations increased rapidly. Doors slammed shut or flew open by themselves; a heavy sideboard slid across the floor without anybody touching

Shared experience: Virginia Campbell's school also saw a number of poltergeist events, which were witnessed not only by her fellow pupils but by her teachers too

it. The disturbances only happened when Virginia was present. When the local vicar was called in he conducted a prayer service, but this produced no effect.

The poltergeist activity then began to go wherever Virginia went. Her schoolteacher, Miss Stewart, noticed this first. At the time she was unaware of the strange events at Virginia's home. One day the child sitting in front of Virginia got up to hand in some work. As she did so her desk rose about six inches into the air. The teacher thought she was seeing things, particularly when the desk drifted back to the ground after a few seconds. A couple of days later Miss Stewart saw Virginia behaving oddly. She was leaning on the lid of her desk, as if to stop it from opening.

Miss Stewart called out, which made Virginia look up. As she did so the desk lid opened slightly, as if something inside was trying to get out, Virginia hurriedly slammed it shut again.

Miss Stewart finally accepted that something very strange was going on when she called Virginia up to the front of the class. The teacher was sitting at her desk, a large heavy wooden affair that she could barely move without assistance. Virginia was standing to one side of Miss Stewart, with her hands folded behind her back. As Miss Stewart was talking she suddenly became aware that the children were no longer looking at her, but at her desk. She had rested the blackboard pointer on her desk when she had sat down and it was now rocking from side to side without anybody touching it. Then it stopped moving, only for the desk itself to start to shake. Slowly the desk began to rise into the air. Confused and alarmed, Miss Stewart put her hands on top of the desk and tried to push it back down to the ground, but without success. As soon as she let go the desk rose higher. Then it began to turn slowly. When it had moved through about 90 degrees it began to descend towards the floor.

ALLOA ADVERTISER, FRIDAY, 2nd DECEMBER, 196

Doctor and Minister see Sauchie girl

THE STRANGE CASE OF VIRGINIA CAMPBELL

FIVE doctors and two leading Church of Scotland ministers have now seen 11-year-old Sauchie schoolgirl Virginia Campbell who is believed to be haunted by a poltergeist. Furniture moves and strange things happen in her presence.

Dr W. H. Nisbet, Tillicoultry, said in an interview: "The child may have telekinetic powers." Dr Nisbet has had to treat Virginia's family—the child resides with her mother, married brother and sister-in-law—for hysteria.

The doctor—tired and worried said: "Things have happened which I do not care to explain—but they do not have any medical explanation.

"The happenings occurred in the girls' school — her teacher saw something—and in her home."

Said Dr Nisbet: "Virginia does not control the happenings verbally, but I do not know whether she controls them from her mind."

Dr Nisbet said he and the other doctors and ministers had visited Virginia to satisfy themselves that things did happen. "We confirmed that they did."

Asked if he thought a leprechaun or poltergeist had invaded Virginia's life replied: "I do not even know what a leprechaun is, a poltergeist?—I looked up the meaning a few days ago and it may or may not apply in this case."

At Sauchie School, the headmaster Mr Peter Hill said: "I have never seen furniture shifting, and we have not got any of our desks tied down. Things may have happened in the girl's home."

Mr Hill suggested that the poltergeist may just be group hypnosis. But Dr Nisbet turned down this theory, "Group hypnosis does not apply in this case," he said.

At the Campbells' council home understandably they do not want to talk.

CHURCH ATTITUDE

Neighbours are guarded in talking about Virginia and her strange powers. They share the family's distress and do not wish to add to it by pandering to the sensation mongers and supplying them with further "stories".

On the question of poltergeists the Church of Scotland is non-committal. Official pronouncements have been avoided by the General Assembly.

At the Kirk's headquarters in Edinburgh an official said: "The girl is entirely in the care of her doctor and minister. Her whole future and mental stability will depend on peace and quiet. This is entirely a personal thing."

The Rev. J. W. Stevenson, editor of the kirk's magazine "Life and Work", recalled in an interview an experience he had a year ago. He had been asked to visit the home of Baroness Kilbride at Fairmilehead, Edinburgh. In her house doors had opened, strange noises were heard, articles moved mysteriously from room to room.

ALVA CHILD FOUND IN TROUGH

A tragic accident took place at the Boll Farm near Alva on Sunday forenoon resulting in the death of 18-month-old Douglas Beatson, infant son of Mr and Mrs James Beatson, who reside at the farm.

The child was found to be missing by his mother around noon and Mrs Beatson went to contact her husband who was working at a hen-house in an adjoining field.

The two went in search of the child who was found in a trough containing about a foot of water about thirty yards from the house.

Medical aid was summoned and Dr Faulkner applied artificial respiration but life was found to be extinct.

Much sympathy will be felt for Mr and Mrs Beatson and also the child's grandparents in the tragic loss they have sustained. The couple have one other child aged four years.

Mr Stevenson and the baroness prayed. The strange happenings completely stopped.

Mr Stevenson discussed it as a simple case of a minister praying with a person and the prayer apparently being answered.

But when asked about exorcism, Mr Stevenson replied: "In the Church of Scotland we do not use that word, although other denominations do."

But while spiritualists and poltergeists are regarded with suspicion by most ministers, a few have become firmly convinced.

One of the most outspoken is the Rev. Thomas Jeffrey—a former Alloa man and brother of Mr R. J. Jeffrey and the Rev. George Jeffrey (an ex-Moderator of the Church of Scotland). Now 81, Mr Jeffrey has been a believer in the spirit world for more than fifty years.

"People scoff about stories of ghosts and spooks, but they have not really studied the subject," he said.

"In the case of this little girl we have examples of well-known phenomena."

Mr Jeffrey explained how John Wesley, the founder of Methodism, had had similar experiences in his father's home. Doors opened before one of Wesley's sisters. Mysterious noises shattered the peace of the house. Then one night Wesley's mother prayed for her daughter to be relieved of the torment. The disturbances ceased.

Said Mr Jeffrey: "But long before this, such phenomena were written in the Bible. When the boy Samuel heard the voices, the old priest Eli did not, but he knew the boy had the gift from God."

Asked what could be done to help Virginia, Mr Jeffrey explained: "Some sympathetic person who knows about these things should go and speak to the spirit, say what they are doing and tell it to be quiet."

Rev. A. Ross Rankin, F.S.A., minister of the Sauchie and Fishcross U.F. Church said, "I have not taken much interest in the affair. Personally I would like to contact the home and have a talk with the girl concerned.

"For unless I see the actual manifestations, I am afraid I can't accept the stories. To my mind it would be a great kindness to the home if the people would leave it in peace."

A DEBUNKER

Finally a debunker — Major Henry Douglas-Home, B.B.C. Bird Man, who has spent years investigating poltergeists. Many years ago he played a big part in exposing the story of Borley Rectory, in Surrey—"the most haunted house in England."

The major said: "Ninety out of 100 cases can be explained. No more mysterious than watching Chan Canasta or David Nixon on TV.

"But the other 10 cases?—Well, some remain a mystery."

THE SEARCH FOR TWO BURGLARS

An appeal has been launched by the Stirling and Clackmannan Police requesting that anyone who can assist in giving

DOLLAR GIRL'S BERWICK

The bridal group after the wedding in Saline Manse, of Mr George Cessford, West Mains, Coldstream, Berwickshire, and Miss Elizabeth D. Sharp, Solgirth Home Farm, Dollar.

Bridesmaid was Miss M. Sharp and the flower girl was Miss Margaret Lauder. Rev. A. G. Downie officiated.

ALVA COUNCIL AND BOYS' BRIGADE
Question Of Rates

Whether—and to what extent—they should extend benevolence to a youth group in the town was a matter which engaged the attention of Alva Town Council at their monthly meeting on Wednesday evening, the particular focus being a plea by Councillor McQueen for a reduction in the rates in regard to the Boys' Brigade premises in Queen Street.

Noting from the Finance Committee minute that relief of rates had been rejected, Councillor McQueen said that what was really asked was a reduction. The young man in charge was doing good work and the Brigade had no specific funds for the purpose. He (Councillor McQueen) asked that the Council consider a slight reduction from £16.

PRECEDENT

Hon. Treasurer Sharp said he felt that to do this would create a precedent. Moreover, the Boys' Brigade could go round the doors to collect funds, but the Scouts couldn't do that. There was no harm in working hard to raise funds.

Cllr. McQueen pointed out that

Struck by m... in lorry ...

TALE OF AN UNGUI...

A 40-year-old Alloa labourer spoke on Wednesday of how he had ... by a milk bottle after the lorry he ... in, was involved in an accident wi... Street Tullibody.

He was Archibald McKnight, 116 Bristol Street, Alloa, and he was giving evidence during a trial in which 34-year-old John Robertson McKinley, milk roundsman, 12 Mill Street, Alloa, appeared on a careless driving charge.

McKinley, who has driven for over ten years, was found guilty by Sheriff Murray. After admitting two previous convictions, he was fined £6 with the alternative of 24 days' imprisonment. His licence was also endorsed and three weeks allowed for payment.

The accident occurred on a Saturday forenoon in August and McKnight told the court that along with Alexander Maley from Glasgow, he was being given a lift in a lorry from Menstrie to Cambus. Maley was to be taken on to ... starting after that.

LIKE A WAVE

While the lorry was being driven along Ochil Street, Tullibody, by David Goodwillie, 2 Glencairn Street, St. Ninians, the driver of a Karrier Bantam milk lorry which was ahead of them, gave a hand signal which appeared to be more like a wave.

McKnight said that he found ...

The story of Virginia Campbell and the poltergeist visitation was reported in the local press as it unfolded. By the time this local newspaper was published, the visitation was being identified as a poltergeist though no explanation could be found for events

Miss Stewart then glanced at Virginia who was sobbing uncontrollably. Seeing the teacher's eyes on her, Virginia began sobbing. 'I'm not doing it, Miss. Please, Miss. Honest I'm not.'

Miss Stewart first calmed Virginia down and then she dismissed the class. After talking to Virginia for a while she learned that similar things were happening at the girl's home. Virginia was adamant that she was not responsible for the events, though she knew that they only happened when she was around. Miss Stewart later summoned her class and explained to them very clearly that sometimes people got ill and that things might then happen that were not really their doing. One child asked if a ghost had been moving the desk. Miss Stewart very firmly put that idea down. She said that there was no ghost and that she would not stay in a room if she thought it was haunted. 'So long as I stay here, you are all right,' she concluded.

Strange things continued to happen at Virginia's school. A bowl of flowers moved across Miss Stewart's desk, for instance. But nothing was ever as dramatic as the moving desk. From then onwards most of the manifestations took place at Virginia's home. Ornaments were moved about – sometimes they floated through the air – and bedclothes were torn off in the middle of the night. Both Margaret and Virginia also felt themselves pinched awake by unseen hands. Annie noticed that the events followed a definite cycle. They built up to a crescendo for a few days and then they faded away. Dr Owen asked Annie to keep a diary of events, which proved that she was right. The cycle was one of 28 days. After about six months the strange phenomena began to tail off and finally they ceased entirely.

The Black Monk of Pontefract

Although the events in Sauchie had been recorded by a responsible researcher while they were in progress, such was not the case during the visitation that became known

Ornaments were moved about – sometimes they floated through the air – and bedclothes were torn off in the middle of the night

as the Black Monk of Pontefract. In spite of the name given to the haunting, the link to any monk living or dead was tenuous. Perhaps a poltergeist was manifesting itself in the form of a monk in order to satisfy the expectations of those it was disturbing.

The visitation took place at 30 East Drive, a street on a fairly modern estate just outside the historic heart of Pontefract in Yorkshire. Living in the house when the disturbances began in August 1966 were Joe Pritchard, his wife Jean and their two children. Phillip their son was 15 years old and their daughter Diane was 12. Joe ran the town's pet shop and was considered to be a steady and reliable sort of a chap. Joe's brother and his wife Enid lived next door and Jean's sister Marie and her husband Victor lived a few doors away. Jean's mother, Mrs Sarah Scholes, lived further away but she was a frequent visitor and she sometimes came to stay.

The housing estate of which East Drive was a part had been built on a hill which had been open farmland when the building work had begun. Until the 18th century

The house afflicted by the Black Monk of Pontefract was built on land that had formerly been an execution ground

a gallows had stood on top of the hill. It would have been some distance away from what is now East Drive. A stream had once run down the hillside. For those needing to cross the stream there had been a footbridge called Priest's Bridge. This bridge stood close to the future site of East Drive. However, when the estate had been built the bridge had been demolished and the drainage system on the hill had been changed.

The stream had then disappeared. None of this was known to the Pritchards in 1966, but they would discover it later and it would become significant.

In August 1966 Jean, Joe and Diane Pritchard went away on a family holiday to the West Country. Phillip wanted to stay at home, so Mrs Scholes agreed to stay with him at East Drive. The visitation began in spectacular fashion on a sunny but none too warm Thursday morning. Phillip was in the garden reading a book and Mrs Scholes was sitting in the living room knitting. Then at about 11.30 am a gust of wind rattled through the house. Soon afterwards Phillip walked into the kitchen and put the kettle on. Then he went through to the living room to ask his grandmother if she wanted a cup of tea. What he saw made him stop in alarm and surprise. The entire room was filled with a cloud of fine white dust, rather like chalk dust. It was drifting slowly downwards to settle over the carpet and the furniture. Mrs Scholes spotted the dust at almost the same moment. She looked up and asked Phillip what he was up to. 'Nothing,' replied Phillip. 'What is this stuff?'

When Mrs Scholes stood up they both noticed that the dust did not actually fill the room but only the lower part of it — so the top half of their bodies rose above the dust cloud. The dust was falling, yet it seemed to be replenishing itself somehow.

A puzzled Mrs Scholes walked over to the house of her daughter, Marie Kelly, and asked her to come over. When Mrs Kelly ran round to East Drive she saw that everything in the living room was covered in a thin layer of white dust, although the dust had stopped falling. She was as puzzled as the others, but she had a practical bent and so she decided that whatever the dust was it needed

In Pontefract, the living room of the house was deluged by a mass of white powder, the origin of which was never discovered

An engineer from the local water company called at the house, but found nothing to account for the pools of water

cleaning up. Mrs Kelly went through to the kitchen to get a duster, pan and brush, but as she did so she almost slipped on a pool of water on the floor. Quickly grabbing a cloth she mopped it up. But then she spotted a second pool of water and a third. She lifted the linoleum to search for the source of the water, but the concrete floor underneath was dry. Enid Pritchard arrived from next door at this point. She turned off the water main tap, but the pools of water continued to form. Finally they called the water company, who promised to send an engineer round. When the water engineer arrived, he soon admitted that he was baffled. He spent a long time checking the pipes, the drains and the taps but he could find nothing wrong. Yet as quickly as the water was mopped up it would reappear. After saying that he would report the problem, he left the house. The water stopped appearing soon after he left.

The next few hours were quiet, but as Phillip and his grandmother were clearing up after supper they heard a clicking noise from the kitchen. They went in to find that the button on the tea dispenser was pushing itself on and off repeatedly, causing tea leaves to cascade over the worktop.

The button continued to operate on its own until the tea ran out. Then it stopped. Seconds later a crash came from the hallway. By now Phillip and his grandmother were thoroughly frightened, but they turned around to see what had caused the sound. The light in the hallway suddenly went on with a loud click. Gingerly venturing into the illuminated space, Phillip discovered that a pot plant had moved from the foot of the stairs to a position halfway up – while the pot in which it usually stood was at the top of the stairs.

Another strange noise now came from the kitchen. A cupboard was rocking back and forth as if an animal were trapped inside. But when Phillip wrenched the door open the movement ceased at once. Totally unnerved by this time, Phillip and Mrs Scholes hastily retreated to Mrs Kelly's house. Called out for the second time that day, Mrs Kelly was now determined to sort things out. She strode over and burst into the kitchen. The cupboard was shaking and rattling again but when she opened it there was nothing there. She checked for hidden wires or strings, but she found none.

Mrs Kelly said that she would stay to make sure nothing else happened. All was quiet after two hours, though, so she went home again. Phillip and his grandmother then went to bed, but no sooner were they under the covers than Phillip's bedroom wardrobe started dancing around his room. The two again fled to Mrs Kelly's house.

Mrs Kelly called the police and they arrived within ten minutes. Although the two constables searched the house thoroughly for signs of an intruder or any trickery they found nothing.

Victor Kelly suggested that they should phone a friend named O'Donald, who had an interest in ghosts and the supernatural. O'Donald went straight over to the house with the Kellys when he arrived. It was freezing cold inside, though it was a warm evening outside. They sat in the house for some time but nothing happened. O'Donald filled in the time by explaining how a poltergeist is different from a classic ghost. As they got up to leave, O'Donald told them that poltergeists often returned to the scene of a visitation. Then he added, 'They are very fond of tearing up photographs, I believe.' This is not, in fact, true, but O'Donald had recently been reading about a visitation in which such a thing had happened. As soon as he finished speaking there came a crash. A wedding day photograph of Joe and Jean Pritchard had been knocked over. When Mr Kelly picked it up he saw that the photograph inside the frame

In the film *Poltergeist* (1982), spirits came into a suburban house and chaos ensued. The film was said to be based on real-life events in the United States similar to the strange happenings in Pontefract

The Pontefract poltergeist had a fascination with the fridge and its contents. On one occasion
it emptied a jug of milk over a guest and it loved to float eggs around in the house

had been cut in half. It seems that the poltergeist could hear what O'Donald was saying.

That was the end of the visitation, or so it seemed. For two years nothing untoward happened at all. Phillip left school and went to work with his father, while Mrs Scholes had taken to spending most weekends at the house. Otherwise, things had not changed much in the Pritchard household. It was August when the visitation returned. Jean was taking a break from decorating Diane's bedroom. As she sat drinking tea in the kitchen with her mother, they heard what they described as a 'swooshing noise'. When Jean went to investigate she found the counterpane of her bed at the foot of the stairs. She carried it upstairs, but a crash made her dash

back down again. This time Phillip's counterpane was lying in the hallway, together with several upturned pot plants. Mrs Scholes began to cry. 'It is starting again,' she sobbed. Indeed it was.

That night Jean woke up for some reason. Then she saw something moving on the landing. She went out to have a look. As she turned on the light a paint brush flew past her face, followed by a pot of paste. The paste pot struck the wall with such force that it splattered its contents everywhere. At the end of the landing a roll of wallpaper was jigging and dancing about. When Jean stepped forward to grab it, it fell to the floor and lay still. Then the carpet sweeper rose into the air and began to sway about. Jean bolted back to her bedroom, pursued by a roll of wallpaper. Joe was awoken by the fuss, as were Diane and Phillip. All four stood on the landing and watched the sweeper bobbing about in midair. A paintbrush was flung at Diane. It hit her on the shoulder, though the blow did not hurt. And then the bizarre events stopped.

An ear-splitting tearing sound drew everyone's attention to Diane's bedroom. The wooden curtain pelmet over the window had been torn off the wall. It hovered for a moment and then it lurched out of the open window to crash into the garden. Joe slammed the door shut, hoping to trap whatever 'it' was in Diane's bedroom. This seemed to work because the door began to shake and rattle as if something were trying to get out. Then silence fell. The family went back to bed. Diane spent the night in her parents' room and they all managed to get some fitful sleep. The poltergeist was back, and it was not going to leave for nine long months.

The visitation soon settled down into a pattern – so much so that the family took to calling the invisible intruder 'Fred'. The poltergeist was mostly active after supper, through to around 1am. It hardly ever did anything during the day, though sometimes ornaments would be found in different places, or even different rooms, from where they had been left. As well as moving objects, the poltergeist specialized in noises. These varied between fairly soft knocks and loud bangs, as if a great drum were being beaten in the room. Sometimes the entire house would shake to the vibrations of the louder thumps, which could be heard up to a hundred yards away. The moving ornaments usually rose into the air and floated around the room for a few seconds before being gently put down. On one occasion a kitchen cupboard opened and dozens of plates and cups floated out, only to be carefully placed on the floor.

Also within the poltergeist's repertoire was the switching on or off of lights. On more than one occasion it actually switched off the electricity at the mains. It would also tear bedclothes off in the middle of the night. Diane was usually the one who suffered this mishap. It was Diane, too, who was sometimes tipped bodily out of her bed to the floor as the mattress floated upwards. A visitor once made the mistake of saying that she did not believe that there was a poltergeist. The fridge door immediately opened and a jug of milk floated out. As the horrified guest watched the jug of milk threw itself at her, drenching her upper body.

The poltergeist seemed to have a sense of humour, too. It once removed a sandwich from a plate and hid it behind the television. When the sandwich was retrieved it bore the clear impression of a set of gigantic teeth. In another incident a pair of gloves came to life and moved around the house as if they were attached to an invisible person. Less amusing for the family was the occasion on which all of the door handles were smeared with jam. The poltergeist annoyed them further by unwinding rolls of toilet paper and stringing them around the house. Perhaps the most inventive of its tricks, though, was when Jean's white mohair cardigan went missing. It was found some time later in the coal shed. Although it was half-buried in coal it proved to be immaculately clean when it was pulled out, though it should have been covered in black coal dust.

About five months into the visitation the family witnessed a very dramatic demonstration of 'Fred's' power. As they all sat watching TV one evening, an egg floated in from the hallway, hovered briefly and then fell and smashed. A second egg did the same thing. Jean ran to the kitchen to find the fridge door open and two eggs missing. She grabbed the remaining four eggs, put them into a wooden box and sat on it. Despite this precaution a third egg floated into the sitting room and broke on the floor. Jean hurriedly opened the box and peered inside. There were only three eggs left. She shut the box and sat

Infernal mess: the Pontefract poltergeist smashed six eggs one after the other

Local legend had it that a wild and evil monk had been executed in Pontefract in the 16th century

The bedroom door swung slowly open. Jean and Joe could see a figure gliding along the landing. It was totally black and it wore a cloak and a hood

on it again. Eggs floated in and smashed on three more occasions. After the final egg had fallen, Jean opened the box again. All of the eggs had gone, even though the box had been held shut by her body weight. It seemed that Fred could move eggs through solid objects.

At other times the poltergeist seemed to be more sinister than playful. Once when Diane was going up the stairs the temperature suddenly plummeted and an ominous black shadow formed on the wall. The hall stand then rose into the air and moved towards her: she stumbled and fell. It finally came to rest on top of her, pinning her to the stairs in a most uncomfortable fashion. Phillip and Jean ran to her aid, but they could not shift the stand, which seemed to be held in place by some force much stronger than they were. A few minutes later the force vanished and Diane was able to be rescued.

About six months after the visitation began a neighbour told the Pritchards about an old legend that was current in Pontefract. Apparently there had once been a monastery there, but like many others it had been demolished in the 16th century, following the

Reformation. According to the tale, one of the monks who had lived in the monastery had been an evil and violent man. His crimes reached a climax when he raped and strangled a local teenage girl. The monk was tried and found guilty. He was then led to the gallows that stood on a hill just outside Pontefract – the hill on which the new housing estate was built. A couple of weeks later 'Fred' was seen for the first time.

Strangely enough, after the Pritchards had been told the story about the monk they began to see him. One night Jean and Joe were in bed. Something woke them up and then the bedroom door swung slowly open. They could see a figure gliding along the landing. It was totally black, it was slightly taller than Joe and it wore a cloak and a hood. The same figure was seen by a neighbour a few days later. A visitor also saw the tall figure in a black robe. Fred began to be called the Black Monk. By this time, the poltergeist seemed to be gaining in power. As became clear later, the visitation was moving towards a climax. The 'Black Monk' began to find a voice. This began as the sound of heavy breathing, which was usually heard at night. Then it began to imitate the sound of a cow or a chicken.

One evening in early May, Diane was walking down the hallway when the lights suddenly went out, leaving her in the dim light of dusk. Then she felt something tugging at the front of her jumper, pulling her towards the stairs. She screamed, which brought Jean and Phillip from the sitting room. By this point the invisible hands had such a firm grip on Diane's clothing that they managed to pull her up the first couple of steps. Jean and Phillip could clearly see the jumper being pulled out in front of Diane, where the invisible hands had a hold.

Jean grabbed her daughter around the waist and tried to pull her back down.

The invisible attacker then grabbed Diane around the throat with what felt like an enormously powerful hand. Diane began to choke. Phillip squeezed past his mother and made a lunge forward, in an attempt to make contact with the invisible assailant. Instantly the invisible force vanished and the three humans tumbled into a heap. But there had been no mistake. The red weals on Diane's neck showed where the invisible hand had gripped her.

> *The invisible attacker grabbed Diane around the throat with what felt like an enormously powerful hand. Phillip lunged forward at the invisible assailant*

Three days later Phillip and Diane were relaxing in the sitting room when Phillip glanced up and saw the black-robed figure moving down the hallway. As he got up to follow it, he saw it pass into the kitchen. When it got there it stopped as if it were looking about. Then it began to sink downwards into the floor, before vanishing altogether. The visitation was over as abruptly as it had begun. This case raises some serious issues for those who feel that all poltergeist visitations must have a focus. The first outbreak took place when Phillip and Mrs Scholes were the only people in the house – the rest of the family were away on holiday. Yet the second and much longer visitation seemed to focus on Diane. Neither of the children appear to have been particularly stressed or upset, nor had there been any dramatic changes in the family situation at around the time of either outbreak.

Otherwise, the visitation seemed to behave in true poltergeist fashion. The second stage began with a number of dramatic events, but they were intermittent and spread out.

It was a while before the poltergeist was able to create manifestations on consecutive evenings. The pace and variety of its stunts increased as the months passed, but it was not able make a sound like a human breathing until the very end of its stay. Nor could it appear as a solid black monk. On this occasion the visitation ended abruptly, which is normal enough, though other visitations have been known to tail off gradually.

The Tropication Arts Visitation

The following events took place in Miami, Florida, which demonstrates the fact that poltergeist activity does not know any geographical boundaries. In January 1967 paranormal researcher Suzy Smith was being interviewed on WKAT, a local radio station, when the radio station received a phone call from a Tropication Arts employee. The young girl claimed that her workplace was being haunted by a ghost that smashed things. Smith decided to investigate. After obtaining permission she visited the company's warehouse, which was full of trinkets, souvenirs and fancy dress novelties. She discovered that the strange events had begun in the middle of December. Some glass mugs had been found smashed on the floor when the staff had arrived for work. As the days went by the damages increased steadily. By the time Smith became involved about a dozen objects were being broken each day. Typically, an ornament would fall off a shelf and smash on the floor when nobody was near it. Just occasionally an object would shatter into fragments as it sat on the shelf.

One of the owners, Alvin Laubheim, had called the police in soon after Christmas. A sergeant had been searching the warehouse when a beer glass had slid off a shelf and crashed to the floor in front of his eyes. The policeman assumed that it had been pushed from behind by somebody he could not see, so he whipped out his pistol and shouted, 'I'll shoot at the next thing to move!' Within the next few seconds, no fewer than 15 objects flung themselves from the shelves. The sergeant holstered his gun and left hurriedly. Smith called in other investigators to help her. Together they carefully ruled out any normal methods by which the objects could have been moved. Meanwhile, Smith noticed that the damage only occurred when one particular employee, 19-year-old Julio Vasquez, was in the warehouse. When

Phone freak: the Rosenheim poltergeist was active in a flat that was used as an office by a local lawyer. It was to be one of the most thoroughly investigated poltergeists on record

he had a day off, or was out on a delivery, nothing happened. Vasquez denied causing the mayhem, but he did admit that he was unhappy in his job. The trouble ceased abruptly when he left Tropication Arts and got a new job elsewhere.

The Rosenheim Visitation

The Black Monk of Pontefract had shown that it was able to manipulate modern electric light switches as easily as earlier poltergeists had moved farm tools and ornaments. However, the poltergeist that struck the office of a Bavarian lawyer was to demonstrate a much greater level of technological ability. As is often the case, the visitation began fairly quietly. It was in the autumn of 1967 that Sigmund Adam began to realize that something was wrong. First of all, several telephone calls were cut off in his office at 13 Königstrasse, Rosenheim, Bavaria. Then the phones began to ring when nobody was calling. Finally, all the phones rang at once, which was when Herr Adam called in the engineers. Working in the office at the time were Herr Adam, a manager named Johannes Englehard, two clerks – Gustel Huber and Anne-Marie Schneider – and a part-time junior named Frau Bielmeier.

First on the scene was an engineer from Siemens, who had installed the office equipment. He found nothing wrong, but the malfunctions continued. The engineer returned and again found nothing wrong, but he

Light fittings in the Rosenheim office swing from side to side, caught on a security camera installed to monitor the situation

replaced the telephonic equipment all the same. When the new equipment malfunctioned as well, Siemens suggested that the fault might lie with the external Post Office lines. The Post Office could find nothing wrong either, but they appeared to think that the fault lay with them. They not only replaced the external lines and the

> *On one particular day the speaking clock had been dialled 46 times in just 15 minutes. It was physically impossible for anyone to dial the clock so often*

telephonic equipment but they also installed a meter that could record all of the calls that came in or went out. On 5 October the meter sprang into life. It recorded an outgoing call even though nobody in the office was on the telephone at the time. Two weeks later the same thing happened. On this second occasion a Dr Schmidt was visiting the office and he signed an account of the event for Herr Adam to show to the Post Office.

The Post Office then produced a log of the calls that had been recorded by the meter over the previous five weeks. According to the log hundreds of calls had been made from the office, many to the same number. In particular, 600 calls had been made to 0119, the speaking clock. Herr Adam and his staff denied making the calls, but the Post Office declared that all the calls that had been recorded were genuine and had been dialled from the Adams office. When they presented Herr Adams with a huge bill he was furious. He studied the list of calls and discovered that on one particular day the speaking clock had been dialled 46 times in just 15 minutes. Given the mechanical dialling mechanism of the phones in the office, dialling 0119 would take 17 seconds, so it was physically impossible for anyone to dial the clock so often in such a short time. The Post Office would not listen, though. They demanded payment of the bill.

Mischievous spirit: Herr Adam points to one of the paintings that was most affected
by the poltergeist. The paintings became involved only after Herr Adam had pointed
out that they had not yet been touched

Herr Adam refused to pay so the Post Office took away all of the telephones except one that had a lock on it. Only Herr Adam had a key yet the mystery calls continued to be made. But the telephones were only a start, because the strange manifestations soon escalated. On 20 October all of the lights in the office went out at once. An electrician, Herr Bauer, was called in. He discovered that all of the light bulbs had been unscrewed. It seemed to be just a question of pushing them back into their sockets so that they all worked again. Herr Bauer had just finished packing up when the lights again went out. Just as before, they had all been unscrewed. Puzzled, he put them back. A few days later all of the fuses popped out, cutting off the electricity supply. Herr Bauer sent for the electricity company.

The light fittings began swinging wildly from side to side. Watching this, Herr Adam remarked, 'All we need now is for the paintings to move'

The electricity company sent senior engineer Herr Paul Brunner along. When he arrived on 15 November he checked the wiring throughout the entire building. Although he found nothing wrong he installed meters to record the electricity usage, voltage fluctuations and changes in magnetic fields. He also replaced the fuses with a more robust, screw-in type and then he sealed them shut. Satisfied with his arrangements he said that he would come back in a couple of weeks to inspect the meters. In the meantime, he asked Herr Adam to call him if anything odd happened. He did not have long to wait.

On 20 November Herr Adam called Herr Brunner, who arrived with a team of engineers and analysts. During the morning the lights had all undone themselves again and a fluorescent tube in Herr Adams' private office had suddenly leapt from its mountings and smashed on the floor. When Brunner checked the meters he discovered that there had been a series of power surges and odd fluctuations. These had occurred only during office hours. The largest surge had taken place when the fluorescent tube had fallen to the floor. Brunner re-seated the meters just to be sure.

Next day Brunner returned to replace the fluorescent tubes with normal light bulbs. While he was there the photocopier began leaking chemicals. On the following day all of the light bulbs blew when a power surge struck. Determined to get to the bottom of the mystery, Brunner arranged for the office to be connected to the local substation by heavy duty cables. The power surges continued, so Brunner assumed that the problems lay with the substation. He moved his team out of Herr Adam's office. They all returned on Monday 27 November having found nothing wrong with the substation. By this time Brunner was running out of ideas, so he disconnected Adam's office from the mains supply and installed a generator. But it changed nothing. During the day all of the light bulbs exploded in turn, showering glass fragments around the office. The generator ran perfectly, but the power surges in the office continued. Next morning it became clear that the problem did not lie with the telephone system or the electricity supply.

The light fittings began swinging wildly from side to side. Watching this, Herr Adam remarked, 'All we need now is for the paintings to move.' Seconds later a painting began to revolve on the wall. It had been hung from a nail by a cord, which was found to be wrapped tightly around the nail. Then other paintings began to move. Two of them fell from the wall and crashed to the ground. At that point Herr Brunner concluded his investigations with these words:

It is necessary to postulate the existence of a power as yet unknown to science, of which neither the nature nor strength nor direction could be defined. It is an energy beyond comprehension.

The electricity company called in two physicists, Dr Karger and Dr Zicha, to examine Brunner's records. The

Anne-Marie Schneider, photographed a few years after events, seems to have been the focus for the visitation

physicists also reviewed the reports about the telephonic malfunctions. They concluded that the strange force was not electrical, sonic or magnetic, but they also believed that it was under intelligent control, in view of the way in which it had behaved.

Herr Adam had already told the police that somebody was trying to ruin him by running up huge phone bills and terrifying his staff. When Brunner moved out, Officer Wendl moved in to begin a criminal investigation. Rather than spend time fruitlessly exploring the 'How?' of the problem, Wendl began investigating the 'Who?' and the 'Why?' He began by assuming that somebody had a grudge against Herr Adam and was therefore trying to make things difficult for him. His method of working was to track back through Adam's past legal cases, financial affairs and past and present employees. At first he drew a blank, but then he realised that one of the

clerks, 18-year-old Anne-Marie Schneider, was unhappy at work. She apparently blamed Adam for the petty feuds and problems that were affecting her relations with other members of staff. Wendl went back over the records of the company and found that the assorted disturbances had happened only on the days when Schneider was in the office. On her days off no untoward events had taken place. To see if his suspicions were correct, Wendl asked Adam to give each of his staff a couple of days off. When it came to Schneider's turn the unexplained events ceased abruptly.

Convinced that he had found the culprit, Wendl decided to have Schneider watched. He thought she must be using some sophisticated trickery to cause the events. The days went by and the poltergeist activity continued, but the police watching Schneider were unable to report anything unusual. Then a massive oak cabinet moved across the office while Schneider and Huber were alone together. The cabinet was so heavy that even if Huber were an accomplice, Schneider could not have shifted it. Two policemen struggled to shift it back into place.

Still convinced that Schneider was the cause of the trouble Wendl presented Adam with his evidence. Adam agreed that it looked very much as if Schneider was to blame, but neither man had the slightest idea of how she was doing it. As a last resort, Hans Bender of the Freiburg Institute of Parapsychology was called in. He persuaded Schneider to spend a few days in Freiburg so that she could undergo a series of ESP (extra-sensory perception) tests. The results proved to be negative – the young woman had no special abilities. Nevertheless, Herr Adam dismissed her from his office. Schneider later moved to Munich and got on with her life. There were no further instance of poltergeist activity, either in Herr Adam's office or around Schneider.

What was noted by researchers at the time was that the Rosenheim visitation had occurred in a place of work, whereas nearly all previous poltergeist events had been experienced in someone's home. However, many of the earlier events had taken place in homes that were also workplaces, such as farms, pubs and workshops. It seems that the departure might not have been as significant as was thought at the time. The Rosenheim visitation attracted the attention of numerous

Called in: Hans Bender of the Freiburg Institute of Parapsychology conducted numerous tests on Schneider, but without obtaining any positive results

technicians, scientists and policemen, all of whom admitted to being completely baffled by the events. In terms of poltergeist effects, however, the Rosenheim case was relatively tame. That was very definitely not the case with a visitation that began in 1977 in the north London suburb of Enfield.

The Harper Visitation

The affected house belonged to the Harper family, which at the time consisted of Mrs Harper, who was divorced, and her four children: Rose aged 13, Janet aged 11, Pete aged 10 and Jimmy who was 7. Mrs Harper's brother, John Burcome, lived in the next street. The Harper family got on well with their immediate neighbours, Vic and Peggy Nottingham and their son Gary.

Their house would attract a number of leading researchers and their experiences would prove to be enormously newsworthy. However, there would be accusations of trickery as well as evidence of genuine phenomena.

The visitation began as the children went to bed on the evening of 30 August, 1977. Pete and Janet, who shared a bedroom, were the first to experience anything strange. The pair came downstairs only minutes after Mrs Harper had switched the light off. They said their beds had been shaking and shuddering. Mrs Harper went up with them but found nothing amiss, so she ordered them back to bed. The next evening the same two called down to their mother. This time they could hear a funny noise. Mrs Harper went up, switched the light on and listened. She could hear nothing so she assumed that the children were playing a trick on her. But when she switched the light off she immediately heard a strange sound. It was like a man shuffling over a wooden floor while wearing slippers, she said later. Then there came four distinct knocks, like someone rapping their knuckles on a wooden board. She switched the light back on and was astonished to see the chest of drawers sliding across the floor. It moved about 18 inches before it stopped. Mrs Harper went over to push it back into position, but it would not move. It was as if some invisible force was pushing it from the other side. 'Right,' Mrs Harper announced, 'everybody downstairs.'

Mrs Harper shepherded the children next door and explained to the Nottingham family what had happened. At this stage they all assumed that there was some intruder in the house. Vic and Gary went back to the Harper household, but when they searched the place thoroughly they found nothing. As they were preparing to leave, the knocking noises began again. They seemed to be coming from inside the walls. Vic searched the gardens, while Gary stayed indoors, following the noises from room to room. At 11pm the Nottinghams gave up trying to find the intruder and called the police. WPC Carolyn Heeps arrived promptly, listened to the story and then ventured into the house. She too searched without finding anything. However, when she entered the living room the knocking noises began again. Heeps stopped to listen, at which point a chair slid across the floor towards her. It moved about three feet and then stopped. She left the house, saying that there was nothing she could do about ghosts. After that she went off to file a written report of the incident. This report would prove to be of great importance to investigators because it confirmed that an independent witness had experienced something odd at the earliest stages of the visitation.

The Harpers slept next door that night and then ventured back to their house on the following morning. Everything was normal until marbles and Lego bricks began to be thrown around in the downstairs rooms. Mrs Harper bent down to pick up a marble, but it was too hot to touch and she had to drop it again. After a few minutes the activity stopped, but it repeated itself each evening for four days.

Mrs Harper called the local vicar, but he was unwilling to get involved, so Vic Nottingham telephoned the *Daily Mirror*. He asked them who should be contacted if the police and the Church could not help. On 4 September the *Daily Mirror* sent a reporter, Douglas Bence, and a photographer, Graham Morris. The two stayed for some hours talking to the Harpers without anything strange happening. Then just as the pressmen were preparing to leave a Lego brick levitated. Morris got out his camera to take a shot but while he was focusing he was struck hard on the forehead by another Lego brick. The blow resulted in a bruise that was still visible a week later.

When Bence and Morris reported back to the newspaper, a senior reporter named George Fellows

Maurice Grosse
of the Society for
Psychical Research
who investigated the
Enfield case

offered to take a hand. He had investigated several alleged ghosts in the past. Although some of them could not be explained, others had been found to have less than psychic origins. Sometimes a pub landlord wanted to get his pub into the newspapers or a teenager was playing a prank. In the case of council house tenants such as the Harpers, Fellows knew that allegations were sometimes made in order to get a better home. So when he went to see the Harpers he asked them if they wanted to move

house. Mrs Harper said they were happy where they were, but they just wanted to get rid of their ghost.

Convinced that the Harpers were genuine, Fellows called the Society for Psychical Research and suggested that they should investigate. The SPR contacted a member named Maurice Grosse. Born in 1919, Grosse had served in the army during the Second World War, before founding a successful engineering business. He had a long-standing interest in the paranormal and

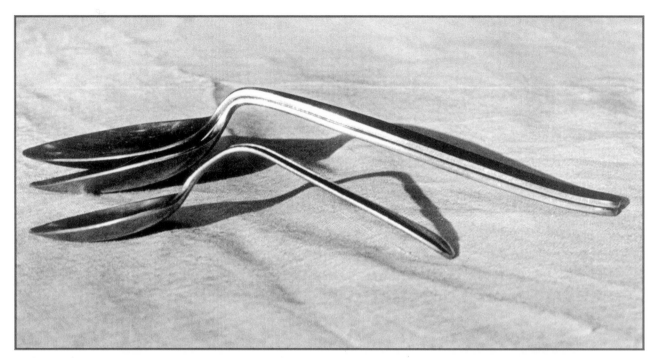

Twisted logic: bent spoons and other metal objects turned up several times in the Enfield house during the poltergeist visitation. The teaspoon above bent on its own while Guy Playfair was seated at the breakfast table. The other spoons were seen bending by Mrs Harper

after his retirement he took up investigating cases and events. Because he lived in north London, the Enfield house was almost on his doorstep.

Grosse made his first visit to the house on the evening of 8 September. He was greeted by a flying marble which had not been thrown by any of the Harper children. A few minutes later, the long brass chimes of the doorbell began to swing back and forth. Then a door slammed shut, flew open and slammed a second time. Later that evening a shirt floated up from a pile of fresh laundry and dropped down to the floor.

Reviewing his notes after getting home, Grosse thought that the most likely focus for the case was Janet. Indeed, he rather suspected her of faking the phenomena. While the others had seemed agitated, upset or frightened, Janet had been quite relaxed about the affair. She was also in the room each time something odd happened. While Grosse had not caught her doing anything, he decided that he would keep a careful eye on her when he returned. He also intended to search for hidden props and wires.

But although he called several times in the next few days he did not witness anything odd.

On 10 September the *Daily Mirror* printed the story, using the headline 'The House of Strange Happenings'. Next day Grosse, Mrs Harper and Mrs Nottingham were interviewed on a local radio station. The media coverage alerted a highly experienced SPR investigator named Guy Lyon Playfair. He called Grosse and asked if he could join the investigation. Grosse agreed. Over the months that followed, Grosse and Playfair would keep a near constant watch on the house between them. They would record hundreds of incidents of poltergeist activity and they would reach their own conclusions about what was going on. The visitation lasted for 14 months in all. During that time the most frequent activity was knockings and bangings that seemed to come from the walls. Early in the visitation, Grosse suggested that they should try to communicate with the poltergeist. One evening when it was banging away, Grosse shouted out that he wanted to ask questions and that the answers should be given in the form of one knock for 'no' and two knocks for 'yes'. Did the poltergeist understand? Two knocks indicated that it did.

Inexplicable events: Grosse's visit to the Harpers seemed to bring the house to life. The long brass chimes of the doorbell began to swing back and forth; a door slammed shut, flew open and then slammed shut again. Then finally a shirt floated in space

In the question and answer session that followed the poltergeist indicated that it had formerly lived in the house for 30 years. The poltergeist then fell silent. Another session a few days later produced the information that the poltergeist had left the house 53 years earlier. That would mean that the spirit had taken up residence 83 years before. Grosse knew the house was not that old and asked, 'Are you having a game with me?' At that, a box of cuddly toys lifted up, floated eight feet through the air and hit Grosse on the head. Later sessions produced nonsensical answers, so Grosse gave up his attempts at communication. On one visit, Playfair and Grosse noticed that several items of furniture had disappeared from the house. They asked Mrs Harper about this. She said that the items had come from a nearby house, where a child had died in suspicious circumstances. The parents had sold up and left soon afterwards. She was worried that the entity causing the trouble had come into her house with the furniture, so she had got rid of it. For the next few days some of the pillows on the beds displayed small indentations, as if a child had been resting on them. As had so often been the case, it seemed that a

The gas fire that was wrenched from the wall and hauled across the floor by the Enfield poltergeist

poltergeist was acting in line with the expectations of its witnesses.

Then in October 1977 the poltergeist became more active. It had previously confined its efforts to moving toys or sliding furniture across floors. Now it began throwing furniture about. A chair beside Janet's bed came in for a lot of attention – it was regularly flung about. Grosse tried securing it to the leg of the bed with a piece of stout wire. A few hours later the chair had been overturned, and the wire had been broken. Grosse then secured it with several twists of the same wire. The chair was again found overturned and the wire was broken a short time later. Rather more dramatic was the fate of the gas fire, a heavy metal contraption that was cemented into the living room wall. One day the family came home to find that it had been torn from the wall and dragged across the room towards the doorway. After that, the furniture began to be moved about more and more often. It was left in ever more bizarre places. The front door could not be opened one day because a bed had been

pushed up against it. Then the younger children began to complain that they could see the face of an old man hovering about, though nobody else saw this.

Increasingly, the events were starting to centre on Janet. She was tipped out of chairs and thrown out of bed and she fell into trances. Finally, in late November, a strange dog-like barking noise began to be heard. It was only evident when Janet was present, but it did not seem to come from her. Over the course of the next few days the bark became a whistle, and then a gasp and finally a harsh male voice. When Grosse and Playfair questioned the voice, it claimed to be two distinct people. The first person was a man called Joe Watson. This was the name of the man who had lived in the house before the Harpers. He had died after suffering a massive throat haemorrhage while sleeping in a chair in the living room. When the voice was claiming to be Watson, it usually uttered a stream of obscenities and made meaningless comments.

The second identity claimed by the voice was that of someone called Bill Haylock. 'Bill' claimed that he was buried in the nearby Durants Park cemetery. He had come to the house looking for his family, he said, 'but they are not here now'. The voice would often ramble on when it claimed to be Bill. It demanded that jazz music be put on the radio and it told people to leave the house. Asked why he was bothering the Harpers, 'Bill' replied, 'I like annoying you.' Many other poltergeists have explained their motives in this way. When Rose asked 'Bill' why he did not move on to where the dead people went, the voice responded rather sadly, 'I am not a heaven man.'

Oddly, 'Bill's' account of his death exactly mirrored the circumstances of the real Joe Watson's last hours. Events were clearly building up to something of a climax as November came to an end. The peak of activity was reached on 15 December. As well as the usual mayhem of flying ornaments, wandering furniture and loud noises, Janet claimed that she had been levitated in her bedroom. This was a special day for Janet in another way, too. It marked the beginning of her first period. The level of poltergeist activity diminished rapidly after this time.

In the spring of 1978 the manifestations began to increase again. This time they were of a rather different kind, though – they rarely happened when anyone was present. Instead, furniture and ornaments quietly moved around in empty rooms. When a new investigator arrived at the Enfield house, she could find no evidence of genuine paranormal activities. She quickly formed the opinion that Janet and Rose were faking the apparent phenomena.

In a radio interview that she gave a few years later, Janet admitted that she and Rose had indeed faked the later phenomena. She insisted, however, that the earlier manifestations had been genuine. Some sceptics chose to believe that her confession meant that the sisters had been tricking Grosse and Playfair from the start. Other researchers gave them the benefit of the doubt.

The Role of the Human Environment

Numerous other poltergeists have been seen in recent years, but little would be gained by examining all of the accounts in detail. The studies carried out by earlier researchers have generally confirmed the usual pattern of poltergeist visitations.

However, some of the more recent investigations have established the importance of the human environment in which the visitations have taken place. This aspect of poltergeist activity was mostly absent from earlier reports. Whether the events have taken place at work or at home, it has usually been the case that people have been surrounded by tension, frustration or even unhappiness. There does not seem to have been outright hostility between antagonists. It is often more of a low-level, simmering discontent. Focus people are usually teenagers and they are more often girls than boys – but that does not seem to be an iron rule. Teenage girls often appear to be associated with the more dramatic events, which is perhaps why they are noticed. On the other hand, young men and teenage boys seem to be more often involved with the less sensational manifestations.

These aspects, and others, must be considered when one is attempting to understand, analyze and explain poltergeist visitations. But before doing so, one other feature of the poltergeist phenomenon must be looked at. In some ways it is the oddest feature of all. Poltergeist activity does not always take place when a visitation is in progress. It can occur in a number of other scenarios as well. It is time to look at them.

Whether the events have taken place at work or at home, it has usually been the case that people have been surrounded by tension, frustration or even unhappiness.

CHAPTER 13

Phantom Nudgers & Other Physical Hauntings

any studies of the poltergeist phenomenon concentrate on full-blown visitations, but in a vast number of incidents only one or two features of a visitation are present. A general pattern is not established.

Very often those on the receiving end of these events do not recognize that a poltergeist-like event is in progress, so they look for other explanations. It is not always easy to determine if a poltergeist is involved or if something else is going on.

The 'Flying Peaches of Shreveport'

Take for instance the case of the 'flying peaches of Shreveport' which occurred on 12 July 1961. Three builders were repairing the roof of a house in Shreveport, Louisiana when they were bombarded by a hail of what they took to be golf balls. The objects were small and round and they hurt when they collided with anybody. Annoyed by the intrusion, the builders looked around expecting to see a gang of teenagers throwing missiles – but they could see nobody. The balls seemed to be falling vertically down from a cloudy sky. Thoroughly mystified, the builders retreated from the roof and took shelter while the bombardment continued. After about five minutes the workmen ventured out. They soon discovered that what they had taken for golf balls were, in fact, unripe peaches. The builders picked up around 200 of the green and hard fruits.

When they reported the incident to the police, it was suggested that the peaches had been scooped up from a nearby orchard by a strong gust of wind. The story got into the local press, and a reporter contacted the United States Weather Bureau for an explanation. However, the organization could not come up with an answer. After studying the weather charts for Shreveport on the day concerned they announced that it had been a calm, normal day. Only something like a mini-tornado could have lifted 200 peaches into the sky – and there was no record of such an event. Again the single shower of peaches was all that occurred. The phenomenon did not progress into a poltergeist visitation.

A Shower of Hazelnuts

A similar event took place on 13 March 1977 in Bristol. This time, though, it echoed a feature of the Bell Witch visitation. Alfred Osborne and his wife were walking home from the Sunday morning church service when they heard a clicking noise. It came from the pavement in front of them. Thinking that a button had come off his coat, Mr Osborne looked down at the ground in front of him. All he could see was a hazelnut. A second or two later another hazelnut fell on to the pavement. Mr and Mrs Osborne looked around, expecting to discover that the nuts had been thrown by a child or a prankster. In that same instant, the two stray hazelnuts had turned into a deluge. Hazelnuts were falling vertically from the sky. About a thousand nuts fell in less than 30 seconds and then the shower abruptly ceased.

'They were coming from the sky, from a considerable height,' Mr Osborne told a reporter from the local newspaper later that day. 'They were peppering all

Flying fruit: builders working on the roof of a house in Shreveport, Louisiana, were assaulted on 12 July 1961 by a barrage of peaches that seemed to come from nowhere. They found over 200 pieces of fruit after the storm was over around on the road, bouncing off cars and rolling in the gutters.' Mr Osborne offered the reporter one of the hundreds of nuts that he had picked up. It was fresh and sweet. The reporter suggested that a gust of wind had picked the nuts up from a local wood. Mr Osborne was contemptuous of the idea. 'I don't know where you could suck up hazelnuts in March,' he said. 'They don't ripen until late summer.' It will be recalled that the Bell Witch deposited a large number of fresh hazelnuts, equally out of season, on Mrs Bell's bed when she was ill one time.

One morning Mr Chickett's workers arrived to find their employer battered to death, with his room ransacked and his money stolen

When It Rained Seeds

A couple of years later there came another curious shower. It was not hazelnuts this time but seeds – hundreds of thousands of them. On 12 February 1979, Ronald Moody was alone in his sitting room in Southampton when he heard a strange 'rushing sound' coming from his conservatory. When he went through to investigate, the room was strangely dark – the glass roof was entirely covered by a mass of tiny seeds. Stepping outside, Mr Moody saw that it was literally raining seeds. Thousands of tiny, pale brown seeds were cascading down from directly above. The shower stopped almost immediately. Mr Moody guessed that the seeds were ordinary cress seeds – as indeed they proved to be when he tried growing some later on – but their sheer number was astonishing. He counted 500 seeds in a space that was only six inches square. The seeds covered his entire back garden, his conservatory and parts of his neighbour's garden as well.

Deeply puzzled, Mr Moody collected up some of the seeds. He then went inside to phone a friend, but at that point he heard another 'whooshing noise'. His garden was now being engulfed by mustard seeds. The sky was black with them. As before, the torrent quickly stopped.

In the two hours that followed vast quantities of everyday seeds fell from the sky on five separate occasions. This event reads very much like the opening salvo of the Battersea House of Mystery affair, but nothing further happened. The strange rain of seeds came out of an unremarkable sky. It was accompanied by snow flurries. All of the seeds fell on one day and that was the end of the affair.

The Haunting of the Brushmakers Arms

Showers of anomalous objects are frequently found in poltergeist visitations, but isolated deluges may or may not be psychic phenomena. However, some incidents feature a wider range of poltergeist-like events. Take, for instance, the haunting of the Brushmakers Arms at Upham, Hampshire. The public house takes its name from the fact that the original building was constructed as part-house, part-brush factory.

About 400 years ago a murder took place there. The victim was Mr Chickett, for whom the original building was constructed. As he grew older, his fortune grew greater. He would sit upstairs in his bedroom counting out his gold and silver coins, before concealing them in a hidden compartment. It was not, however, hidden well enough. One morning his workers arrived to find their employer battered to death, with his room ransacked and his money stolen.

After such a heinous crime Mr Chickett's spirit could not rest easy. Four centuries later it appears that he has still not left the scene of his murder. A witness to the physical manifestations recalls his experience:

Saw it myself in here. A few years back now. I was sitting at the bar, about where you are, when the bottles started moving. Two of them fell off the shelf on to the floor. Then one flew across the bar. It was like someone was throwing it, but it didn't break. Just shot across the room and landed on that table there by the window.

The distance indicated was about 15 feet. Glasses, bottles and other objects are moved around the bar about once a month, though it is unusual for anyone to see them move.

Just as often, footsteps are heard moving out of the room in which the murder took place. They go along the corridor and down the stairs and then they stop in the hall. Rather less frequently the sound of chinking coins is heard from the same small room. The ghost himself is seen only rarely. In 2002, Jill the landlady recalled:

Last time was about three years ago. I was upstairs doing some paperwork in the office. Suddenly I heard the door to the front bedroom [where the murder was committed] slam shut, very hard and loud. I looked round and there was the outline of a man, like a shadow on the wall, moving off. Only it couldn't be a shadow as the sun was not out. And it was not a shadow on the wall, not as such. It was more like a shadow in the middle of the corridor – oh, I am not explaining it very well. It was definitely a man moving down the corridor. Mind you, we haven't seen him since. People hear him of course. But I think he must like us. We get no trouble.

Here, we can see quite a wide range of poltergeist activity: noises, objects moving and a sinister black shape. Other elements are missing, no knocks or voices and the only objects to be moved around are small and light. The level of activity is very low, with an inexplicable event happening only once or twice a month, rather than several times a day as is more typical.

What really makes this case different from a more usual visitation is that the activity has been going on for at least 50 years. There are locals in the village who can remember the strange activity at the pub as far back as the 1950s – and they say that it was nothing new then. Maybe the activity really has been going on since the time of the murder. This long period of time would seem to rule out the possibility of a focus person. The landlord of the pub has changed at least six times since the 1950s, while staff come and go even more frequently.

The Haunting of the Crown Inn at Lea

A similar situation exists at the Crown Inn at Lea, Herefordshire. It became a pub when two houses were knocked together in about 1930. The activity in this building is restricted to the downstairs back room, which was formerly the kitchen of the more western of the two houses. It now forms part of the restaurant area of the

pub. In particular, the manifestations centre on the rear window that overlooks the pub garden.

Those who have encountered the ghost say that he sits quietly on an equally spectral chair, looking out of the window. He is never seen, but he can be clearly sensed. There is little doubt about his general appearance. Those who have sensed it are very definite about the fact that he is an elderly man. On the whole, this spirit – if such it is – is no trouble at all. He will be sensed now and then by members of staff, but those who have worked here for

Hurriedly returning she saw that the Christmas tree had been overturned and all of her carefully arranged baubles were scattered over the floor

any amount of time have learned to ignore him. There are times when the old boy seems to get quite irate. That is when anything is placed where he likes to sit. Then a range of poltergeist-like activity will break out.

In 2005 a new member of staff was given the task of putting up the Christmas decorations. She thought that an empty spot next to a window would make an ideal location for a Christmas tree. So she set up the festive tree and went to work decorating it. The job was finished to her satisfaction so she went off to make a cup of tea. She had only taken a couple of steps into the kitchen when there was an almighty crash from the restaurant area. Hurriedly returning she saw that the Christmas tree had been overturned and all of her carefully arranged baubles were scattered over the floor. The landlady quickly put her right and advised her to place the tree elsewhere. She did and no further mishaps occurred.

It is, of course, usually customers who are new to the pub who interfere with the window space. They may move a chair to the area, or leave a drink on the window sill. Inevitably the drink will be overturned or the chair will be moved. On at least one occasion a person unwary enough to sit at the window has been

The corner of the Crown Inn at Lea where the ghost of an elderly man has visited for many years

nudged or pinched by some invisible hand.

'Phantom nudgers' have been recognized as a separate category of ghost by some researchers. They frequent public places, such as pubs or railway stations, where they creep up on perfectly unsuspecting humans before delivering a nudge, a shove or a pinch. Always invisible, they persist in their activities for years on end.

A 'ghost' is effectively a hallucination projected by those who believe in it. It can be picked up by other people, whether they share that belief or not

The Philip Experiment

Another outbreak of poltergeist-type activity occurred in Canada in the early 1970s. It took place in the most unusual of circumstances. The train of events began in 1972, when Dr George Owen of the Toronto Society for Psychical Research decided to test the theory: 'Ghosts have an objective reality but they are created out of the minds of those who see them.' In effect, a ghost will appear and will haunt a particular place if enough people believe that it will do so. A 'ghost' is effectively a hallucination projected by those who believe in it. It can be picked up by other people, whether they share that belief or not.

In order to test the idea, Owen recruited a group of seven volunteers who agreed to meet once a week. They would concentrate on an invented ghost in order to see if they could make him appear. Owen created the basic character, though the group collectively wrote his life story in the hope that this would increase the strength of their belief in him.

The character they invented was named Philip. He was imagined to have lived in Diddington, Warwickshire, during the mid-17th century. Philip was a fairly wealthy landowner who had married young for money. His marriage to Dorothea was unhappy, though, so he had embarked on a passionate affair with a beautiful gypsy girl named Margo. Tragedy struck after some months of wild abandon with his tempestuous lover. Dorothea discovered the affair and denounced Margo as a witch. Philip's wife fabricated enough evidence to have Margo convicted and Philip did nothing to save her. He was afraid that he would be accused in his turn. Margo was then burned at the stake, sending Philip into a deep depression that resulted in his suicide. The group drew pictures of Philip so that they could visualize what his ghost should look like.

It was felt that this dramatic, romantic and ultimately tragic story was just the sort of thing that should lead to a haunting. The group began to meet regularly. They sat around a table to discuss Philip's life story, they added details and they concentrated hard on the existence of his ghost. When one of the group visited England he made a point of travelling to Diddington, so that he could take photographs of the church and other old buildings. It might create a link to Philip. Nothing happened – the ghost of Philip did not appear.

Then one of the group found a report written for the British Society of Psychical Research by DW Hunt and KJ Bachelor in the 1960s. It described an investigation into the old 19th-century parlour game of table turning. The investigators had apparently been very successful in their efforts to produce phenomena. There were some guidelines for anyone who wanted to repeat their experiment:

Nobody must feel responsible for, or pressured into making, phenomena happen; everyone taking part must believe in paranormal events being possible; no surprise should be shown or, if possible, felt when something does happen; a light-hearted, jocular atmosphere should be encouraged.

The Philip group decided to adopt these guidelines in the hope of getting the spectral Philip to appear to them. They cracked jokes, swapped banter about Philip and his amorous exploits and chatted about their own lives while they were waiting for the ghost of Philip to appear. After barely a month something happened. A ghost did not

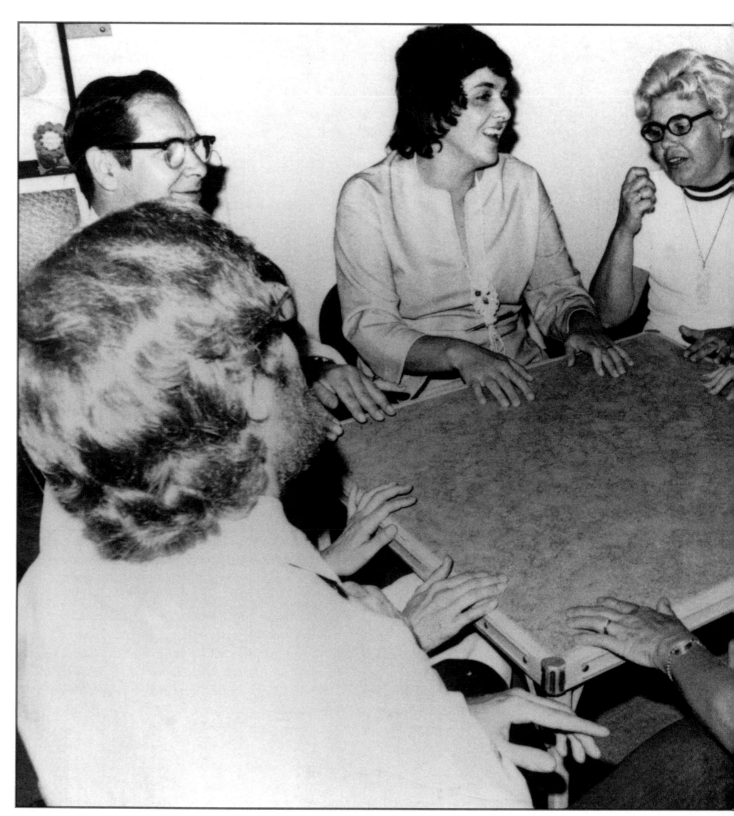

The Philip Group during a session. The table around which they are
sitting would later move – apparently of its own volition

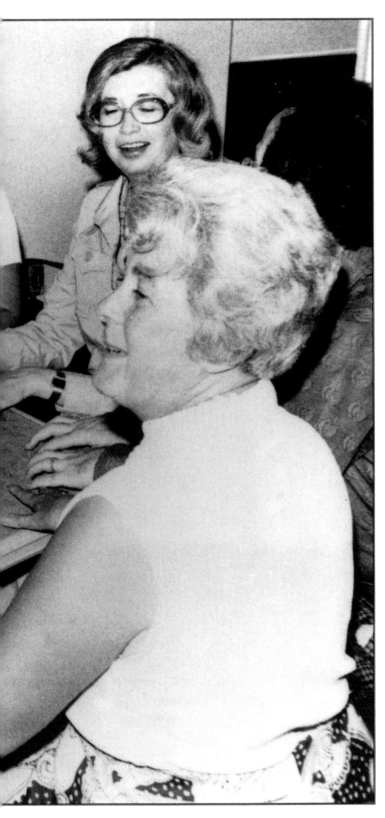

materialize, but the table vibrated. At first the tremors were light and uncertain, then they gathered in strength over a matter of weeks until the table was juddering and rocking from side to side quite visibly. There was still no ghost, but then one of the members had a thought. 'I wonder if by chance Philip is doing this?' she asked. There was a single loud knock on the table.

It was decided to call out questions to the invisible knocker. They began by instructing it to give one knock for 'yes' and two knocks for 'no'.

It was 'Philip' himself who devised a signal to indicate that he either did not know the answer or he refused to give it. This signal was a scratching sound. Each session would begin with the group members calling out, 'Hello, Philip,' in turn. As they spoke, each person was rewarded with a knock on the table in front of them. When they said, 'Goodbye, Philip,' at the close of each session each person again got a personal knock on the table. When the group began to question the knocker, the invisible entity at once identified itself as Philip. In answer to a series of questions 'Philip' gave a version of his life and death that tallied exactly with that which had been invented by the group. When the group asked questions about things that they had not included in their fictitious background for Philip, the knocker would give clear and direct answers. These answers were always internally consistent with the invented story, but they were not always historically accurate. Interestingly, the historic errors were not known to any of the group at the time. They came to light only when research was carried out into 'Philip's' claims.

As the weeks passed by the knocks got louder and more definite. Owen went to great pains to ensure that no one in his group was indulging in trickery. He checked the table over before and after each session, he frisked the group members and he kept a look out for any tricks. But he never found any. Each of the group members was asked to keep their hands fully in view of the others, preferably letting them rest on top of the table. By late 1973 the meetings began to get much livelier as 'Philip' began to display the sort of tricks that were common among poltergeists. The table began to bounce up and down – it rose several inches into the air before falling back down again.

Collective hallucination: Dr George Owen of Toronto who organized an investigation that would become known as The Philip Experiment and which may offer some clues into the nature of poltergeists

When asked to do so, 'Philip' would cause the lights to flicker. Eventually the table took on a life of its own – it danced around the room and floated up into the air. On one occasion it became stuck in the doorway as it tried to escape the room. It sometimes did this even when not a single member of the group was touching it. This ruled out any chance that a group member might be pushing it about, even unconsciously.

In the early months of 1974 the group decided that it was time to carry out some tests. They recorded the knocks, along with the sounds of themselves knocking on the table, and had them analyzed. Although the knocks seemed natural to the human ear, they had an unusual sound profile. Knocks produced by human hands began loudly and then died away gradually, as the vibrating wood became still. On the other hand 'Philip's' knocks began loudly and then dropped off to silence very quickly. Then the group decided to try taking movie film of the events. 'Philip' did not seem to mind.

Later the group moved the table into a TV studio, where the bizarre events were recorded as a moving TV image

The raps, knocks and table movements all happened as frequently as before – and all was caught on film. Later the group moved the table into a TV studio, where the bizarre events were recorded as a moving TV image.

The Philip group concluded that their attempt to create a visual ghost of Philip had resulted in an auditory ghost instead. However, the experienced poltergeist researcher will have realized that many of 'Philip's' antics are typical of a poltergeist visitation. In particular, a poltergeist will usually claim to be whatever its human observers believe it to be. It could be a witch, a demon or an invented ghost called Philip.

The Skippy Experiment

Since the Philip Experiment became public there have been several attempts to replicate its success. One of the most productive of these imitations has been the Skippy Experiment – a series of ongoing sessions in Sydney, Australia. The Australian team closely followed the methods of the Philip team. They created a sensational life history for their invented ghost and then they hoped for poltergeist activity. The Australians invented a teenage girl named Skippy Cartman who entered into a passionate but illicit love affair that resulted in her pregnancy. Her tragic tale ended when she was murdered by the father of the unborn baby. So far the team have heard some soft rapping and scratching noises while they have been sitting around their table. However, none of the more dramatic table moving events have yet been replicated.

It can be seen that the range of manifestations that are generally associated with poltergeist visitations are not confined to those events. Some of the features of a visitation can be observed in a range of other situations: conventional hauntings, showers of anomalous objects and entirely invented experiments. Whether this indicates the origin of the poltergeist phenomenon or merely serves to cloud and confuse the issue depends on the viewpoint of the investigator.

It is time to turn to the explanations that have been put forward for the existence of poltergeists. We will be looking at the different viewpoints of researchers, be they sceptics or believers.

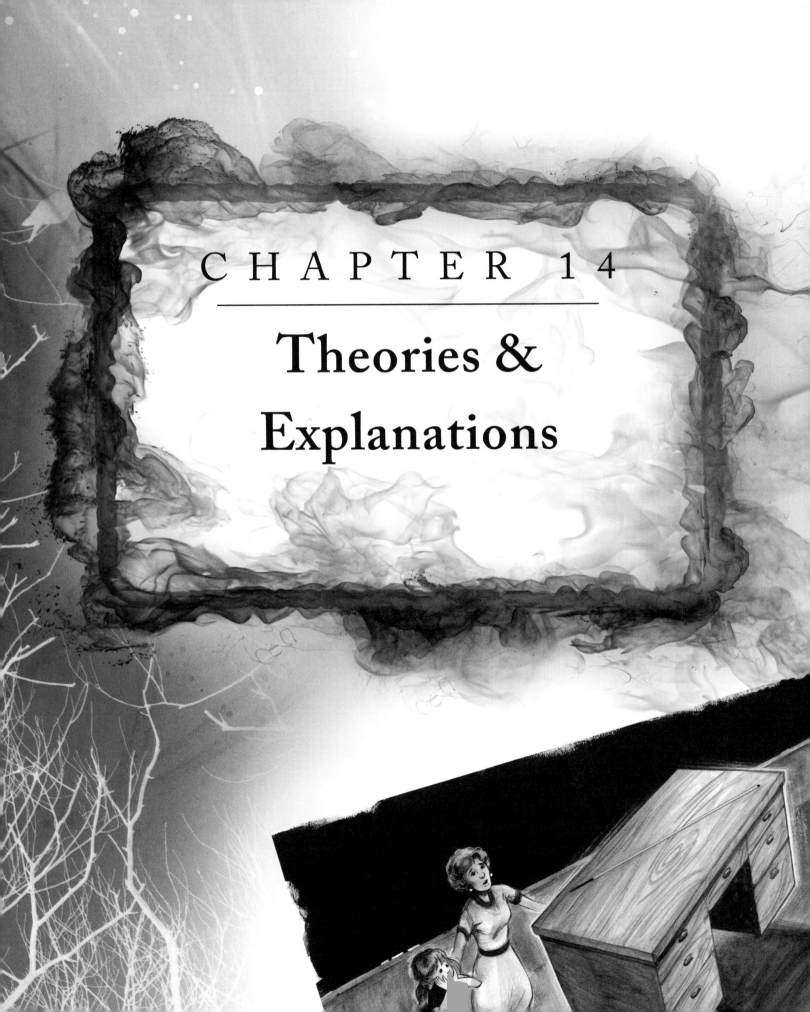

CHAPTER 14

Theories & Explanations

Having surveyed the poltergeist phenomenon in its many and varied guises it is time to draw some conclusions. From the cases studied so far in this book it will be apparent that poltergeist visitations can be varied and diverse or they can follow a common pattern.

The Stages of a Poltergeist Visitation

A hypothetical idealized poltergeist visitation would follow a set course, though it should be noted that any visitation might end at any point during this progression of stages.

Stage One: Beginnings

A poltergeist visit usually begins with low-volume household noises. Before the Second World War people usually assumed that these noises were made by mice and rats, or any other animals that had found their way into the house. This was probably because such animals did sometimes get into houses in those days. These days we are more likely to interpret such noises as air-locks in the central heating or malfunctions in electrical equipment. Very typical of this first phase is scratching, as if an animal is clawing at a door or a wall. The sound of scratching can at times be abnormally loud, though, far louder than any dog or rat could possibly produce.

During this stage most witnesses are not aware that anything odd or unusual is happening. They typically believe that there is some mundane explanation for the noises. Plumbers, electricians or pest-control experts are called in, but they find nothing that can explain the

The noises continue, despite all efforts to discover their source. They will increase in volume, variety and frequency as time passes

sounds. The noises continue, despite all efforts to discover their source. They will increase in volume, variety and frequency as time passes.

Stage Two: Noises

Once the occupants of the building have become accustomed to a variety of apparently normal noises, the visitation moves on to a series of noises that are quite clearly not normal. The most characteristic of these is usually described as a knock or a rap. It is frequently likened to the sound of human knuckles knocking on wood. This sound comes from walls, furniture, doors and other objects around the house. In the Ballechin House visitation two men heard it coming from the same door when they were on opposite sides of it. Both men assumed that the cause of the knocking was on the other side of the door from themselves, when obviously it was not. In the Cock Lane visitation, the knocking sounded as if it was coming from behind the wooden panelling that lined the rooms – that is, from within the walls. Sometimes the surface that is being knocked can be felt to vibrate, just as if it really has been rapped by knuckles. In other instances this vibration is not present.

Odd fact: most poltergeists occur in perfectly normal houses inhabited by normal families

In addition to the knocking, other noises are frequently recorded. Some of these may well be variations on the knock. There can be the sound of a cricket ball bouncing on the floor, for instance, or clapping. The sound of cracking also seems to be common – some have compared it to dry wood being snapped in half. Bangs and explosions are heard less frequently, but they can be extremely loud. In the Amherst visitation the witnesses thought that a cannon had been fired just outside the house – they ran out to look for it.

In the Battersea Mystery House case, the crowds in the street could hear the bangs and thumps quite clearly up to 150 yards away. The timing of the inexplicable noises is interesting. They often manifest themselves in the evening. In the case of the mill at Appleby, the noises always came during, or just after, the family ate supper. In the case of the Fox Sisters the noises began when the girls went to bed. At Ballechin they began at around midnight. In a country house of the period that would have been when most of the people in the house went to bed. The lower-key noises of Stage One are

often heard at night, too. Once the noises have become an established part of the visitation they often, but not always, abandon their evening timing. They may then be heard at any time of day or night.

In those visitations where the first stage is missed out, the events will start at Stage Two, but only if the male head of the household is away. The Demon Drummer of Tedworth visitation began in truly spectacular fashion when Mr Mompesson was away on business. Many other visitations show a similar pattern.

Stage Three: Moving Objects

Once the repertoire of noises has been established, the poltergeist may get busy moving objects about. This stage will sometimes begin concurrently with Stage Two.

Rather more dramatic is the throwing of stones. Stone throwing is such a common feature of poltergeist visitations that a name has been coined for the manifestation: lithobolia. The frequency, scale and violence of stone throwing may vary considerably. At the Appleby mill only two stones were thrown, but they were large and heavy and they caused considerable damage. At the Battersea Mystery House hundreds of stones were thrown and again they caused a lot of damage.

Stone throwing is such a common feature that a name has been coined for the manifestation: lithobolia. The frequency, scale and violence may vary

through the air and then fall suddenly. They usually smashed on the hard floor. Conversely, the objects that were moved about in the Sunderland household of Dr Wilkins were always placed very carefully and neatly, without anything breaking. Sometimes, but not always, these objects are warm or even hot when they are picked up.

One feature shared by all outbreaks of lithobolia is that the poltergeist uses stones that are readily to hand. The stones at Appleby quite obviously came from the river bed outside while those at Battersea were pieces of coal, probably from the family coal shed.

Although stones are usually the most noticeable objects to be moved, the poltergeist seems to be able to move almost anything. At first smaller household objects are moved about.

Ornaments and utensils are the usual choice – they are very often found in the wrong place. In a number of instances the objects are moved so that they are placed very carefully indeed. In one case in Hertfordshire in the 1990s a china duck ornament was moved repeatedly so that it sat on the floor facing directly towards the door. It would then be looking at anybody who walked into the room. Other objects are placed exactly in the middle of a table, or teetering on its edge.

The majority of poltergeists are not so fastidious. They apparently prefer to throw objects about more or less at random. Some poltergeists seem to develop a fixation with one particular object, or type of object. It may be that a particular ornament will be moved day after day. In the Black Monk of Pontefract visitation it was a candlestick that came in for the most frequent moves.

It is rare to see a moving object. More often than not objects move when nobody is around to see them. However, witnesses who have seen an object being moved often say that it looks as if some invisible person has picked it up and carried it at a walking pace. This 'invisible carrier' description is also consistent with what happens when the item is put down. Sometimes objects are put down carefully, but at other times they are dropped. The wine bottles in the Turin wine bar that was investigated by Professor Lombroso would float gently

Stage Four: Apports and Disapports

On rare occasions objects are not just moved – they appear from nowhere. These are known as 'apports'. Objects that disappear into oblivion are termed 'disapports'. Not many

In the Black Monk of Pontefract visitation it was a candlestick that came in for the most frequent moves

Curiouser and curiouser: the moving eggs of Pontefract were an interesting form of 'apport' as they moved from within a sealed wooden box, having apparently dematerialized and then rematerialized outside the box

Colourful pasts: poltergeists usually claim to be linked to tales of murder, sexual debauchery or other dramatic crimes

poltergeist visitations reach this level of activity, but the effect can be dramatic.

In the Bell Witch visitation apports happened on at least three occasions. Hazelnuts were brought shelled and then unshelled to Mrs Bell. Then Betsy was presented with a basket of tropical fruit. There may be a crossover between apports and moving objects. In the Pontefract case eggs were moved from the kitchen to the sitting room by the poltergeist, where they were dropped and smashed. However, the eggs had started their journey from inside a sealed wooden box, which was kept shut by one of the witnesses sitting on it. The poltergeist was apparently moving the eggs through solid wood. That is, it was disapporting them from the box and apporting them in the living room. Perhaps all apports are actually being transported from somewhere rather than being created out of thin air.

Stage Five: Communication

Some poltergeists are capable of communicating with the humans that they are infesting. In the majority of cases the communication is by means of raps and knocks in accordance with a code. Such communication only begins if it is initiated by humans. After instructing a poltergeist to answer with a different number of raps or scratches to indicate 'yes', 'no' or 'don't know', humans then proceed to ask questions. The poltergeists at the convent of St Pierre de Lyon and at Amherst seem typical of those spirits who use such forms of communication. Most instances of communication remain at a basic level, but the Fox Sisters seem to have been almost unique in having devised an alphabetical code. This allowed their poltergeist to spell out names and words, thus facilitating a rather more complex series of messages.

Rather fewer poltergeists appear to have gained the ability to speak directly. The voices seemingly come from thin air and are usually described as being disembodied or phantom. Typically, the ability to speak is acquired gradually by the poltergeist. In the case of Gef on the Isle of Man, the speech began with barks and whistles. The Bell Witch began with slurping sounds and a noise akin to the smacking of lips. These noises progress on to mutterings or whisperings, where the sounds of human

voices can be discerned but actual words cannot be distinguished. Then the voice will begin to enunciate audible words – but its tone is still rather odd. Earlier observers have often said that the voice is gruff, cracked or stilted. A more modern witness has described the voice as being robot-like. Finally the voice will become more like that of a normal human. It becomes perfectly audible, with a range of tones that is able to convey emotion. It is as if the poltergeist has been slowly learning how to talk by a process of trial and error.

> *The desire to shock is apparent. Poltergeists will often use swear words; or they will insult people or make outrageous allegations*

Whether the means of communication is coded knocking or a disembodied voice, poltergeist utterances have a lot in common. The desire to shock is apparent. Poltergeists will often use swear words; or they will insult people or make outrageous allegations. Most of the allegations are false, but some are apparently lifted from local gossip about a person's private life. Poltergeists also seem to know a lot about what is going on in the vicinity. Both Gef and the Bell Witch would repeat things that had been said by a member of the family when they had been well away from the house. The Irvings assumed that Gef had scampered off to follow the person, before hiding in the place where the conversation had taken place; the Bells imagined that their witch could travel far and wide invisibly, in order to spy on them.

A poltergeist's statements about itself usually follow a set pattern. Most noticeably the poltergeist will often make a claim that fits in with how it is being viewed by humans. Gef said he was a mongoose after the Irvings had become convinced that he was a small animal; the Fox Sister's poltergeist claimed that it was the ghost of a man after the girls had said that the noises were caused by a ghost; and the poltergeist at the convent of St Pierre de Lyon claimed to be the spirit of Alix de Telieux only after a nun had suggested that this might be the case. When asked why it is causing such the nuisance, a poltergeist will typically reply that it is doing so for sport, for a joke or for fun. The response is almost universal when the question is put.

Another feature of the claims made by poltergeists about themselves is that they are almost uniformly sensational, exciting and salacious. The poltergeist claiming to be Alix de Telieux seemed to delight in regaling the nuns with tales of Alix's debauched sexual escapades, while the Cock Lane poltergeist claimed that it was the spirit of a woman who had been murdered by her husband. Claims of murder are common among poltergeists, as are tales of crimes, immoral behaviour and daring deeds. If poltergeists are to be believed then none of them are humans who have led routine lives of normal activity. They have either perpetrated the most appalling and outrageous crimes or they have been victims.

When the claims made by poltergeists are checked out, they usually turn out to be false. If they are true, the claims relate to events that are generally fairly well known in the area. It is extremely rare for a poltergeist to be in possession of any information that is not already known to its human witnesses.

> *It is extremely rare for a poltergeist to be in possession of any information that is not already known to its human witnesses*

Stage Six: Climax

After a poltergeist case has built up gradually over a period of time there will often be a sudden and distinct increase in the level and frequency of activity. Typically, it will increase even further for a day or two, until a climax is reached. For a few hours the level of activity will be far greater than it has ever been. Then it will drop off rapidly, returning to the level it was at before the climax began. When the poltergeist is communicating with its human witnesses it might announce that it is going to leave. Sometimes it might even set a date and time for its departure. These announcements, unlike most other statements made by poltergeists, generally turn out to be accurate.

Stage Seven: Decline

As we have seen, after the climax of the visitation has been reached activity will tail off and then cease. Sometimes this will be immediate, or nearly so. In other instances the decline might be spread over several days. During this phase it is usual for the various types of activity to continue much as before, but with increasingly less frequency and violence. Sometimes, but not always, the poltergeist will follow a process that is the reverse of its build-up. First it will lose its voice and then it will lose the ability to move objects. Finally, it will cease making noises at all. The decline is almost always much shorter than the build-up.

Stage Eight: Endings

The majority of poltergeist visitations simply peter out as the decline nears its conclusion. A few end rather more spectacularly. The Bell Witch visitation, for instance, went out with a bang. A gigantic ball of smoke erupted from the fireplace and exploded loudly and then the voice declared that it was leaving. However, some poltergeist visitations are brought to an end by humans. The visitation that plagued Miss Sharpe at Bethony ended temporarily when the local vicar carried out a prayer service in the house. Although the activity later began again at a lesser level, a second prayer service was enough to end the visitation completely. Other clergymen have been far less successful. Some poltergeists have thrown objects at them while they have been conducting services.

A good number of poltergeist visitations end abruptly when there is a change in a person's personal circumstances.

The visitation that affected the offices of Sigmund Adam at Rosenheim ceased instantly when the clerk Anne-Marie Schneider was dismissed. The poltergeist neither returned to the offices nor to Anne-Marie. Similarly, the Battersea Mystery House visitation ended when Mr Robinson's teenage nephew went to stay with relatives in the country. These, and other cases, would indicate that poltergeist manifestations are activated by the presence of a particular human in a particular place.

As well as this progression of stages, an idealized poltergeist visitation would incorporate some other features.

Features of a Poltergeist Visitation

Focus person

In all of the cases that have been studied in the past few decades, it has been clear to researchers that one particular person is often at the centre of a visitation. Manifestations will occur more frequently when that person is present. They might not even take place if the person is not there. The visitation usually commences in the bedroom that is used by that person. Or it might be connected with a favourite possession of theirs. In poltergeist cases from past centuries, it is often easy to see that a focus person was at the centre of the disturbances. Someone like Elizabeth Parsons, for instance, who featured strongly in the Cock Lane Ghost affair. On some occasions a focus person cannot be identified in a past case. However, it might be fair to assume that those who wrote down the account were so busy trying to identify a witch or a ghost that they simply did not notice something that would have been obvious to a modern researcher.

The focus is very often a teenager or a young adult and it seems to be a girl more often than a boy. This is not always the case, though. Grown adults are sometimes found to be the focus – sometimes even retired folk.

If focus people eventually realize that they are somehow related to the visitation, they are both puzzled and distressed by the fact

Indeed, the general presumption that the focus is always a teenager can sometimes mislead the researcher. In the case of the poltergeist that afflicted the house of Dr and Mrs Wilkins in Sunderland, Harry Price assumed that the focus was the newly married teenage daughter Olive. But she was never present when the manifestations took place while her mother usually was. Perhaps it was Mrs Wilkins who was the focus, not her daughter.

In most cases it is clear that people are not always aware that they are the focus of a visitation. Most families believe that it is just their house that is being haunted, not themselves. If focus people eventually realize that they are somehow related to the visitation, they are both puzzled and distressed by the fact. When Ann Kidner was found close to a burning hayrick she was sobbing almost hysterically. She repeatedly said that she was not responsible. Similarly Virginia Campbell was obviously distressed and upset when her teacher's desk levitated at her school. She broke down and sobbed, 'I'm not doing it, Miss. Please, Miss. Honest I'm not.' Whatever role a focus plays in a manifestation, it would seem that on most occasions it is unconscious. Some focus persons, on the other hand, almost seem to enjoy events. Janet Harper, who was at the centre of the Enfield visitation, seems to have fallen into this category.

Emotional turmoil

It is often said that focus people are usually in a stressful situation of some kind. The clerk Anne-Marie Schneider did not enjoy her job and she had a grudge against her employer; Esther Cox had just experienced an attempted rape; and Virginia Campbell had suffered the trauma of her parents' divorce before being forced to move from Ireland to Scotland, where she had to share a cramped bedroom with a cousin. Focus people are not always obviously distressed by their situation, but there is usually some sign of underlying worry or frustration.

Classroom nightmare: the Scottish case that saw a teacher's desk rise into the air in front of an entire class of children seemed to centre around a teenage girl who had recently moved house

The type of raw emotion that has just been described does not have to be confined to the focus. It is often felt by all or most of those in the affected household or workplace. Indeed, it is sometimes the case that focus people are not only the centre of the poltergeist activity, but they are also the cause of the emotional problems. Or at least other humans in the vicinity might think so.

Explanations for the Poltergeist Phenomenon

There are six different explanations for the poltergeist phenomenon. Each has its merits and its problems. They will be dealt with in some detail below, but in outline they are as follows:

by a supernatural entity such as a ghost, a demon or a spirit.

4. *Repeated Spontaneous Psychokinesis* (RSPK) – the events are truly paranormal and are caused by the subconscious use of psychokinesis by one or more of the humans involved.

5. A combination of two or more of the above.

6. Something else as yet unknown to humanity.

In the remainder of this chapter I will compare these suggested explanations with the recorded events.

Fraud or fakery is often alleged in poltergeist outbreaks. It is certainly true that a proportion of those who have reported a visitation have been found to be faking some or all of the events. Elizabeth Parsons was most certainly faking the later manifestations of the Cock Lane Ghost and Janet Harper admitted faking some of the Enfield events. Whether either girl had faked the earlier manifestations in either case is open to doubt. Parsons was caught faking the knocking noises only after other witnesses had reported a diminishing in the activity of the poltergeist.

She had a very clear reason for doing so – her father had been threatened with legal action if the ghost did not perform on cue. Janet Harper was again only caught out in the later phases of the visitation. Her frauds at this time were quite easily spotted. Furniture moving about in empty rooms was unconvincing, to say the least. It must be acknowledged, however, that some researchers felt that the Enfield case showed signs of fraud in the very early stages.

People do strange things, sometimes for the oddest of motives. There are cases on record in which people have made claims of ghosts and hauntings in order to be re-housed by their local council. Others have done so in order to frighten a relative whom they dislike. It is not entirely implausible that a person would seek to manufacture a poltergeist outbreak in their own home for such motives. Many of the more spectacular events – those that would be impossible to fake – are witnessed

1. *Fraud* – the supposedly paranormal events are faked by humans.

2. *Mistake* – the supposedly paranormal events are entirely natural occurrences that are falsely assumed to be paranormal.

3. *Entity* – the events are truly paranormal and are caused

by only one person, or at most only by the family concerned. When the six dining chairs in the Battersea Mystery House lined up like soldiers on parade and marched out of the dining room, the only person to witness the event was Mrs Perkins, a member of the affected family. The events that were witnessed by impartial outsiders, such as the policeman, would have been easier to fake. The lump of coal that hit the policeman on the back of the helmet could have been thrown by any member of the family acting as an accomplice to Mr Robinson. It seems unlikely, however, that families or individuals would seriously inconvenience themselves for frivolous reasons. The Robinsons suffered substantial financial loss because of smashed furniture, broken windows and lost rent when they were driven to move to another house. At the same time, it must be said that some people behave extremely oddly even when there are no supernatural forces at work.

People have sometimes persecuted neighbours to distraction for imagined slights. Newspapers often print stories about 'neighbours from hell' who play loud music, hack down hedges, swear and curse and generally make life intolerable for individuals against whom they have a grudge. So faking a poltergeist visitation in order to persecute a neighbour is not impossible. Looking at the Battersea case again, the idea that the neighbours were causing the damage was at first raised as a real possibility. This was entertained only during the early stages, when most activity took the form of coal being thrown about and windows smashing. Once furniture inside the house started dancing about, the idea had to be discarded.

So there can be no doubt that fakery and fraud are involved in some cases. However, other visitations have defied all attempts to discover any trickery. Most cases merely rest on the uncorroborated word of the families involved, but a few have been investigated by people of the highest reliability. On occasion they have

> *There can be no doubt that fakery and fraud are involved in some cases. However, other visitations have defied all attempts to discover any trickery*

witnessed things that they simply cannot explain. When Professor Lombroso watched wine bottles float through thin air at the Turin wine bar he was at a complete loss for an explanation. And then there was the policeman in the Ann Kidner case. He was impartial, sober and disinclined to imagine things but when he watched the loaf of bread levitate he was totally bemused. As soon as it stopped moving he inspected it thoroughly, but he was quite unable to discover what had caused it to float around. He arrested the hapless Kidner simply because he felt that she was somehow to blame. The lack of any evidence is demonstrated by her subsequent release.

All too often a sceptic will allege that an incident must be faked because otherwise it would not conform to the laws of physics. But just because something seems to be impossible does not mean that it is impossible. Until the late 19th century scientists did not believe peasants and farmers when they reported that large rocks sometimes fell from the sky. 'How did the rocks get there?' scoffed the scientists. 'Did a gust of wind lift a 20lb lump of rock up only to drop it on to the pigsty of an unsuspecting farmer?' The whole idea seemed impossible. Then somebody recognized that the lumps of rock were meteorites from space. Suddenly the impossible became not only possible but mundane.

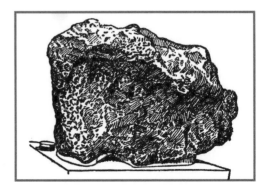

Hard evidence: a meteorite, a lump of rock that has come to Earth from outer space

Out of nowhere: meteorites crashing to earth from the sky were reported several times by witnesses over the centuries, but were consistently dismissed by scientists as superstition and nonsense until a rational explanation was found

The Rosenheim Poltergeist: solicitor Sigurd Adam displays the phone bill for his company, which rose colossally after a poltergeist started playing tricks with the phones in his office

Sceptics often suggest that a witness to poltergeist activity is mistaken. The idea has some merit. We have already seen that most of the families and individuals who report a poltergeist are living under conditions of stress. People who are distracted or upset are not the most reliable of witnesses, so some of the antics of a poltergeist could be explained in these terms. Mrs Wilkins, for instance, reported that she would often come home to find her daughter's bedclothes turned back, or toys moved about. It is at least possible that she had moved the toys herself and then forgotten about the fact. She may even have turned down the bedclothes when she was thinking about her daughter, without actually realizing she had done so. As for a poltergeist allegedly moving a bunch of keys from a hook to a table, most people have experienced this phenomenon. Forgetfulness and absent-mindedness are far more likely culprits.

However, the level of activity that surrounds some visitations is too intense for it to be blamed on forgetfulness. And while commonly used objects, such as keys, may be accidentally put in the wrong place it is more difficult to explain the movements of other objects. Consider the model duck that was repeatedly left in the middle of the floor, for instance.

It has also been suggested that apparent poltergeist visitations are caused by natural phenomena. For example, some houses in London are subjected to regular vibration strong enough to make pictures on the wall shudder noticeably. There is nothing supernatural about this, it is simply underground trains passing by immediately underneath. Similarly, forces such as magnetism, static electricity and infrasound have been suggested as explanations for some manifestations. This might be the case, but the sceptics have been unable to reproduce the effects in laboratories.

Electrical devices are a favourite of the sceptics. Theories abound as to how lights can be switched on or off, how radios can malfunction – the list goes on.

However, in the Rosenheim case several highly qualified technicians spent weeks investigating malfunctioning telephones and electrical systems. They could find nothing physically wrong. Indeed, they concluded that some energy not yet known to science was to blame. This natural phenomena argument also falls down when it meets the more spectacular exploits of poltergeists, such as dancing chairs and floating bottles of wine. It is impossible to account for chairs dancing around a room or bottles floating through the air. Hallucination might account for it – but not for the broken bottles and furniture that remains.

Finally, the most hardened sceptic must admit that a large number of poltergeist visitations have many features in common. So much so, that the possibility of fraud or error seems relatively remote. In fact, a researcher who is comparing accounts of visitations that occurred thousands of miles from each other and hundreds of years apart can easily confuse one with the other.

If the poltergeist phenomenon is genuine – and the weight of high-quality evidence would suggest that it is – then a solution must be sought. In past centuries the favoured explanation was that a hostile entity had entered the house and was causing the mischief. This entity might have been a ghost, a witch or a fairy of some kind, but it was generally believed to be intelligent, invisible and powerful. If one examines the reported phenomena, this solution has merit – provided that one is willing to accept the reality of such disembodied entities.

Many observers have likened poltergeist activity to having an invisible person in the room. Objects are moved just as if they are being carried by a human, except that there is nobody there. There is also the undeniable fact that many poltergeists exhibit both intelligence and personality. Those who are able to communicate do so with obvious intelligence. They respond to questions in a manner that is usually rational and logical – even if it is often untruthful. Even when direct communication is not established, the poltergeist seems to be aware of the people with whom it shares a house or a workplace. It will react to what they say and do. The Rosenheim poltergeist, for instance, did not move any paintings until Herr Adam commented on the fact and then it would not leave them alone.

Other poltergeists do not show such a high level of intelligence. The poltergeist at the mill at Appleby displayed enormous strength when it was shifting things about, but it did not have any obvious motive. It would stack boxes, smash windows and heave stones about, but it confined its actions to a single room and it never seemed to achieve a great deal. For all we know, though, it fulfilled some strange ambition of its own. It does seem very much as if the majority of poltergeists are distinct entities. But the case is not without its problems. If poltergeists were some disembodied entity that for some reason or another decided to take up residence in a house or office, it might be expected that they would come fully prepared to cause mischief. That is not the case.

Poltergeists do not suddenly arrive in a house with all of their future skills in place. They are not immediately able to talk, apport nuts, throw furniture about or perform any of the other spectacular manifestations. Instead, each poltergeist starts off slowly and builds up its repertoire of abilities over a period of time.

Fairies and other supernatural entities have been blamed for poltergeist visitations in the past

If poltergeists are demons or fairies, we can assume that each poltergeist is an entirely new demon that has never done anything similar before. This may be the case, but it seems unlikely. Having learned how to scare humans witless, a demon would surely seek to move on to the next house to enjoy its sport again. They do not seem to do so. In any case, suggesting that a disembodied spirit of some kind is the cause of poltergeist activity only complicates the situation. We know that there are humans involved because we can see them, but the existence of a demon, an angel or a fairy is entirely theoretical. There is no evidence for their existence other than the poltergeist activity. It would be much simpler to assume that the visitation was caused by the humans themselves.

If we examine poltergeist activity in those cases where the human background is fully known, the outbreaks make some kind of emotional sense. At Rosenheim the focus person did not enjoy her job and she resented her employer. It was the office equipment that was sabotaged, not the personal belongings of the other staff. And the constant telephone calls to the speaking clock suggest a desire to know what the time was. If the agent causing the events was the subconscious mind of the focus this makes sense. She would want to know the time, so that she knew how much longer she had to stay in the hated office. And she would want to damage the employer's property, but not the belongings of her fellow workers.

The case of the Wilkins poltergeist is also open to an emotional explanation. Olive had recently married a wartime pilot at a young age and had quickly fallen pregnant. These circumstances must have made her yearn for the simpler, safer times when she had lived at home with her mother and father, who had cared for her needs as parents do. Whether it was Olive or Mrs Wilkins who was the focus, the emotional desire would have been the same – for Olive to be home, safe and snug. This would explain why Olive's bed was turned down, why her favourite toys were apparently played with and why her mother heard her come home so often.

Esther Cox went through the ordeal of an attempted rape. The poltergeist at first attacked her in physical terms and threatened to kill her. It then proceeded to act in a more disorganized and chaotic fashion, lashing out at anyone who got near.

This sort of emotional train is not unknown among rape victims. They first blame themselves for foolishly trusting a man, or for getting drunk in a nightclub; then they move on to become angry at the unfeeling world that does not seem to sympathize with their predicament. Again and again, the poltergeist seems to be lashing out in a purely emotional way, not in a logical way. It is not always possible to correlate the poltergeist's actions with the focus person and their problems. Sometimes it seems as if the person is being targeted rather than doing the targeting. It may well be that the focus is not the the person with the emotional problems, but the one who is causing them. The emotional attack would then be centred on the person who was blamed for the problems.

This would suggest that the poltergeist phenomenon is unwittingly caused by a person who is unable to sort out their emotional problems by conventional means. Perhaps Anne-Marie Schneider was unable to get another job and so was stuck in Herr Adam's office. Virginia Campbell was certainly unable to move out of her cousin's bedroom. But that leaves the huge problem of how a person's subconscious mind can cause chairs to march around and stones to be thrown. And can somebody create a communication from an apparently intelligent entity?

This is where the Philip Experiment should be brought in. The evidence from that experiment, and those that have followed it, would indicate that people can cause physical effects by mind power. The Philip team discovered that the table knocking and other effects became less powerful if they were not all present. When one of the team members reminded his colleagues that they had invented Philip from nothing, the activity ceased for a couple of weeks. If the Philip Experiment, ongoing table turning experiments and other studies are taken at face value it would seem that it is possible for humans to move objects using mind power alone. This process is called psycho-kinesis, or PK. Mainstream science does not recognize that PK exists. Consequently it is virtually impossible to find any reputable scientist willing to research it. It is even more difficult to find an institution that is willing to fund such research. But then there was a time when scientists did not believe that great rocks fell from the sky.